THE PSYCHIC PATHWAY

The Psychic Pathway

A Workbook for Reawakening the Voice of Your Soul

Sonia Choquette

THREE RIVERS PRESS
NEW YORK

A CAROL SOUTHERN BOOK

Published by Three Rivers Press, New York, New York.
Member of the Crown Publishing Group.

Random House, Inc. New York, Toronto, London, Sydney, Auckland
www.randomhouse.com

THREE RIVERS PRESS is a registered trademark and the Three
Rivers Press colophon is a trademark of Random House, Inc.

Printed in the United States of America

Library of Congress Cataloging-in-Publication Data
Choquette, Sonia.
The psychic pathway: a workbook for reawakening the voice of your
soul / by Sonia Choquette. —1st edition.
Includes bibliographical references.
1. Psychic ability. 2. Intuition. 3. Parapsychology. 4. Choquette,
Sonia.
I. Title.
BF1031.C52   1994
133.8—dc20   94-40628

ISBN 0-517-88407-0

20 19 18

This book is dedicated to my loving family
who have created a circle of guidance,
protection, teaching, and joy in my life.
It is with deep appreciation and love
that I thank you all for sharing
the pathway of soul with me.

ACKNOWLEDGMENTS

I would like to thank my mother, Sonia, for starting me out on the psychic pathway at the beginning of my life and supporting me spiritually throughout it all. I would also like to thank my father, Paul, who lives the meaning of unconditional love and acceptance and has been the loving foundation of stability in my life.

To Lu Ann Glatzmaier, my best friend and "soul" sister, thank you for exploring all the dimensions of the psychic pathway with me. To Joan Smith, thank you for charting our course with your astrological calculations and commonsense savvy. To Kathy Churay, thank you for your talent, humor, and grounding and for letting me be a part of your transformation. To Cuky, my sister, thank you for being like a second mother to me, nurturing me during the difficult passages and celebrating my victories.

To Gene and Mary Tully, thank you for being great grandparents and caring for my daughters while I wrote this book, and for your great son, Patrick. To my children, Sonia and Sabrina, thank you for being patient while I was working and for your humor and love when I needed inspiration.

And finally, thank you to the souls of my teachers, Charlie Goodman and Dr. Trenton Tully, for the guiding light and road maps on my spiritual journey.

Also, thank you to the wonderful people at Transitions Bookplace who first brought my manuscript to the public; to my agent, Susan Schulman; to my editor and publisher, Carol Southern, and her assistant, Eliza Scott; to Penny Simon, my publicist; to Camille Smith, Joy Sikorski, and all of the other people at Crown who worked behind the scenes to make the book a success.

And a special thank you to my dear friend, fellow psychic, student, and teacher, Julia Cameron, for her vision—and insistence—on my bringing *The Psychic Pathway* into the world. It was *her* psychic knowing that first noticed this book inside me seven years ago, and in her artist's way, she helped me lead it safely into the world.

The psychic pathway led Julia to create *The Artist's Way*. *The Artist's Way,* in turn, led me to create *The Psychic Pathway.*

CONTENTS

FOREWORD

It has been my privilege to know Sonia Choquette, and travel with her on the psychic pathway, for the past decade. I have long admired the artistry and creativity in her work. In my own work I have found her support joyous and invaluable.

Several years ago, seated at my writing desk, I received a telegram: "Call Sonia Choquette and ask her about her book." I call such telegrams my "marching orders," and I know better than to ignore them. So I called Sonia and asked about her book. . . .

She was horrified.

If I was a closet psychic, she was a closet writer! It's a toss-up whose closet was darker and scarier. After a little telepathic arm-twisting, I convinced her to show me "It."

"It" was the nub of the book you hold in your hands.

From that day to this, my job has been to welcome Sonia's book into the world. This was easy: I read it in nightly installments like a thriller. I got to ask all the questions I wanted. She had the answers. We had the adventure of shaping this book together.

I have found *The Psychic Pathway* and the world of knowledge it contains to be magic.

I envy you your first steps.

—Julia Cameron
Taos, New Mexico

IN THIS SPIRIT

What lies before us, and what lies behind us, are
tiny matters compared to what lies within us. . . .

—Ralph Waldo Emerson

An Exciting Adventure

My name is Sonia. I was named after my mother, Sonia, a psychic, and I am psychic. For twenty-five years I have given psychic readings. For a decade and a half I have taught psychic development.

Perhaps more important, I have lived my own life on what I call the psychic pathway. I have developed my own psychic gifts, and I have learned to develop them in others. This means I have lived my life publicly as a psychic. The book that follows is a practical sourcebook, a developmental guide to nurturing your natural psychic gifts. It is the fruit of my life experience—and it works.

Let me tell you a little of my story before we begin.

I like the word *psychic* because no one knows exactly what that means, and it doesn't mean the same thing for any two people. For me, being psychic means being able to look at someone and know who they really are. I can see past the facade people stand behind. I can recognize their soul. I understand where their fears are, where their dreams lie, and where they must concentrate their growth. Most of all, I can see the ancient and beautiful self lying deep within the personality of each person I meet.

I've always been able to see the real soul inside each person, but it's been a long learning process for me to come to the understanding that that is what I had been doing all along. Even I wasn't really aware of what I was seeing at times, especially when those around me didn't know what I was talking about and laughed at me. I have done psychic readings for people ever since I was a young child, starting as early as age eleven.

I didn't think about it in terms of being strange or out of place. Instead I looked at it as a family trait. Since my mother, Sonia, is also psychic, our own family experiences were anchored around her psychic feelings about things. My mother's "vibes" determined everything we did as a family—whom we made friends with, where we would go. It was a way of life. My father, Paul, was a calm, loving man. He adored my mother and deeply valued her psychic feelings. None of us ever disputed my mother's intuition. She was always right. We felt safe and somehow protected from harm, and this psychic awareness began to manifest in me.

I was one of seven children, but perhaps because I was named after my mother, I really identified with her. I loved how she responded to everything around her on a very soulful, feeling level, and I wanted and tried to do the same from the youngest age I can remember. It never occurred to me not to look for or listen to my "vibes." Life without vibes would be like being blind or deaf. It was my primary sense, my primary way of experiencing life around me.

People frequently ask me how I came to realize I was psychic. I never remember realizing I was psychic, but after I began first grade it became apparent that what was obvious to me was hidden from others. It took me a few months to realize that my perceptions were different from those of others. I was constantly trying to fit my reality into the more limited framework of those around me.

For example, I recall that one day in May I woke up and felt as though I were going to be crowned princess. I was very happy at breakfast and told everyone what a special day it was. I was going to be crowned princess.

"Mom," I said, "please sew me a beautiful gown because I am going to need one for the special ceremony."

My brothers laughed at me. "Yeah, princess of the stupid-heads!"

What an insult! I just ignored them.

"*You'll* see! I will be crowned princess!" I put on my blue plaid uniform and skipped to school. I was so happy.

The morning went as usual. Sister Mary Ellen, my first-grade teacher, didn't seem aware of my big event, so I figured she wouldn't have anything to do with it. I just waited.

At noon, right after we returned from the lunchroom and right before nap time, Sister Mary Canisius, the school principal, came into our class with three beautiful eighth-grade girls. Sister Mary Ellen had all the first-grade girls line up against the wall, and the three eighth-grade girls studied us. Then each one walked over and picked a girl. My best friend, Susie Cain, was picked. A girl I didn't like, Stephanie Montoya, was picked. And finally, the most beautiful girl of all picked me!

Then Sister Mary Ellen and Sister Mary Canisius told us that our school was having a May crowning ceremony for the Blessed Virgin Mary. The three eighth-grade girls were the May queen and her attendants. We, the three first-graders, were the May princesses. We were to dress in formal dresses, wear beautiful flowers in our hair, and lead the school parade in the May Day pageant.

This was it! I was picked to be a princess! And by someone I had never seen before in my life! Needless to say, my brothers heard about this one.

Another useful discovery from my school days was that I knew whenever our teachers were planning any sort of surprise test. It was never like a light bulb going on. It simply occurred to me on the walk to school. I would just be walking along, thinking of nothing in particular, and it would float into my head—test today! I loved it.

The hardest thing about being psychic when I was young was that I was always conscious of the thoughts of my classmates, especially those about me! As you might imagine, some of them thought me quite weird.

In retrospect, perhaps we were. I grew up in a crowded sensual house. My mother was an artist in many ways. She painted and sewed, did photography and interior design, and raised seven children, all the while maintaining an elegance and grace. My father was artistic, too.

Over the years he completely remodeled the home we lived in.

Our home emphasized the creative, the beautiful, and above all, the imagination. We all worked hard to reach within ourselves and pull out something extraordinary. My brothers and sisters became musicians, artists, designers, travelers, and inventors of the beautiful. I simply became psychic and used my creativity to look for and guide people to find the beautiful and extraordinary in themselves.

When I was a teenager, I became particularly clairvoyant and began to see future events around people. When I held an object that belonged to someone, visions came across my mental screen, a little like a movie. I could see, feel, even hear future events or distant occurrences as if I were right there. It was exciting but inconsistent, so I began *trying* to stabilize or control my psychic abilities through concentration.

Even though I was getting psychic information, I pressed deeper into things. I read. I studied. I practiced. I apprenticed myself to master teachers. Eventually my readings reflected my discussions about why certain events occurred. First I saw only events. Next I could see how events were set up, offering me a bigger picture.

For example, I wouldn't just see a person getting married next year. I would see that person going back to school and marrying someone he or she would meet there. I would see that the marriage would occur because they had common goals.

Gradually, with much work, I went from what, to who, to how events unfolded, but I still yearned for more understanding. Ultimately I kept on pressing until I could see *why* life formed for each person as it did.

I began to see the deep soul behind all the layers of self-consciousness we wrap ourselves in. By continuing to look deeper and deeper into how life unfolds, I found myself seeing into the very essence of people. I saw what they longed to express, what they feared, how they were going about things, where they struggled with values, and how their creativity was manifested into the events of their life. I recognized the beauty of their life and worked to show them how to tap into their joy. These abilities have been mine for many years now.

Of course, I can still predict the future, but now that prediction comes from seeing creative energy set up the future. It's the same as seeing a cut tulip in a vase on a table or seeing a tulip bulb being cultivated into a beautiful flower. The more I try to see, to know, to understand, the drama of each person's life, the more apparent it becomes to me who the soul is that I have the privilege of meeting that day.

For example, today a woman came to me at noon. She had white hair and pretty skin and was dressed casually in slacks and sensible shoes. Everything in her tone, her movement, her demeanor, indicated she disapproved of herself for letting herself come to my door. In fact, she seemed angry. That was the surface energy, and I ignored it. I have long ago let my ego step aside in this process. She had allowed herself to be here. It was that self I would address.

She was so edgy that I asked her to shuffle my tarot cards. I didn't intend to use them, but the task would distract her mind. I closed my eyes and saw a flaming red bull, the red of anger and pain. I could tell she was a retired social worker. She had never married, lived alone, and was poor. She was depressed, even suicidal, and terribly trapped by the unfortunate condition of her good health. She had become paranoid. Being poor, she lived in a low-rent situation amid crime. The city frightened her, and being in her seventies, she had no opportunities, or so it appeared.

My Higher Self said this woman was sad because she'd come to earth to do spiritual, even religious, work to help people. Instead she'd turned down the road of the mind and become a social work administrator and become caught up in an endless bureaucratic nightmare that denied the sacredness of life. She'd adopted a contemptuousness for those whom her soul had come to heal. Consequently she'd found herself stuck in a sea of lost souls, with no viable way out. At seventy-one she still had a chance to fulfill her soul dream of spiritual ministry if she would only stop calling herself "social worker" and start calling herself "soul worker."

Gently I began to ask her questions along the lines indicated to me.

She did admit that she had spent twenty-five years studying yoga, Buddhism, service to others, and really had wanted to be a nun, but her family had scorned such an urge, and she'd substituted social work for the convent. It hadn't worked. Her life lacked gratification because on a soul level she wanted a spiritual, even sacred, life, not an intellectual, analytical one.

The good news was that it was still possible for her to find peace. It meant she had to stop scorning the souls around her hooked on drugs, reproducing countless babies, living on welfare. Instead she had to minister to their souls, give them dignity by showing basic love and kindness. Her mission was not to save them, help them, change them—just simply to salute the good within them. That is the job of a soul worker. And when people do their job and fulfill their spiritual goals, they become peaceful and secure. Joy wells up from within.

I added the unimportant details of a coming change in apartment, money from a rebate, and a trip to San Antonio at Christmas, details that amused her. But what helped was not the details, but allowing her to reframe her perspective on life so she could see where her work needed to be done.

Helping people see their souls' work is *my* soul work. The psychic details now serve only to get their attention. My real work, after gaining their attention, lies in teaching them to look into their own experience with a wide-open heart and helping them to become content.

I do readings three days a week, three times a day. I also teach psychic development workshops and write. That's all I can do without taking away from my family, and it works. I see my readings and teaching as part of my responsibility. (The writing is part of my delight.) I still must go through all the cycles of personal work and growth as well. It's a constant juggling act.

When I am finished with my three clients a day, I have lunch, put away the laundry, pick up my children, and simply become a mom again. Oh, I also find my way to an aerobics class three times a week. My work is so esoteric that for balance and grounding I do something with my body. It shuts off my hyperawareness and brings me home to my own responsibilities to my marriage, my children, my body, my life.

My life is normal, but extraordinary. Normal in that I face all the challenges, hassles, upsets, and responsibilities that any married person faces who owns an old home and is raising kids. Extraordinary in that I am very conscious of the point to all this effort—to learn to love others and myself, to honor my true soul desire, and to enjoy myself. I'm not gilded in glitter, twirling around a crystal ball. I wear jeans and T-shirts, like to watch *Seinfeld,* and listen to REM.

In other words, being able to see the soul doesn't require you to dress for the prom. That's silly—harmless, but silly—and usually a way of substituting drama to compensate for lack of substance. True psychic sense is founded in common sense above all.

BUT WHAT IS THE PSYCHIC PATHWAY?

When I talk about psychic ability, people conjure up widely differing ideas and beliefs about what "psychic" means. Some people imagine that it bestows upon a person extraordinary abilities to know all things at all times. Some think it's like having X-ray vision. Some people think it gives one the ability to know the future or the past, including past lives. Some people believe it means seeing ghosts or talking to dead people. Some people believe it's a great power. Others feel it's an evil affliction. What we can all agree on is that rarely do any two people hold the same beliefs on what "psychic" means, so let me begin by establishing what I mean when I say "psychic ability."

The word *psychic* comes from the Greek word *psyche,* meaning "soul." Therefore psychic means "of the soul." In following the psychic pathway, you are following the pathway of the soul.

What is the pathway of the soul? It is the pathway of life lived with the belief and understanding that you are a soul, and that spiritual growth is your primary purpose. It is the understanding that your true essence is spiritual, and that your physical body is your instrument of expression, just as a piano is an instrument through which music is expressed. The piano is designed to be capable of expressing beautiful music, but without the understanding and discipline of a talented and developed musician playing it, the piano may sit silent or worse yet, if played carelessly, will send out awful and discordant noises. The piano expresses the creativity and awareness of the musician. It does not create the music, it channels the music.

An evolved and knowledgeable musician creates beautiful sounds that soothe and inspire all who hear its vibration. The same holds true for people. We are souls, here on earth to express our divine gifts of creativity. Our physical body and our mind are our tools, our instruments of expression. The creative force behind these miraculous instruments is our soul. If we are knowledgeable and conscious of our true spiritual essence, we too send out beautiful and soothing vibrations that inspire and heal all who are around our vibrations, including ourselves.

The psychic pathway is the pathway of learning how to express our highest degree of creativity and love in this lifetime. It is the pathway of living life receptive to spiritual assistance and conscious of all the planes of energy we share with each other, with higher planes, and with God. The psychic pathway is not the usual pathway so many follow, focused on the ego, feeling alone and frightened by others. It is a spiritual pathway focused on connection to God, on our creative purpose, and on spiritual growth. It is the pathway of the extraordinary life.

Psychic development is training your awareness to expand and receive more information from others, from astral planes, and from God than it receives now. It is learning how to expand your consciousness and to better understand how your instrument of expression—your body—receives energy. It is the art of evolving your physical body into a highly sophisticated receiver of vibrations, thus giving you much more accurate information to work with as you interact with others in life. It is training your mind to be open and receptive to the subtle planes of energy that constitute psychic activity. It is living a life that communes with spirit, sees into things rather than looks at things, and is open and responsive to the guidance of God at all times.

If you walk the psychic pathway, you live in the world differently from the ordinary person. You look at life differently and respond to it differently. You know that you will be helped with each experience you face, however difficult. It is the pathway of trust and belief. That is what we mean when we talk about psychic ability.

Different psychic skills, such as clairaudience, clairvoyance, telepathy, and precognition, are like different melodies a pianist plays on the piano. Each is beautiful, and some may be more appealing to you than others. You will learn to play all these "melodies," to express all these psychic faculties naturally, if you remember that the musician, the creator, the true you, is divine soul, a beautiful reflection of God.

THE BASIC PRINCIPLES

 1. Psychic gifts are gifts of the soul.
 2. We are all souls; therefore we all have psychic gifts.
 3. The development of our psychic gifts is our birthright.
 4. Psychic gifts are messages from a divine source, directing us toward our own divine nature and its highest creative expression.
 5. The development of each soul's psychic gifts is not selfish; psychic gifts benefit us all.
 6. Psychic gifts bring light and healing to us all.
 7. The psychic pathway is born in love and results in understanding.
 8. The psychic pathway is gentle, powerful, and *always* noncoercive.
 9. The psychic pathway does not flatter the ego; rather it supports the soul's true essence.
10. Exercising psychic gifts is fun.

HOW TO USE THIS BOOK

First of all, I encourage you to use this book playfully. Psychic exploration is best undertaken with a spirit of adventure. I will be sharing with you a variety of tools that I have learned, discovered, and invented over time, both as a psychic and as a teacher. These tools have worked for me, and they can work for you. As you will soon discover, the pathway is laid out carefully and has a predictable and natural progression. Psychic development is predictable and natural—as long as you remain willing to be surprised.

Of course, many of you reading this book already suspect that you are psychic. Unfortunately your experience of these gifts may not have been pleasant or consistent. This book offers you a foundation upon which to build and a course that is safe, reasonable, and guided. While we will go slowly, each step will offer you immediate feedback and visible results. Each step builds upon the previous step—the process itself will encourage you onward. Throughout the text I will be sharing with you stories of my experience as both a teacher and a student, as well as the experiences of my students and clients.

As you set out on the psychic pathway, it is important to be both lighthearted and serious in your commitment. The rewards of the journey are exponential to your efforts.

While the psychic pathway is intense, it is not *time-intensive*. You will find that this journey asks of you only about a half hour each day. Additionally, about once a week you will need to commit another hour-long block of time for further "explorations" and to chart your progress.

In the first part of the book, you will acquire basic tools for balance and strength. Next, you will clear away the past and present obstacles to your psychic growth. Then—and only then—you will get down to the nuts and bolts of building your psychic tool kit.

You will eventually learn the full psychic repertoire of skills: how to see auras, clear auras, balance chakras, work with guides, do readings, and more. We will, however, move into this work carefully. As I tell my students, "You have to build a platform before you can have a show."

Allow yourself to work with me in trusting this step-by-step approach. Psychic energy is powerful, and I have seen too many people rush into psychic work without laying a foundation. Such a full-speed-ahead approach actually throws them backward. As you will discover, the pathway is built on a twelve-week course that I have developed and refined—initially solo and later with my husband, Patrick—over fifteen years.

Please know that the psychic pathway will give you a new perspective on old issues and emotions and will ask you to draw new conclusions. It is also reasonable to believe that you may encounter resistance from others. Therefore, commit to discretion and self-protection using the tools in this book, including excellent self-care—adequate sleep, diet, exercise, and recreation—for the duration of the journey.

I do not believe in "quick fixes," but I do believe in miracles. As a teacher, it has been my great joy to witness the spiritual awakenings of my students. I have witnessed the miraculous unfolding of many lives.

My greatest reward comes when my students remember who they really are. In this sense they become teachers, reminding me of our essential unity as each of us journeys toward the true magnificence of our souls.

For too many years—perhaps centuries—the psychic pathway has been shrouded in mystery and cloaked in secrecy. Fear of persecution and a misplaced sense of exclusivity have often distanced my colleagues from the central truth that we are *all* psychic. I hope this book will open the gateway and welcome all souls who wish to develop their natural gifts.

With this understanding of what the psychic pathway is, let us begin our walk.

THE PSYCHIC AWARENESS SURVEY

As you begin, it might be helpful for you to recognize how psychically aware you already are. Complete the following questionnaire, checking one choice after each statement.

		Rarely	Some-times	Often
1.	When I am with someone I am aware of how they feel.			✓
2.	If I meet someone for the first time, I form an accurate picture of what they are like.		✓	
3.	I am able to make decisions easily.	✓		
4.	I am aware when someone is manipulating me.		✓	
5.	I can tell if someone is lying.		✓	
6.	I can tell if someone is giving me a true account of a situation.		✓	
7.	I get involved with others' problems.			✓
8.	I can see clearly why people have a problem with something.			✓
9.	I can change my plans easily if I get bad "vibes."		✓	
10.	I can stand up to dominating energy.	✓		
11.	I am able to know what I want.	✓		
12.	I can say no to someone.		✓	
13.	I can express myself easily.		✓	
14.	I trust myself to make decisions.	✓		
15.	I ask others for advice.			✓
16.	I conform to win approval.		✓	
17.	I take care of my body.		✓	
18.	I eat/drink/sleep to escape my feelings.		✓	
19.	I knew something was going to happen before it did.		✓	

		Rarely	Some-times	Often
20.	I think of people, and they call me the same day.	____	✔	____
21.	I sense things before they happen.	____	✔	____
22.	I have "vibes" but ignore them.	____	✔	____
23.	I am afraid of my intuition.	____	____	✔
24.	My life has lots of coincidences.	____	✔	____
25.	I believe I have a Higher Self watching over me.	____	____	✔

When you have completed the questionnaire, go back and look at your answers. Give yourself:

> 1 point for each "Rarely"
> 2 points for each "Sometimes"
> 3 points for each "Often"

If your score was 25–39:
You are not in the habit of reflecting on how people and situations affect you—this will change rapidly. As you open to your intuitive self, your sense of adventure and vitality will increase.

If your score was 40–59:
You are already quite tuned in to psychic energy, although you may not call it that. You may just consider yourself "hypersensitive." As you work with the tools on this pathway, you will experience an increasing sense of safety, guidance, and well-being.

If your score was 60–75:
You probably realize that your awareness is exceptionally developed, but you may not trust it completely. Your work with these tools will help you develop confidence as you fully integrate your psychic ability into your daily life. You will learn how to drive the car instead of push it.

A Journey Inward

In order to initiate psychic development, you need to tell your subconscious mind that you intend to be psychic. The best way to communicate this intention to the subconscious mind is through gentle repetitive suggestions.

The four necessary decisions you need to make and convey to your subconscious mind are that:

- you are *open* to psychic guidance,
- you will *expect* psychic guidance,
- you will *trust* psychic guidance, and
- you will *act* on psychic guidance.

BE OPEN TO PSYCHIC GUIDANCE

The first intention you must establish is, *"I am open to my intuition."* This sets up your frame of mind to be receptive. Intuition and psychic energy are subtle. You need to create a mind-set that allows for these subtle influences to enter your field of awareness. Ask yourself: Am I open to psychic feelings? Am I comfortable thinking of myself as psychic? Am I mentally flexible enough for psychic energy to influence my behavior?

An attitude of openness is the beginning of psychic development. Psychic energy and psychic feelings are repressed by a closed mind. If you are reading this, you are probably interested in psychic ability, but are you truly *open* to it occurring for you?

It is important to see yourself as a *naturally intuitive receiver* of psychic guidance. The truth is, you are presently being psychically influenced all the time. It happens when you are around strong-minded people. It happens when you think about someone, only to have them call the same day. It happens when you spontaneously change your plans for no reason and chance upon a very important discovery by doing so. It happens with every "coincidence" you experience. If you reflect on your own life, you may recall many events that were psychic, that you may have not acknowledged consciously. Therefore you can see how being open to psychic energy is positioning your mind to allow you to acknowledge psychic energy when it does occur rather than dismissing or minimizing its significance, as you may have done up until now.

Being open to your psychic ability is the first step on the psychic pathway. It is the beginning of what will make your experience different from that of the close-minded person. It is the shift that will allow your life to be assisted by psychic ability and by the divine assistance of angels, guides, teachers, and God.

EXPECT PSYCHIC GUIDANCE

The second step is even more bold, more intentional, than the first. Once you are open to psychic guidance, you must move on to expect it! This may seem presumptuous to the old conditioning of your mind, but if you realize that your soul is living in a psychic receiver, the instrument called your body, it makes perfect sense that you should expect psychic communication. You are designed to receive this communication. It's natural.

Imagine for a moment that your body is like a radio receiver. It is designed to pick up and relay psychic vibrations, just as a radio is designed to receive and relay sound vibrations. Being open to psychic ability

urning on the radio receiver. Expecting psychic communication is
ning the dial, the tuner, to a clear band of communication with
your Higher Self.

The dial that tunes this band of psychic guidance is your attention.
When you tune your attention to the realm of psychic activity, you can
expect to receive this relay. If a radio is turned off, it will not receive and
relay sounds that are being transmitted even though the sounds are always being sent. By being open, you turn your field of awareness "on" to
psychic energy. By expecting it, you tune your attention to a particular
band of psychic vibration called your Higher Self.

Ask yourself:

- How often do I check in with my intuition when faced with a decision?
- Do I expect my intuition will be available to me as I need it?
- When I do experience a psychic feeling, how do I react? Am I comfortable with it? Does it feel natural? Am I surprised? How does this
  feeling come across?

By making the decision to expect your Higher Self to guide you, you
are placing both your attention and your intention directly onto your
conscious station to your Higher Self. This shifts your orientation away
from the energy outside of yourself coming from other people or from appearances as the basis for your decisions and places it primarily on the
guidance coming from your Higher Self and your guides. By making this
shift, you become a person who responds to life, rather than one who
reacts to it. Expecting psychic guidance realigns you with your natural
heritage and affirms that you are a spiritual being directed and assisted by
God at all times.

TRUST PSYCHIC GUIDANCE

The third step on the psychic pathway is to *trust* what your Higher Self
conveys to you. This step may be harder for some people to take. You
may have a difficult time or struggle with your intuitive feelings because

these feelings may not be supported or confirmed by appearances or by your beliefs. Or you may not want to trust your psychic feelings because they are telling you something you may not want to hear.

For example, suppose you meet a new man or woman for the first time, and you are really attracted to him or her for reasons of appearance, personality, or charm. And suppose that in spite of your strong attraction to this person, your psychic feeling is *not* as enthusiastic and warns you to be careful, cautious, and to get more information before you open yourself to this new person.

What would you do, especially if you are lonely and want a new friend? Would you ignore your feelings and proceed ahead enthusiastically, wearing blinders? Or would you slow down your emotional enthusiasm and take more time getting to know this new person before you become attached?

I know that can be a difficult choice. People, especially sensitive people, are very easily carried away with their emotions. They make decisions based on first appearances or on a strong desire to see everything through rose-colored glasses. Being psychic requires that you refrain from jumping to conclusions before "checking in" with your Higher Self—and it means trusting your intuition, even when your desires and appearances urge you to do otherwise. It is the act of listening to the relay you have gone to the trouble of turning on.

Psychic guidance is God's gift to you. It is the collective voice of your Higher Self, your guides, your teachers, your angels, and the divine. To receive such a gift and have it work for you, you have to value it by listening. You have to accept that your intuition is there to help you, guide you, inspire you, protect you, teach you, lead you, and support you. It is a loving and beautiful force. But it is gentle. It will *not* override your free will or your emotions or manipulate you in any way. You have to listen to this influence and recognize that these psychic feelings, although inconvenient at times and frequently confusing, are a sacred counsel and should be not only trusted, but, even more, appreciated.

Walking the psychic pathway takes courage. It takes courage to let go of the egocentric viewpoint of appearances that says we are made up only of body and mind, that our worth is measured by our acquisitions, that we must fight and fear other people and strive to gain power over others. To walk the psychic pathway means to trust in yourself, in your psychic ability, in the counsel of God's helpers, to strive in every way to recognize that your soul is a true essence, and to see the soul in everyone you encounter.

To lead the psychic life takes courage to stand apart from the majority and to direct your life from within, focused on your inner counsel. It means taking risks and being patient as things unfold. It means making the decision to put your trust in the spiritual direction you receive.

Reflect on your own past psychic experiences and ask yourself:

- Did these feelings turn out to be accurate?
- Did this psychic feeling help me?
- Did I trust it? If not, what did I trust?
- Would I have been better off had I trusted my intuition? How?

For all the years I have been teaching psychic development, and for all the years I have lived on the psychic path, I have never known intuition to have harmed me or anyone else. True intuition, the natural voice of the Higher Self, seeks only to assist you in your growth. Most people acknowledge, in hindsight, the unhappy consequences of ignoring their intuition, but when they do trust it, it almost invariably is to their advantage.

Psychic feelings sometimes make us aware of our own shortcomings, and this recognition enables us to do something about them. Psychic ability supports your growth, but not at the expense of other people. Psychic guidance seeks only to return you to your divine heritage. Psychic ability can be trusted to guide you and help you in every way to express your creativity, but it won't be there to manipulate others on your behalf. So, in being willing to trust your intuition, you must also be willing to give up wrong beliefs or erroneous conclusions. You must be spontaneous and flexible and be willing to redirect yourself midstream if your Higher Self suggests that you do so. Trusting your psychic voice will change the way you are in the world. It requires that you be willing to stop, change, redirect, or even abandon a plan completely if your intuition suggests it, without letting your ego get flustered about it.

If you were on an expedition in a foreign land, didn't know the terrain very well, and had a limited time to achieve your goal, would you welcome an expert if he or she unexpectedly volunteered to show you the best and most beautiful way to explore the territory? Or would you reject the guidance, stick to the map, and fumble on? Either way would be okay, but the guided tour would be a lot easier, more fun, and more enlightening.

You are given that kind of opportunity when you choose to trust your intuition. And your experience in trusting this guidance will verify for you that it is indeed trustworthy! The final decision you must make and convey to your subconscious mind is that you are willing to *act* on it.

ACT ON PSYCHIC GUIDANCE

Acting on your psychic feelings is the leap of faith that will propel you forward into the world of the extraordinary. Every time you make a decision to act on your intuition, you are telling your subconscious mind that you are serious about your psychic faculties, and you are telling your Higher Self that you trust and value its counsel. You are affirming to your guides and teachers that you will incorporate their guidance into your affairs. But above all, you release yourself from living your life through the limited power of your ego and place the power of your life into the hands of your soul and into the hands of God.

Acting on your intuition is an act of surrender on the part of your ego—not an unreasonable or foolish resignation, but a conscious and wise leap into the counsel of an infinitely higher form of reason than that of your limited personal awareness. Acting on your intuition is making the choice to allow your life to be directed from a divine source, as opposed to being directed by your small, fearful ego.

Choosing to act on your intuition in no way relieves you of the responsibility of doing your work in life. I must stress that psychic energy will not be available to those who are manipulative. Avoiding responsibility is a form of manipulation. Rather, you must continue to focus and concentrate as hard as ever on any goal you may be working on, but the reward of this effort is that psychic ability becomes an added assist with which to move you toward your goals. Psychic ability, the Higher Self, becomes a partner to your reason, leading you to faster, more efficient ways to achieve what you set out to do.

Choosing to act on your intuition is the final shift into being in the world differently. It is the necessary step toward setting up an extraordinary life. Going back to the analogy of the radio receiver, when you are open to it, you turn on your receiver. When you expect it, you place your attention like a tuner onto the band of energy called your Higher Self. When you trust it, you pay attention and value the psychic guidance being relayed. You "listen," if you will, to the music. When you act on it, what happens is like what happens when you listen to beautiful music coming from a radio. You find yourself moved by it, and you allow yourself to express it. You begin to dance.

Acting on psychic energy is dancing the "dance of soul." Your life becomes a spontaneous flow of movement, carried by the beauty of the transmission. It becomes a life where you are carried from moment to moment with a conscious awareness of the spiritual vibration of divine energy. Life is free of self-consciousness, anxiety, and fear. A life lived on the psychic pathway is a life lived in peace and inner security.

WHERE PSYCHIC ENERGY COMES FROM

It is easier to train your senses to notice your intuitive impulses if you have an understanding of where those intuitive flashes originate. In every psychic development class I teach, I ask the students where they think psychic or intuitive feelings and impulses begin. Some answer, "From my subconscious mind." Others say, "From my Higher Self." Some believe, "It's dead people talking to you," or, "Your guides."

If you are going to convince your mind to listen to your intuitive feelings, your mind has to value those feelings. Your mind requires an acceptable reason to value psychic feelings. The best way to convince your mind to pay attention to these feelings is to introduce it to where these feelings come from. After all, there is a big difference between listening to Joe Nobody's opinion on something and listening to a highly knowledgeable expert. Whom would you listen to?

Ask yourself:

- Where do I think my psychic information comes from?
- Why should I listen?
- Do I think it's trustworthy? Do I think it comes from a helpful and knowledgeable source?
- Am I comfortable tuning in to it?

It's important to ask these questions. The good news is, the answers are very specific and enlightening.

Actually, psychic energy comes from various sources. Our conscious minds have been trained to focus on one broadcast on our sensory radio—the broadcast of our five-physical-sense relay. But there are other relays broadcasting that we can, and spontaneously do, tune in to now and again, which give us our psychic information.

The first of these psychic relays comes from our own *subconscious* minds. Our subconscious minds are like giant computers taking in thousands of bits of information every day, information that slips past our conscious attention yet nevertheless is perceived and saved for a future moment. Every detail of every experience that we've had since the beginning of our lives, and in our past lives as well, is stored here and held unless released spontaneously by some necessity. It would be overwhelming for our conscious minds to process every detail of every event, so the mind allows unneeded information to slip unnoticed into this huge storage library. But if the subconscious is jogged by need, or by visualization or relaxation, the subconscious will release back to the conscious mind necessary and helpful information.

An extreme example of this is in the case of an accident or crime witness. The events witnessed may have occurred too quickly or have become clouded over by the attendant wave emotions of surprise or shock, and the details were lost. But if this same person were to relax through hypnosis, his or her recollection would become nearly perfect because the subconscious memory can be accessed.

This also occurs in everyday events. Perhaps you have been mulling over a problem for weeks, coming to no specific solution. Then suddenly, when daydreaming during another task—watering the lawn, taking a long drive—a solution will pop into your head. This relaxed frame of mind is a *receptive* frame of mind, and in this receptive state your subconscious can scan its stored information for possible solutions. If it does find one—"Eureka!"—you'll have a psychic flash.

This type of psychic experience happens most often in your work, or in an area that you've spent a great deal of time learning or reading about, or in an area of natural interest. The fact is, you may have acquired bits and pieces of useful knowledge along the way, information that would provide an answer or solution. Your subconscious mind can take in and rearrange these bits and pieces and create new and significant relationships among these bits of understanding. The solution lies in finding new relationships to old information.

All this occurs below your conscious awareness. Can you believe that your subconscious mind not only records your experiences perfectly, but can also combine different records, thus creating solutions that couldn't be found just in examining the pieces? Yet it does, naturally. Through proper training, you can develop a far greater access to this stored information than you ever believed possible.

The second type of psychic experience is with *telepathic* connections to others. How many times in your life have you found yourself humming a tune silently in your head, only to have someone next to you start singing the same tune out loud? How many times have you been thinking about someone and had them call within a short time? How many times have you taken up a new interest, like skiing, cooking, or sewing, only to find people with the same newfound interest popping up all around you? Psychic? Yes—*telepathic!*

We are all silent radio stations, broadcasting our own tunes, and even though we are not conscious of it, we do like to harmonize with one another. We gravitate naturally toward people playing "our tune," and together we amplify our broadcast. One of my spiritual teachers once told me that we are always telepathically tuning in with many, many others—up to six thousand people at any given time—even though it is usually not conscious. It sounds incredible, but this is what creates mass consciousness. Groups of people band together and "group think" about things: pro-lifers, animal rights activists, rebels, and fundamentalists, to name a few. People think in blocks all around the world, and these blocks of mental energy float and move in space, influencing political ideas, religious beliefs, and social and moral values.

Telepathic connections can be useful and amusing, as in the case of the telephone call from the old friend you were concentrating on. If you are lazy and undiscerning about your thoughts, however, you can become a psychic garbage pail, in which all sorts of negative or mass beliefs settle and take over your mind. An example of this is the telepathically relayed belief that cities are now extremely dangerous and suburban areas are safer. Many people telepathically accept this belief as fact. In reality, some aspects of city living are dangerous, and some are vitalizing and marvelous. The fact is also that many suburban areas are riddled with dangerous people, and one is not really in any more or less danger in one area versus another. Safety is governed by awareness more than geography. If you are susceptible to negative mass beliefs, you will overcome this problem when you begin your psychic development. You cannot be psychic if you are mentally lazy.

You'll need to snap out of your dreamy state and *be here now*. If you have a sharp focus to your mind, telepathy will automatically become more specific, filtering away unnecessary and unconsciously unexamined "group thought," and will attract only what is helpful to your focus. One way to do this is to set goals so that you will focus your attention and eliminate mass thought influences. Setting goals keeps you free of collective negative emotion and attracts telepathic support. As part of our work on this pathway, we will be working to set and refine your goals.

The third and most interesting source of psychic energy is from the *superconscious* plane of energy. Every one of us has, as our spiritual birthright, access to a Higher Source of knowing and loving guidance.

This Higher Source is actually composed of several distinct levels of spiritual guidance. These types of psychic impulses influence your future and the present choices you make that will set up your future.

This level of psychic guidance influences your perspective and helps you look at your choices from a new point of view. These kinds of communications are felt as warnings, urgings, new ideas, inspirations, breakthroughs in understanding, desires to redirect your life, a need to stop or let go of what you are doing, or a need to commit or go forward with what you are hesitant about.

Remember, these types of psychic experiences are loving but not flattering to your ego; stable, consistent, and unwavering but not coercive; subtle but distinct. They will always leave you feeling reassured, relaxed, and certain of yourself, in spite of appearances, if you listen and pay attention. Additionally, these types of psychic feelings help you with questions in love and relationships, health and well-being, and creativity and purpose in life and above all will help you find inner security and spiritual peace of mind.

Let's face facts. Your conscious mind will be more amenable to listening to these impulses if it is given a reason to listen. After all, your conscious mind would like to consider itself reasonable. If it accepts and understands the reasonability of listening to your intuition, it will do so far more easily. You would not ignore the advice of an expert if you were building a house, would you? Especially if the advice were free? And painless?

It is just as foolish to ignore the assistance of your psychic guidance as you build your life, especially knowing that your psychic sense is offering you a solution from your subconscious mind, from a telepathic relay, or from the loving guidance of your superconscious. The psychic experience comprises all these sources of assistance.

Essentially what psychic development involves is becoming keenly aware of what is going on around and inside you, here and now. By tuning in to your little psychic impulses, you will notice what you heretofore may have ignored. Once you make this realization, you can begin your development.

Have you ever had a hearing test? If so, do you recall (when wearing the headphones) that all your senses perked up to hear the barely audible beep that sounded for but a split second? Or an eye test, where you wore a patch first over one eye, then over the other, while scanning a screen for a teeny blip of light moving over the area? These exams are designed to test your ear and eye sense acuity. The more acute, the more subtle the beep or flash you noticed.

Psychic development requires the same acuity. Relax and enjoy, notice impulses you otherwise overlooked. Don't worry that you are imagining things. You aren't. You are just redefining your sphere of awareness and allowing it more room to play.

Once you understand where your intuition and psychic feelings come from, you need to learn how to gain freer and easier access to these channels of the subconscious, telepathic, and superconscious broadcasts, so that they are available when you need them. That is the purpose of this book.

Getting Ready

Always remember that psychic awareness ultimately means trusting in your own experience. As you enter this process, I am here to serve as your guide. Don't trust me—trust your experience. You will be working with my tools, but in time they will become your own to refine and expand.

Although the psychic pathway is a spiritual practice, for many people it is best to approach it scientifically. For this reason, I do not ask you to *believe* anything. I ask you only to experiment and chart your progress. The results will speak for themselves, and you will have a chance to draw your own conclusions.

During this journey you will be working with two basic tools. The first of these is meditation. Many of you may have an aversion to the very word. What people don't understand is that there are many different forms of meditation. You will be asked to practice a very simple form, essentially a daily fifteen-minute break.

Once you prepare yourself to receive psychic guidance, the next step is to clear away unwanted noise or distractions in your mind so you can hear your Higher Self when it does communicate. The noise or chatter constantly going on in your mind makes it difficult to hear your inner voice. The Higher Self is very subtle and does not intrude or overwhelm your mind's dialogue. You must quiet your mind's chatter and listen for your Higher Self if you want to hear it, and the way to do this is to teach yourself to meditate.

Learning to meditate sharpens your awareness, increases your concentration, and assists in shutting off mind chatter, the endless drone of voices that run through your brain. You will slowly learn to become more aware of the voice of guidance within. Meditation will also sharpen your awareness. Being psychic means paying attention far more keenly to the world around you, and meditation will help you.

HOW TO MEDITATE

Meditation is quite simply the art of relaxing your body and quieting your mind. Meditation is a learned skill. Training your mind to be still is like training a puppy to sit. The mind likes to jump around and needs to be told many times in a firm but friendly tone to sit still. Meditation is learning to hold your attention on one thing, to the exclusion of all else, for about fifteen minutes. This breaks mental patterns of vibrations, opens up awareness, and allows the soul to speak to you.

You begin by concentrating your awareness on your breath. Start by taking in a slow, deep breath right now. Notice how much your awareness expands simply by taking in a large, deep breath and then exhaling. This simple act seems to stretch the boundaries of your world a little farther, giving you room. Exhale to the count of four. Hold to the count of four. Inhale to the count of four. Continue this until a comfortable, slow pace is established. I find listening to music, and especially to Baroque music, extremely helpful when learning to meditate. Its slow tempo is compatible with the breathing exercise I just discussed, and you can establish a naturally relaxing pattern with the music.

Fifteen minutes a day of closing your eyes and clearing your mind is all that you will need to expand your awareness. All of you know your own life patterns, and you should place this break where it occurs naturally in your life. For some of you, this will be after the kids are off in the morning; for others, a break at lunch hour at the office; for still others, the fifteen minutes before bed. You will know best.

You may need to change some of your habits in order to make a place for meditation. This may mean forgoing the fifteen-minute conversation with a friend on the phone, folding the laundry at night, or watching the ten o'clock news. Experiment to find the time that works for you.

When you stop to meditate, tell yourself this is your time to recharge your battery. It is a time to remember that you are a spiritual being. It is a time to rest your emotions and your mind and to feel the divine presence of God. It is not a time to receive specific guidance from the spiritual plane. Instead it is a time to train your awareness to check in with the spiritual plane, a time to relax, refresh, renew. It is a time to stop the drone of worry, of other people's voices, of doubt, fear, or meaningless mental chatter, and to enjoy the quiet calm of silence.

Meditation is the foundation of psychic ability. Without it you will not be able to train your awareness to expand. It is indispensable. Most of my beginning students say they can't—or don't—meditate because they don't feel they are doing it right.

Personally I think people make it too hard. Meditation is tricky because it is so simple. We expect valuable experiences to be a lot of work. Meditation requires discipline and concentration, but it isn't complex. Quite the opposite, in fact. It's very simple.

All you must do is sit in a comfortable chair, place your feet on the floor, and put your hands in your lap. Close your eyes and inhale deeply. Then slowly exhale. After a few deep breaths, allow your breathing to slip into an even rhythm. Let your head rest in a comfortable position or against the back of your chair.

Concentrate all your thoughts on one idea. You can say, "I am at peace," over and over, or, "I am still," "I am relaxed," or any other simple repetitive mantra.

In the beginning, your mind will wander. But when it does, gently direct it back to the relaxing exercise. Don't be impatient. Don't expect to blank out, lose consciousness, or have some mind-altering experience. Just expect to relax and think of nothing but relaxing and being quiet for fifteen minutes.

If you are having a hard time meditating, allow yourself to close your eyes and listen quietly to a piece of classical music instead, preferably Handel, Vivaldi, Pachelbel, Telemann, or Bach. These are Baroque composers, and their music is particularly calming to the mind. Concentrate on your breathing, keeping it even and slow during this time. There are also many pieces of meditation music available, sold as New Age or meditation music. I enjoy both synthesizer and classical music when meditating. Choose what appeals to you. Pick what matches your mood. You don't have to use the same selection all the time. Entice yourself.

The important thing is that you not skip this very important part of your psychic training. During this time you are shutting out the outside world and connecting your awareness to your Higher Self. You are turning off the distracting chatter of the mind, and you are going into a restorative, listening mode attuned to your Higher Self. There is no way you will be able to develop psychic ability if you don't do this.

You must see the absolute necessity of and benefits to this practice so you won't push it aside. Be practical. Find a time each day that will accommodate this short break. Find a quiet place. It is as easy as it is important to you. For me, it's like breathing. I couldn't live without this time.

You may have to overcome some stubborn leftover conditioning that says self-care is selfish. That's ridiculous. Self-care is loving. It will help you heal, open up, and become loving to others instead of being needy and manipulative. Self-care is wise, and the self-care of fifteen minutes of meditation will be what ensures your breakthrough in psychic awareness.

You may also have to overcome the belief that if you stop for a moment, everything you are doing will unravel. This, too, is an illusion. A few moments of daily meditation will actually increase both your energy and your efficiency.

That's it. That's all it requires. Now try it.

The greatest benefit to training yourself to shut off your mind chatter through meditation is that you slowly learn to turn your awareness inward and listen for the voice of your Higher Self. You will come to enjoy the relief you get from the endless drone of voices in your brain. After meditating you learn to distinguish the voice of your Higher Self from other voices in your mind. The voice of intuition is subtle and very calming. The other voices are loud and inconsistent!

After meditating every day for a week, you should be able to feel the benefits and will look forward to the quiet time in your day. Another thing you will become aware of is that your awareness is getting sharper. You should begin to notice the world in a much more specific way than before. In my psychic development class I teach that psychic awareness is a heightened awareness of the here and now, not a vague awareness of some nonspecific future.

This brings us to our second tool, recording.

KEEPING A PSYCHIC JOURNAL

Many times throughout this book I will ask you to explore your beliefs and attitudes with journalizing, games, and exercises. The first thing you'll need is a small, portable notebook. Carry this journal with you everywhere, and record all psychic activity as it occurs. This includes all impressions, impulses, and what you might call coincidence. Do not censor, edit, or dismiss anything. *Everything counts.* (Also, the phrase *as it occurs* is very important. Most of us tend to forget or ignore our psychic impressions.)

It is essential in developing psychic ability to become aware of your natural psychic activity occurring now. Don't worry if you can't recall any psychic experiences. Simply be willing to notice and write down any and all unusual, weird, funny, bizarre, coincidental, surprising, odd—indeed, *psychic*—occurrences over the next few days. You are probably so in the habit of ignoring or denying these occurrences that you actually block them out. What you need to do at this time is take a fresh and open look at what goes on around and inside you and pay attention to every little thing.

Additionally, remember and write down any past psychic experiences you can recall. Don't censor or disqualify certain ones because you don't feel they are important enough. Every single psychic impulse, however trivial, counts. Remember as many as you can. Write over several days as certain psychic memories return. Try to discern which of these experiences were from:

- your subconscious storehouse,
- a telepathic connection, or
- a higher plane of assistance.

Trust your feelings as you try to discern the differences among various types of psychic activity.

This type of concentration and focusing is new to you, so be patient and allow yourself to muse over the different experiences. Do not force yourself to find the right answer. Let it be *fun* to notice these psychic impulses. They have been occurring all along in your life, just below your present level of awareness. By recording your experiences, you are gently beginning to expand and broaden your level of awareness.

By recording in your psychic journal what occurs in your life over a period of days, you can begin to see how many times intuition pops up and struggles with other influences as it tries to sound off. By doing this, you will become conscious of the times and ways you stop yourself from really benefiting from the guidance of your Higher Self.

Last, I will ask you to chart your progress each week by reflecting on your explorations and answering the questions at the end of each chapter. In doing this you will be able to report your successes, note any difficulties, and integrate your intuition solidly into your awareness.

At times you will be asked the same questions over and over. What is exciting is to see how the answers change from week to week. This journal will become your greatest cheerleader, as your own documented experiences serve as proof that you are moving ahead on the psychic pathway.

EXPLORATIONS

Reflection on being psychic will change your life. As you keep a daily journal of feelings and thoughts, and even conversations you have about psychic development, you will study your deeply rooted feelings and beliefs about being psychic. Are they supportive? Or do they need to be changed? In what way? The answers will become clear to you in the following quizzes.

Reflections

Before we go forward, let's explore your past to find what hidden beliefs influence your psychic receptivity. Do not overthink on this exercise. Reflect on these questions and answer as honestly as you can.

What does being psychic mean to you? _Knowing Things w/out having a reason, my grandmother, future, tarot,_

Was your mother psychic? Or intuitive? _Could be intuitive — Grandmother_

Did your father get hunches or "gut feelings"? _don't know_

Could you openly discuss intuitive feelings in your home and be taken seriously? _– No –_

As a kid, could you freely share your feelings about people with your parents? _Not so much_

What did your religious training teach you about people who were psychic? _____ — not in keeping w/ God _____

_____

Why do you want to be psychic today? _I'd like to_

be able to trust my own counsel - and
know what it was

Where would you apply this ability in your life? _relationships —_

work

Do you carry any fears about sharing your intuitions with others? _____

Seeming silly _____

Psychic Heebie-Jeebies

Many people carry very negative images and ideas about psychics that interfere with their natural development. Make a list of your worst fears about psychics.

Psychics are _will know only "bad" things_ .

Psychics are_____.

Psychics are_____.

Psychics are_____.

Psychics are_____.

The General Consensus

Do not be surprised if your list looks pretty frightening. Among the common negative beliefs I've encountered in my life as a psychic are notions such as these:

Psychics are fakes.
Psychics are Gypsy scam artists.
Psychics are scary.
Psychics are mind-readers.
Psychics are delusional, unstable human beings.
Psychics are weird.
Psychics put curses on you that are very expensive to lift!

The Surprising Truth

What you will come to discover as you walk the psychic pathway is that being psychic can be:

helpful	inspirational	protecting
safe	healing	prosperous
kind	creative	balanced
spiritually affirming	practical	fun

The Reward

List some areas where being psychic can make your life easier.

Being psychic will help me _Know what my own counsel is – connected w/ The universe._

Soul-Searching

Do you see yourself as a soul? _____ yes _____

How do you feel about seeing yourself as a soul? _____ The spiritual
part - interesting _____

If not, what do you see yourself as? _____

Truth (No Consequences)

Answer the following questions as honestly and as definitely as
you can.

What keeps you from trusting your intuition? _____ I feel it's
often wrong _____

What do you believe will happen if you do trust your intuition? _____
make big mistakes. _____

Does your intuition come to your attention when facing a decision? _____
I don't feel its reliable _____

Does your intuition come to your attention at all? _____
I can't tell what my
intuition is — _____

Do you feel comfortable telling people about your psychic feelings? If yes, why? If no, why not? _____

No - I don't feel they are

reliable

_____

If yes, how do people respond to your intuition? If no, what kind of response do you think you'll receive if you let people know what your intuition tells you? _____

_____

_____

_____

Do you like the word *psychic*? What kinds of feelings does this word evoke in you? _OK - sounds a little more_

supernatural than intuitive

_____

Do you listen to other people's intuition? _depends_

on the person

On a scale from one to ten, how important would you rank your intuition when dealing with issues in your life? _3_

_____

What is number one in terms of influencing your behavior?_____

_____

When faced with a problem, what is the first thing you do?_____

Try to think it out rationally

_____

Do you try to solve problems by yourself, or do you take them to another
authority?_ _both –_

_____

If you go to someone else, who is it? Husband? Wife? Boss? Friend? Therapist? Clergyman? Whoever is there at the time?_ _Friend_

Susan, Jerry

_____

Why do you go to these people for help? Are they helpful?_____

Insightful

Do you agree with their opinions?_ _often not_

_always – They often have a different
way of perceiving things_

Do you feel relaxed taking a problem elsewhere, or do you feel it makes
matters worse?_____

depends on the problem.

What kind of religious training have you had? _____

_____Catholic –_____

_____Buddhist_____

Are your spiritual beliefs fixed, or are they changing? _____

_____changing_____

How do you feel about this? _____

_____fine_____

_____

_____

CHARTING YOUR PROGRESS

Continue to reflect on the above explorations over the period of this entire week. Review them every day and see if the answers change depending on circumstances. Then answer the following questions.

How many days this week did you meditate? If not every day, what kept you from it? _____3/4____getting up early for work_____

_____

_____

_____

How many days this week did you make entries in your psychic journal?
What was your favorite entry?_____

_____

_____

If you didn't make any entries, what kept you from it?_____

_____

Clearing the Path

If it is natural and beneficial to become psychic and more spiritually aware, why aren't more people psychic now? This is a question I pose to people in my psychic development workshops. The answer is, quite simply, people are blocked.

I call anything impeding your psychic and spiritual awareness a *block,* because that's what it is. Over the years I've really watched and studied the various psychic blocks, and I find they can be narrowed down to two categories: blocks from the past and blocks in the present. Let's start with the most obvious blocks, then zero in on the more insidious and hidden ones.

THE RELIGIOUS TRAINING BLOCK

The first and most unconsciously pervasive block from the past is what I term the religious training block. Many of us have been raised to believe in a powerful authoritarian God and to respect the "powers that be." This message often also implies that we are fundamentally flawed and untrustworthy beings, that we should seek our authority outside ourselves.

It follows naturally that the block that comes from such a conservative religious and ethical orientation creates an unconscious anxiety about trusting yourself. At its most toxic level, we are taught to believe that psychic ability is the work of the devil or his maleficent forces. In its more subtle form, we are taught that the autonomy that psychic abilities confer is somehow immoral. (This despite the fact that Jesus Christ himself said, "Don't you know that ye are gods?")

Growing up in a religious school system, I endured much of this kind of disapproval and discrimination. I felt it necessary to go underground with my own psychic abilities as early as the age of eight or nine. The sad fact is, the world is full of many fearful souls who are most comfortable being led by outer spiritual authorities, who do not really understand what psychic energy is, and who therefore categorize it as a wholly unsavory and unspiritual activity. Fortunately, I had strong affirmation outside the church.

I have had the benefit of three great teachers in my life. The first was my mother, who established the framework and gave me permission to delve freely into the realm of spirit. The second was Charlie Goodman, a gifted psychic who taught me how to discipline my mind and fine-tune my sensory awareness so that I could receive psychic energy. From ages twelve to fifteen I apprenticed with Charlie, who taught me the skills of clairvoyance, clairaudience, and psychometry, as well as how to do psychic readings.

The third, and perhaps the most transformational in many ways, was a man named Dr. Trenton Tully.

Dr. Tully was the director and primary teacher of an organization called the Metaphysical Research Society, consisting of about thirty-five men and women dedicated to the study of ancient mystical texts, the Dead Sea scrolls, the Kabala, numerology, astrology, and the mystical meaning of the tarot. The MRS was also affiliated with an ancient worldwide organization called the Brotherhood of the White Light, a group dedicated to the study and practice of spiritual consciousness and to the goal of ushering in a higher degree of love and balance for the planet.

I was first introduced to Dr. Tully when I was sixteen by a man named Pat Adamson, a good friend of our next-door neighbor. Pat was in his early twenties and deeply dedicated to the study of spiritual matters.

He often came over to talk with my mother. At least twice a week after I came home from high school, the three of us would sit at our kitchen table, drink coffee, and discuss metaphysics and religion with each other.

Pat was not a psychic, but I found him fascinating and knowledgeable and wanted very much to be like him. He often talked about reincarnation and was personally committed to the study of tarot.

When I asked him how I could learn more about these things, he said, "You can come with me to listen to one of my teachers, Dr. Tully. He's a brilliant guy, and I've learned a lot from him."

I arranged to have Pat take me to hear Dr. Tully speak the following Sunday.

The group operated out of an old mansion up high on a hill, in a central part of Denver where there was "old money." I had never been to such a beautiful home in my life. It's funny, but both of my teachers, Dr. Tully and Charlie, lived in mansions. I thought of Jesus's teaching: "There are many mansions in my father's house." I now knew of two.

This mansion was a spacious two-story structure with classical columns and grand ballroom–style windows. We had to walk up the stairs to the front door, a solid oak door with a brass knocker. I remember feeling *severely* underdressed as we approached. We knocked, and a short woman who looked like Aunt Bee on *The Andy Griffith Show* answered the door, opening it up just a crack.

"Hello, Virginia," said Pat. "I brought a friend." She mouthed the word *hello,* but no sound came forward as she opened the door and let us in.

As we entered, the sweet smell of fragrant incense wafted to my nostrils. We were in a foyer facing a grand oak staircase. At the very back wall was a marble fireplace with elaborate brass candlesticks on the mantel. In the corner was a stand full of printed transcripts of past lectures given by Dr. Tully. I surmised from the logos that the group had some affiliation with the Rosicrucian mystery school, an ancient sect of Gnostic Christians.

There was classical music playing in the background, and there were about a dozen people, all finely dressed, standing around whispering.

Apart from Pat and me, the average age of the group was about fifty. Everyone seemed to know one another, yet I didn't feel like an interloper. They were warm, and the atmosphere was serious but friendly.

I noticed everyone had a notebook. Pat explained that Tully was a teacher and we were sitting in on a class. People were starting to move toward a room on the far side of the foyer.

We crossed the foyer and walked into a much smaller room, with chairs lined up seven rows deep and a central aisle in the middle. In the front of the room was a small stage, and painted on the back wall of the stage in gold against a blue background was a twelve-pointed star. Toward the front of the stage on the left stood a huge brass Chinese gong, and to the right was a lectern with a glass of water on it.

The music stopped and there was silence. The Chinese gong was sounded, and a rich, deep tone filled the air and reverberated across the walls for several lingering seconds. When it was completely quiet and everyone was sitting up straight with eyes wide open, out walked a tall, elegant-looking man wearing a white robe and white slippers, with a golden rope belt wrapped several times around his waist. He was about six feet four, had very white skin, a full head of thick black hair, and a balanced, handsome face. It was hard to tell his age. I guessed him to be in his early fifties, but I couldn't be sure because his skin was so firm. Pat told me later that he was closer to seventy. It was hard to believe when looking at him.

He stood in the middle of the room, opened his arms and stretched them out, and with palms facing forward said, "Let us close our eyes and begin with a healing vibration."

We closed our eyes, and moments later Tully began to sound a mantra. It started as a light, quiet "Oooo," then proceeded to become the deepest, clearest, loudest, *longest* "Ooooommmm" that I had ever experienced. It pierced my brain. It penetrated every cell in my body. It commanded my full attention.

After holding the note for at least a minute, he stopped suddenly and paused. Again he spoke, in the most beautiful, rich voice.

"Great Ones, mighty masters of light, truth, and wisdom, open thou the way and the gate that lies between this temple and the hidden shambalas, that the light, truth, and wisdom of the Great Ones may be opened unto us. So mote it be." Then silence.

He had a powerful presence. His aura was radiant, almost like the sun glowing off his skin. He approached the lectern and opened up a book. "Let us continue with our studies."

He began to talk about psychic power as awareness and nothing else. He discussed at great length and in detail how we are being helped from the masters of light to raise our consciousness and attune our minds and bodies, so that we can receive this vibratory healing. He talked about the way the earth is shifting and how each of us must strive to increase the amount of light in our bodies.

Tully continued to teach for two hours, referring to the great teachers—Jesus and Buddha—and he often referred to the teachings in the Bible and their spiritual meaning and interpretation. He was focused, specific, and filled with metaphysical detail. I wished I had a notebook. I was completely entranced.

After two hours he said, "Let us finish for today. Everyone close your eyes, and we will do a closing meditation."

I closed my eyes. It felt good to shut off my sensory awareness for a minute. After a moment of silence, again he started to sound a mantra, first quietly, then much louder, until the tone was sinking clear into my bones.

It stopped. He spoke again. "Light is eternal. O Soul of the Cosmos, fill us, light the darkness of night. Go with us through all of life's journeys, help us to be one with the light. So mote it be. Thank you."

When I opened my eyes, he was gone. The music started again, gently drifting across the room.

The whole experience was deeply impacting for me! I just sat for a moment and didn't move. Slowly people were getting up and leaving the room. No one spoke. I turned and looked at Pat.

"He's a fabulous teacher," I whispered.

Pat just shook his head and said, "Yes, he's pretty amazing, isn't he?"

We got up and walked into the foyer. Virginia, the woman who looked like Aunt Bee, was saying soft good-byes to everyone. Tully never came forward. We said good-bye and left. It was obvious that Tully was a Gnostic scholar. I was greatly moved by his talk.

"Pat," I said as we walked down the front stairs, "can I come and listen to him, even if I'm not with you?"

"Sure. The society is open, but you must be introduced by someone the first time."

I was thrilled. There were no membership dues, no binding agreements.

Tully was a scholar, a healer, and a mystic. I went every Sunday and Tuesday with few exceptions until I left Denver. Then I continued to receive his written lectures until he died in 1992.

Through studies with Tully I learned about balance and the negative effects the energy of ignorant and fearful thinking has on the body. I was taught how to focus thought and to use thought to create physical conditions. It was very complementary to my work with Charlie. Tully discussed past lives, karma, and reincarnation in great detail. We were taught mantras for healing, balance, protection, and absorbing more light from the Higher Forces in the universe. We were taught over and over and over again to study and ultimately control emotions. We were taught not to judge anything, only study it. Tully said a thousand times, "Nothing is good or bad. Only thinking makes it so."

Awareness was everything in our study. We were taught to be aware of and study in great detail every situation we found ourselves involved with. We used both Jesus and Buddha as examples of spiritual mastery. We were told tales about the masters that were not commonly known. For example, we learned that men cast lots for Christ's robe before the crucifixion because they were seamless garments of India and very expensive; that Jesus's "lost years" between the ages of twelve and thirty-three were spent studying with the masters of India, Asia, and China.

I learned that the "fall of man" meant the loss of consciousness of man's divine self, and that reawakening to this truth was our mission. I also learned we are being assisted by Higher Beings, all over the world.

Tully traveled occasionally to discuss spiritual encounters with other master teachers around the world, from Finland to Findhorn to China and back. I am sure this is one of the reasons I developed, and still possess, a great passion for travel.

I spent over eighteen years taking classes or reading lectures given by Tully. I complemented much of what I learned with readings from other great metaphysical texts, some by the Rosicrucians, others by published authors of the Theosophical Society, such as Ann Besant and Madame Blavatsky. I read the Tibetan Book of the Dead, and whatever I could about the Dead Sea scrolls. My thirst for knowledge, spiritual knowledge, was insatiable, and Tully was another gift from God to me. He was an impersonal, nonmanipulative teacher. With him I never gave up freedom, free will, power to choose. He always said, "A real teacher sets the student free."

Because of my total involvement in learning about esoteric teachings, I used to feel indignant at the presumption that all religious orientation counter to psychic development was wrong, stupid, and paranoid. But I have matured and grown to understand the need behind the conventional, sweeping rejections of psychic ability by the church.

Unfortunately there *are* many manipulative and unscrupulous people posing as psychics in the world, con artists who cleverly take advantage of vulnerable people, manipulating them out of large sums of money and creating unnatural dependencies on the psychics for counsel. These people, to greater or lesser degrees, can seriously manipulate the minds and emotions of the weak.

I'd like to tell you another story from my own past that greatly influenced my life.

When I was sixteen years old, I was introduced to several psychics in Colorado who became aware of my abilities. One woman, Phyllis, a trance channeler, and a man, Howard, a psychic and astrologer, in particular took a very big interest in who I was and how I worked. They focused lots of attention on me, and being a teenager, I was impressed. I believed they knew better than I. I loved all their fussing over me, although my mom did not like or trust them. I dismissed her disapproval as jealousy and made myself available to Phyllis and Howard as much as possible.

Phyllis had a very dramatic personality and claimed she was frequently able to talk to spirits. Sometimes her attention drifted off in midsentence, tuning in to who-only-knew-what coming through. She lived alone, had no friends, and talked constantly about "them," or the beings from other planets who would be coming to get us at the end of the world. She seemed ominous, even slightly paranoid, yet fascinating, offbeat. And she appeared to be very kind and protective toward me.

Howard was a fiftyish, eccentric, professorial man who carried around his astrology ephemeris everywhere he went. He continually asked me questions about the outcome of various business schemes he was forever dreaming up, and when I gave him my thoughts he would say, "Just my feelings exactly," and smile.

After a few months with these two, however, what had struck me at first as fascinating and dramatic began to seem bizarre and overbearing. But I was young and immature; I wanted them to like me, and I continued to spend time with them even though I felt slightly trapped and uncomfortable.

One beautiful fall morning Phyllis called me, excited and breathless. The police had contacted her and wanted her to do some psychic detective work on an unsolved murder in Salida, Colorado.

She said, "This is your big chance at fame, Sonia. You must go with us. You can get lots of recognition for helping solve this case."

I said, "Great! Count on me," not thinking at all about the seriousness of the situation. I was a naive sixteen-year-old who obviously watched too much TV.

My mom was not at all in favor of my getting involved. She said, "Do this if you must, but this is not a game."

I wasn't listening. This was my big chance. Big chance for what, I wasn't sure, but I was convinced that Phyllis and Howard knew more about my destiny than I did, and I must be there.

In retrospect, it *was* my big chance, but not in the way they projected.

They picked me up the next morning, and we drove for what seemed like hours to a small mountain community just west of Red Rocks, Colorado. Eventually we wound back off the road and reached a hidden, lovely home, where two sheriffs and the family of the elderly couple who had been murdered stood on the porch.

I'll never forget the look on the faces of the family members. There was the son, around forty, the daughters in their thirties, and the sister of the murdered man. They all wore a shattered look of horror and grief, mixed with such hope in us that I was completely overwhelmed.

Seeing them, I felt suddenly ashamed that it had never even occurred to me to think about them, about their sorrow and loss, about their fear. For the first time in my life, I stopped to think that my psychic feelings might really influence people.

Before I had time to dwell on my feelings, Phyllis and Howard were shaking hands, introducing me, and asking the family to show us into the house where the murders had occurred. The two sheriffs walked in first, then Phyllis, Howard, and me, followed by the family—everything took on a slow-motion feeling inside me.

We entered the living room, where apparently the couple had been sleeping in front of the fireplace. There was the outline of the man's body drawn at the base of the fireplace in white chalk. Blood was splattered all over the fireplace, wall, and floor. Apparently he had been shot ten or fifteen times.

The woman had managed to get up and run to the basement stairs, where she was shot from behind, again many, many times. There was the outline of her body sprawled over four or five stairs leading down. Again blood was all over, with a particularly large stain of blood where her head would have been.

Never before had I witnessed such a horrible scene, and I was not at all prepared for the emotional impact it had on me. I was speechless. Not so Phyllis.

What followed seemed like a scene from a bad horror film. Phyllis was carrying a huge black purse with her, which she picked up and placed squarely in the middle of the room. She turned to the police and family and in her typical bizarre and dramatic manner told them that they must leave for a while so we could work.

I watched them file out one by one, then turned to her, feeling totally helpless and afraid. "Now what?"

Phyllis threw open her bag and pulled out a two-foot wooden crucifix, which she grabbed and held as she closed her eyes. Then she started to jerk and gyrate. Howard began to hum at this point, then chant some garbled words.

I stood there with my mouth open. All of this was just too much to process.

Then Phyllis started screaming intermittently, reciting the Lord's Prayer, then screaming again that the house was full of evil, evil, *evil* energy. Howard by now was wailing away at full volume, following Phyllis, who was stalking through the house with the crucifix, thrusting it out into the air randomly and screaming, "Out! Out! Get *out!*" to the evil spirits she was seeing.

All of a sudden she swung around, looked straight at me with crazed eyes, and said, "Oh, my God! The evil spirits here are taking over your body! You are too young! You are not protected! You are becoming possessed! Here! Take this black box! It has a crystal in it. You can pay me later! Take it or you will be possessed! Run! Run! *Run,* before they overtake you!" Then she started waving this crucifix all around me.

Needless to say, I was terrorized. Never had I been so frightened, so totally and completely lost in the bizarre. Clutching the box for dear life, I turned and ran out the door, past the sheriffs, past the family, down the driveway, and onto the mountain road. I ran and ran.

I had run for maybe twenty minutes when the sheriff drove alongside and stopped me.

"Get in," he said. "Are you all right? What the heck is going on?"

I couldn't even begin to explain. I was psychic, but what I had felt in that house was sorrow, grief—not evil spirits. I had experienced devastation, loss—not drama. The only evil in that house belonged to Phyllis. She and Howard were exploiting the vulnerability of the family in a most heinous way—I was shocked far beyond words.

"Can you get in?" the sheriff asked again.

I got in. I told him I was sorry I was of no help to the family, and I hoped I hadn't upset them more. (It would be years before I fully realized that I, too, had been exploited.) Shaking, I asked the sheriff to take me to the station, where my parents could pick me up.

When my mom arrived she didn't even ask what happened. I cried all the way home.

She finally said, "Sonia, being psychic is not enough. You must also be spiritually educated and spiritually ethical or you'll get into big trouble. You should have listened to *your* intuition, Sonia, instead of being motivated by flattery."

I look back at that event as my spiritual initiation. It had a deep impact on me and was a profound turning point in my life. I no longer was impressed with merely being psychic, with seeing visions of the future, with showing off, knowing who was on the phone when it rang or where to find a parking spot. More important, I was no longer impressed with know-it-all outside authorities. I had learned two things: first, the danger of ignoring my own inner voice and repressing my natural instincts; and second, that unscrupulous people—some posing as psychic authorities—do exist and do prey on vulnerable people.

This experience has stood me in good stead. Having been preyed upon personally has made me sympathetic to the protective guidance of traditional authority. It has also, however, made me wary of yielding personal authority to *any* outside authority.

Because unscrupulous people do exist, I understand why many churches have made it a matter of policy to disavow *all* psychic activity as deviltry. This oversimplification effectively eliminates the more difficult and complex task of specifically defining what is considered "good" psychic activity and what isn't. It is easier for them to take an overall approach and say, "Stay away, and let the clergy remain the authoritative voice of influence for the people." I can see their point. This kind of sweeping guideline is very good for those souls who haven't yet developed the spiritual good judgment and confidence to lead their lives safely.

Many people have advanced beyond this point yet have lingering doubts about their own motives and integrity. This subtle shadow is the cloud of negative religious conditioning.

I agree with conservative religious thought that it is unwise to naively place one's well-being into the hands of strangers, as some people do with storefront psychics. Developing your own ability to become aware of the spiritual guidance of your Higher Self is another matter entirely. This is what we are working on.

When you develop psychic ability, you will naturally overcome a vulnerability to manipulation by others, be they unscrupulous storefront psychics or less obviously manipulative people; your Higher Self will alert you to any lack of integrity on the part of people you deal with. Your Higher Self can then take over from outside spiritual teachers the responsibility of protecting you. I find that all people, if they genuinely want to, are competent to undertake guidance of their own spiritual journey. What it takes is a willingness to be responsible for your choices and decisions in life.

As you begin to awaken spiritually and look into the world more responsibly, you will wish to act rather than merely react to the world. You will develop a spiritual maturity that will allow you to have more confidence in your judgment and your intuition.

Another reason this block is so troublesome is that religious beliefs for most people are formed at a very young age. As children we were taught to follow the rules of older and wiser authorities—our parents, our teachers, our religious and political leaders. For a lot of people, starting to listen to your "inner counsel" over the voices in your head of past authorities stirs up a childish anxiety about being "bad," "naughty," or, worse, "sinful." This is what we are out to overcome.

Whatever religious training you may have had as a child may have been necessary for your development and protection at the time. Ideally it guided you to develop a balanced sense of right and wrong, helped develop conscience, and taught you how to respect others.

But as an adult, the restrictions imposed upon you as a child may be outgrown. It may be time to investigate a little more, spiritually and religiously. Conclusions drawn as a child will not necessarily serve you as an adult, especially if those conclusions are heavily based on shame, guilt, or the need to control. Intuition is the loving voice of God operating in your heart. As a person evolves and matures spiritually, he or she can become self-regulating rather than regulated from authorities outside.

If you have conflicts about religious beliefs versus personal intuition, the block can be overcome with an effort on your part to reopen the question of what is morally and spiritually appropriate—for you. As an adult, you have the right and opportunity to investigate and learn more and to draw conclusions not possible when you were a child. In developing your intuition, you actually take a huge step toward leading a sacred and blessed life. True psychic guidance is guidance for the good of all concerned, not just for you.

Read, ask questions, then turn the various ideas over to your soul and trust what rings true for you. Seek out more information. Clear understanding of psychic ability and a focused intention on your part to overcome your block will help dissolve it. And remember, this kind of block is indicative of your growth. If you weren't growing spiritually, you wouldn't be questioning the rules laid down for you as a child. Each person has his or her own unique spiritual style on the pathway of life.

If you reflect back on the teachings of all the greatest spiritual masters, you will recall, repeated over and over again, "The kingdom of Heaven is within." The still voice of God is the most *direct* personal affirmation of God's love in your life. Your experience will let you know if it is good and sacred.

All the great spiritual masters—Jesus, Buddha, Mohammed—became great because of their revolutionary teachings and beliefs. It is good to question all, for truth endures scrutiny very well.

THE UGLY DUCKLING BLOCK

Many of you are reading this book because you already know you are psychic and you don't find it very comfortable. You may sense things sooner than other people. You may read situations more accurately than other people. Your feelings often differ from the general consensus and prove to be accurate. This isn't comfortable for you, and it's often not comfortable for others. Their discomfort becomes your discomfort. It makes you feel self-conscious—like an ugly duckling.

Until you accept your psychic abilities, realizing they are in your best interest, you may feel burdened by being different. You are not so much "different" as you are more awake. Being psychic has far-reaching and deeply gratifying rewards, but it does carry along with it special problems and challenges. Let me again cite a personal example.

I once attended an opening at the Steppenwolf Theater in Chicago. There was a woman there who looked very familiar to me. I smiled and said, "You look very familiar." After I introduced myself, she asked me what I did.

"I'm a psychic," I said.

You'd have thought she was being electrocuted. Her whole face turned white, and she seemed to jolt, backing away from me. It was obvious not only to me, but to my husband and my sister, that she was frightened and repelled. My first impulse was that my feelings were hurt. It brought back many memories of my years as a teenager.

After I got out of school and left my "psychic" home, being psychic created challenges for me socially. For one thing, it definitely killed off my prospects for dating. Though I am tall and slender, with a nice-looking face, and even did some modeling over the years, I was rarely asked out. I'm sure it was because I told the men I met that I was psychic.

I learned the hard way that telling people that I was psychic or "a psychic" made them almost universally uncomfortable. Men generally either laughed, then ran—or just ran. Besides thinking of the "Gypsy rip-off" image, people often interpret psychic to mean "I have X-ray vision and I *know* who you are and I saw what you did and I'll use it against you."

No wonder people are uncomfortable. Their misconceptions are scary. To be psychic requires that you be willing to be different, to stand apart from others and live your life as a self-directed person. Most people in life fall into two camps—dominant and passive. Dominant people push passive people around. Passive people submit to dominant people. But there is another group, small but growing, that is balanced. That group seeks neither to control nor to be taken care of. People in that group are directed by creativity, work with love, and manipulate no one. To be psychic and spiritually aware puts you in that group.

It's important to recognize that psychic awareness is a gift, and that in order to receive this gift, you must agree to the accompanying responsibilities. For one, you must accept that psychic development is not something people in general share, agree upon, or even support—although fortunately that is changing.

In order to be psychic you must be willing to walk through the gateway to the psychic pathway and join this third group. This means walking out of the ordinary world and into an extraordinary world—but you must walk through the gate alone.

Once through, you'll find others like yourself, but on approaching it, you will definitely feel—and, indeed, be—alone. The words on the door into the world of the extraordinary are clearly marked: "Enter Only If Taking Responsibility for Yourself." To go through this door, you must surrender all false notions of worth and fully assimilate your true identity and your spiritual self.

When you approach the spiritual and psychic pathway, you will be met with tests. Unless you pass these tests, you will not be firmly on the path. You may have to pass the tests of:

- unpopularity (being psychic may cause you to go against the group consensus)
- ridicule (people mock what they fear or don't understand)
- rejection (some people will think you are simply weird)
- criticism (people criticize those who are different)
- lack of support (very few people support psychic feelings)
- being misunderstood (you often will be)

Let me tell you a story that happened to one of my students. Working with me, she had begun developing her psychic gifts to the point where she could give accurate and helpful readings. I encouraged her to follow this as part of her spiritual work.

"You have earned the gift of being able to do this," I told her. "Use it with people who take it seriously and treat you with respect."

All went well for a while. She read for a number of people, and enthusiasm grew for her work as people were being genuinely helped. Several women with unsolved medical problems were aided in finding proper care for their healing. In several cases she had seen uterine tumors that had heretofore been undiagnosed. Lives were saved, and in two cases infertility was cured. Needless to say, these women were grateful and respectful of my student's gifts and eager to tell the world about her ability.

So far so good, but this student belonged to a "close-knit" spiritual community centered around a progressive church. She was friendly with one of the ministers whom she thought was open minded. When the minister was enthusiastically informed of my student's intuitive activities, however, he reacted negatively and strongly suggested she stop. "I don't think you should try to be a guru. I have psychic abilities too," he said, "but I don't go around using them!"

My student was confused and thrown into self-doubt. Was she arrogant? Was she trying to play God? She stopped giving readings and fell into depression, feeling she had wandered somehow from her spiritual path. She lost all sense of being connected to God and to herself. People kept calling her for help, but she was very reluctant to read for them. Finally she called me for advice.

I advised her to look at reality. I said she had been met with misunderstanding and superstition, which is very common. I told her to ignore his reaction and stay true to her intuitions. "Remember the good you've done. Look at the people you've helped with your insights." That is the truth, and the truth holds its own in the universe. Learn to discern the difference between fear and truth. Don't let one opinion override the truth in its many manifestations. "There is nothing negative in using your intuition to help others when asked to do so. Simply be certain that your heart is in the right place, and know your limits!"

Although it took her several months, I am happy to say my student regained her sense of self and integrity and resumed her spiritual work to the benefit of hundreds of people. She had encountered one of the tests on the psychic pathway.

It is only reasonable to expect that there will be those who will make you, too, doubt your psychic integrity. Doubt goes with the territory. It is the watchdog against arrogance.

When you begin to use your intuition, you begin to exercise your personal power, and if people around you have been holding your power for you, plan on a little struggle from them before they give it back. Sometimes the people closest to you will be the most antagonistic when you begin relying on your intuition. This reflects their insecurity, not your ability.

On the other hand, don't invite drama into your life as you embrace your intuition. True intuition is subtle and graceful and will leave you secure if you listen. Don't try to convert anyone to your beliefs. Remember how hard it was for you to change. Let each one awaken at his or her own pace.

Using intuition allows you to operate in the world differently, but first you must decide to channel this energy effectively. Start off easily and in small ways. Then gradually, as your psychic experiences multiply, your mind will allow more psychic impulses into your awareness, making them more and more apparent to you.

Remember, the best way to overcome the ugly duckling block is to know that you are (perhaps secretly) a psychic swan. Attach your worth to your spiritual nature, not onto appearances or the opinion of others. Hold your own counsel. Don't advertise. Let your truth advertise for you.

THE INTELLECTUAL CENSOR BLOCK

Some people play psychic fireman with themselves. By this I mean that your mind may censor or disqualify many truly psychic experiences by determining them to be coincidences, chance, or luck and therefore not indications of true psychic ability.

The last time I asked the students in my class to describe a psychic experience, I was met at first with blank stares, and no one out of a group of twenty-five would dare to share with the others a personal psychic experience. Why? Because they were all busy disqualifying and minimizing all their wonderful events; they didn't consider them grand enough! After a little coaxing, a few people finally ventured forth.

One student, Eileen, started with, "This is probably not a psychic experience, but I was thinking about my old college boyfriend a few days ago and that same day I ran into him, after not seeing him for five years."

"Why isn't it a psychic experience?" I asked.

"Well, it wasn't any big deal," she replied.

"So?"

It doesn't have to be a big deal to have a psychic event. In fact, it *rarely* is a big deal. Psychic awareness is more often a series of unending "little deals" that make life easier and more magical.

Another student, Bob, said, "Well . . . I *don't* know if this is a psychic event, but at the last minute, before I went to work the other day, I decided to make a lunch instead of eating as usual in the work cafeteria. Strange, but I did. Turns out there was an outbreak of food poisoning in the cafeteria the same day. About twenty-five people got sick. But I brought my lunch that day. The first and only time I ever did that until then. Spared me a bellyache."

Why not call that a psychic event? What should Bob call it? Luck? Chance? Coincidence? When you begin to wake up to your soul, you become aware of just how much you are being guided and protected by Higher Planes at all times. Such guidance *is* psychic—it is a communication of the soul. Sometimes these soul communications will directly conflict with your reason. When they do, don't be surprised if the still, small voice speaks up loud and clear. In my case, it shouted.

Some years ago I had returned to school at the University of Denver after a two-year break, and I wanted to go to Paris as an exchange student. I made an appointment with the French department.

The person in charge, a Parisian named Mrs. Holz, was a short woman of about fifty who wore half glasses on a chain and had a curly red wig. She listened to my request for application as an exchange student, but upon reviewing my records, she said, "Absolutely not. You must apply one year in advance, and you must be a French major. You are a religion major, and the deadline was two weeks ago. I'm sorry. *Ce n'est pas possible!*"

I listened to her, heard her words, understood why she was saying what she was saying, but my intuition, my psychic feeling, was that this did not apply to me. "No" was not no. I left her office a little annoyed with the pleasure she took in sending me away. I could just hear her thinking, How dare she even think . . . ! Somehow I simply did not feel that what she said was the last word.

It was a beautiful day in April. Once again I was in a quandary. My psychic feeling absolutely told me that Paris was the next step. The grass on the campus was like a rolled-out emerald carpet. I walked to the middle of it, lay down, and closed my eyes. I could hear the voices of students drifting all around me, but I was lost in thought when right in my ear I heard a deep male voice that said, "Go to the dean!"

I opened my eyes to see who had sat down beside me. I fully expected to find two students sitting somewhere near my head. I was embarrassed to have been lying there. I looked around, but there was no one within a hundred yards of me in any direction—not one soul. Yet I had heard this beautiful, rich voice clearly say, "Go to the dean!" It was my spirit guide, a new one, and I hadn't heard any clairaudient voices in months. I smiled and said, "Thank you."

I got up and started walking. My heart was beating fast. I headed for the dean's office with no idea of whether the dean was a he or she, what this person was like, or whether this person would see me, but I had been told to go. That was enough for me.

When I arrived I was greeted by a surly secretary in the outer office. "Yes," she said, not looking up, "can I help you?"

"Yes, I would like to speak with the dean."

She winced. *"Everyone* would like to speak with the dean. Do you have an appointment?"

"No," I said. "Can I make one?"

After shuffling through a daily planner, she said reluctantly, "Yes, in two and a half weeks, on May sixth."

Two and a half weeks! It would surely be too late by then!

"Why not earlier?"

"Mr. Frank is leaving on vacation. He will be *out of town!*" She emphasized each word.

"Oh, I see." I paused. I didn't know what to do. I was searching for some sort of guidance from within.

Just then a nice-looking middle-aged man walked into the office and stopped at the desk. The secretary looked at him and smiled, which was quite a change of expression, but before she could speak he said, "Finish what you're doing. I'll wait."

"Well, young lady," she said to me, "would you like to schedule for May sixth? That is the *very earliest.*"

"I guess so. I just think it'll be too late. I had really wished he could talk to me sooner. This is so important." I was half talking to myself because I knew she wasn't listening.

"Can I help you, young lady?" the man said to me. "You look really let-down." I turned to him. "I'm Dean Frank," he said. "I'm on my way out the door for vacation, but if it won't take long, I can give you five minutes."

I couldn't believe it! I couldn't have arrived at a better moment. A few minutes later and I would have missed him. As fast as I could speak I told him my story. I had been a student, quit to be a flight attendant, lived in France, learned French, and now felt a French degree would be the right one for me, I was *sure* of it. Could he bend the rules, please? I told him the whole story in five minutes and was out of breath and panting by the time I finished.

He was quiet. After a minute he said, "What airline?"

"TWA."

"I like TWA. Let me think about it. My office will get back to you."

We shook hands and I left.

That was Friday. I spent a long quiet weekend and a restless Monday. On Tuesday Madame Holz called. Could I please come in immediately? Yes, *bien sûr,* I said. When I arrived she was waiting. Her jaw was tight, her expression grim. She definitely didn't like me.

"We've reviewed your case. Apparently there was more to it than we understood in the beginning. We have agreed to accept you to the program, and I was told to give you this package from the Financial Aid Department."

I opened it up. It was a full scholarship for the year. I wanted to scream for joy.

"Thank you," I said. "I'm very grateful."

She smiled. This time she meant it. I think even *she* felt my joy.

Joy is a landmark of the psychic pathway. One very important decision to make if an intellectual block is your problem is to lighten up, back off, take it easier, and see how *everything* counts that comes from spirit, however insignificant, every subtle magical twist in your day, every thought, every impulse, every notion. It's *all* psychic. None of the million and one various ways a soul expresses itself, from a whisper to a gusting wind, no impulse that comes from the soul should be disqualified. Not one!

Again, here is where your psychic journal comes in handy. Every time you have a psychic impulse or experience, write it down, even if you consider it ninety-nine percent imagination. Remember, psychic ability arises out of the imagination. It won't be long before you are forced to see just how frequently you are psychic and how accurately you are guided. It's an eye-opener!

Being on the psychic pathway is being in the world differently. It is being in the world, able to see beyond appearances and into the true relationship between you and your life's experiences. It is being receptive and aware of subtle guidance from God, from your Higher Self, from your guides. It is being conscious of making choices that further you on your spiritual path and ensure your deeper well-being. Intellectual blocks are mostly bad habits, inherited perceptions, and insecure disqualifications. They are usually cured through a sense of humor, of wonder, and of awareness. So if this is your block—laugh, lighten up, and *pay attention.*

It all counts!

EXPLORATIONS

Oh, My God!

Many of us were raised to believe in a God who was not very tolerant. Were you? Double-check by filling in the blanks below.

My childhood God was ___fearsome unforgiving –___

___personal___

_____.

What were you taught about God? By whom? Did you believe it? _____

___Catholic church – yes___

_____

Your beliefs may have evolved during the course of your life. Describe the God you believe in today. Or do you? _____ _____

___Divine Spirit –___

_____

Now describe the kind of God you would like to have. _____

___Divine Spirit – connected.___

___connection with, guided by –___

_____

_____

For All You Ugly Ducklings: The Times You Felt Like a Quack
Please list three people you knew better than to trust . . . and trusted anyway.

1. _Darryl_____

2. _T_____

3. _____

Please list three times you "knew" something and you didn't trust your intuition.

1. _____

_____

_____

2. _____

_____

_____

3. _____

_____

_____

Please list three times you distrusted your own intuition and trusted someone else instead.

1. _____

   _____

   _____

   _____

2. _____

   _____

   _____

   _____

3. _____

   _____

   _____

   _____

For All You Ugly Ducklings: The Times You Knew You Weren't a Quack
Please list three people you knew you could trust . . . and you were right.

1. _____

2. _____

3. _____

Please list three times you "knew that would happen" and acted accordingly.

1. _____

_____

_____

_____

2. _____

_____

_____

_____

3. _____

_____

_____

_____

Please list three times you trusted your intuition over someone else's opinion.

1. _____

_____

_____

2. _____

_____

_____

_____

3. _____

_____

_____

_____

For All You Rational Beings: Get Over It
Please fill in the blanks with some "coincidences" you've experienced.

It was probably just a coincidence, but __I was talking__
__about being in a suspended animation —__
__next day's sermon = missing years__ .

It was probably just luck that __I found the__
__two Jack London books in the closet__

_____ .

I'm sure it was my imagination, but __I asked for__
__The song — and it playing on The__
__radio__ .

It's a little weird, but I had just decided to _____ break a $20.00 _____

_____ when _____ I saw the lifesavers _____

_____ + bought 2 packs + Joyce asked _____.
for them

I've never had a *psychic* experience, but _____

_____

_____.

I was just thinking about _____

when _____.

I had this weird dream that _____ said "it's gonna happen _____

and then _____ I saw the same scene on TV _____
The next day _____.

I was looking for _____

when _____.

I had just heard about _____

when _____.

I had just said I'd like to _____

when _____.

CHARTING YOUR PROGRESS

Reflect on your experiences this week when answering these questions.

How many days this week did you meditate? Was it any easier? How did you feel afterward? _____

_____

_____

How many entries did you make in your journal this week? _____

What was the most difficult part in getting started? _____

_____

_____

What was the most surprising experience you had this week? __ ____

_____

_____

Tying Up Loose Ends

Now that we've taken action to clear away the past, let's look at where you find yourself today—if you *can* find yourself. For many of us, life is so chaotic and demanding that we lose our focus as we move through each day. This is a problem that is often reflected in our physical surroundings.

"Where did I put that scarf? I can't find my keys. Where are my gloves? What did I do with that report? Did you happen to see my notebook? Where's that novel I had last night? Who took the *TV Guide*? Where did you put my tennis shoes? What do you mean, they're under the bed? How did this place get so *messy?!*"

THE DISORGANIZATION BLOCK

The most concrete block to a person's intuition is having a disorganized life. Intuition or psychic ability is the ability of a person to perceive and be aware of subtle direction coming from his or her Higher Self. In order to perceive this guidance, you must have keen awareness. If you live in a constant state of disarray, with unfinished business, chances are you'll fail to perceive even the most obvious circumstances around you, let alone the more subtle, higher psychic influences.

If you are not organized, you won't be able to become consistently psychic. Psychic ability is a moment-to-moment relay between your conscious mind and your Higher Self. In order for that relay to occur, you have to be able to reflect on your present situation before acting. If too many responsibilities and demands are burying you alive, there will be no opportunity for reflection, as you will be too busy frantically holding everything together.

Organization is something that goes back to your intentions. Organization will follow true intentions, those objectives you really care about in your life. Organization is the by-product of clear intentions, and psychic guidance is the by-product of organization. Frantic, disorganized, dramatic people have very low levels of awareness. This kind of chaos creates an emotional anxiety that shuts down all intuitive ability.

A friend of mine, Mary, a Chicago public school teacher, had been procrastinating about cleaning her classroom. It had accumulated a whole year's worth of paper, old books, broken desks, and assorted debris. Feeling overwhelmed and ineffective, she finally decided to devote some serious effort to the project. For an entire weekend she stacked, moved, recycled, and donated the material she no longer needed. On Tuesday morning the following week, she was informed that her classroom was one of only a few to receive a grant for new books and desks for the following year.

You may call this coincidence. Dr. Carl Jung called this kind of event *synchronicity*. I call this psychic awareness in action. As Mary organized herself, she created a place to receive something new. As she organized and cleared her consciousness and her classroom, she created a space to be filled—and stimulated a flow of energy into her life that had not existed before.

Organization unclogs the drains in your life, the things that take your attention away from your Higher Self. How many of you, when faced with writing an important paper for college, found yourself cleaning and clearing your desk and calling it procrastination? That it might have been, but it was also an unconscious psychic preparation for guidance. How many of you, when facing an important presentation at work, find yourself cleaning the garage or scrubbing the kitchen floor? This, too, is psychic preparation—"As within, so without." As you free your attention from the distractions in your surroundings, you expand your awareness and sensitivity to your psychic ability exponentially.

To put it bluntly, disorganization is an energy leak. Look at your physical surroundings and notice whether they reflect order, balance, and organization. It is very important to have outside order to support your inner order. For most people this means doing a big purge, a spring cleaning, a letting go of the unnecessary.

Remember that everything in your life requires attention and energy. Are your attention and energy being drained away on vast accumulations of old, unnecessary, outdated, disorganized, useless stuff surrounding you? If so, realize that all the disorder in your life steals your awareness, your most precious commodity.

Remember that everybody places different degrees of sentimental importance on *stuff*. Even bearing this in mind, though, ask yourself how much of your stuff is truly reflective of some important life experience and how much is just junk accumulated thoughtlessly and for no purpose?

Realize that this is the time to recognize the importance of simplicity in your life and clear out of your life what really contributes nothing. My teacher, Dr. Tully, once said to me, "If you haven't used something in one year, chances are you never will."

Resolve that if you have something that no longer serves you, donate it back to the universe, where it can benefit another soul and continue to do some good. All spiritual masters live simply. I don't mean you need to live as austerely as they—only that you need to keep out the unnecessary or useless so it won't clog up your awareness.

In my case, the hardest part of my psychic and spiritual development was getting physically grounded and organized. I was like an antenna in an electrical storm without a grounding post. The greatest difficulty for me was to admit that all the psychic activity happening in my body, without the necessary grounding or balanced diet, emotional stability, and proper rest and relaxation, just about killed me. I was a receiver picking up all levels of psychic activity at once. I felt as though a hundred thousand volts of psychic energy were running through my hundred-watt body. I was literally fried.

This happens to many people who are psychic but not conscious of it. I believe it's the root of chronic fatigue syndrome and many other nervous system disorders, including depression. The psyche uses the nervous system to relay information. If the nervous system is overwhelmed by too much energy flowing into it and too much chaos around it, all sorts of unpleasant results occur.

Life these days is demanding, hectic, and intense at its best, but if you are sloppy and inattentive in your daily life, you are intuitively doomed. A life lived that way is a life lived in drama and frustration.

I am thinking now of a woman I read for named Lois. An extremely talented designer, Lois was forging out on her own. She was very ambitious, but terribly disorganized. She had a very charming personality and easily persuaded clients to give her projects. Her trouble was that she started so many projects at one time that she was unable to maintain her focus and finish what she had started. Everybody in town was mad at her.

When she came to me, she was frantic. She was exhausted and barely able to get out of bed each day. What started out as creative ambition had turned into an overwhelming game of catch-up. Her exhaustion was her attempt to run away from her responsibilities. Her creativity had long ago dried up, and her freelance career had turned into an endless hassle. Her marriage suffered from lack of attention, and her husband left her. She had no friends to fall back on because she had long ago burned them out with endless requests to save her.

All this had happened simply because she was so disorganized. She still had as much talent and creativity as ever, but it had been buried under a mountain of unfinished business. Her only recourse was to stop making new commitments and fulfill the ones she already had.

Taking Care of Business

My job with Lois was to help her find her focus and organize her life. Your job is to do the same with your life. But in addition to simplifying and purging your life of the unnecessary, you need to take responsibility for your past obligations and commitments. Recognize what is yanking on your awareness because of neglect and clean it up. Take care of old business so that you can be free to move on to new business. Let go and complete the past so your soul can guide you onward.

This is hard if you have vague or nonexistent goals. This very lack of clear direction is what creates a clogged existence. The more specific you are about your goals, the easier it is to identify what supports these goals and what doesn't. Clearing away the old and completing old responsibilities comes naturally if you are focused on where you are going next.

When I speak of clearing, I really mean on all levels. If you are going to walk on the psychic path, you have to travel lightly. Anything that encumbers you, you must let go of. Some people don't even know what encumbers them until they set their goals. You can't just walk away from responsibility, however.

The only way to free yourself from encumbrances is to ask yourself if they are:

- unnecessary baggage from the past,
- unfinished business in the present, or
- sabotage.

If it's unnecessary baggage from the past, let go and give it up. If it's unfinished business, finish it. If it's sabotage, see it for what it is and get away from it fast.

Psychic Sabotage

Psychic sabotage occurs when conditions, people, or even your own mental misconceptions actually work against your achieving your goals. Sabotage from the outside is most easily eliminated by guarding your goals carefully and keeping them secret, or at least sharing them only with truly supportive people.

Sadly, you can count on lots of people telling you that your intuition isn't real or accurate or reliable if you give them the chance. The best way to avoid this is—*don't tell anyone!* Just know where you are going, and don't let unsupportive people confuse you.

Once you begin to focus on your goals, anyone in your life who works against you will be exposed. It's natural, but remember, it's not that old friends want to hurt you (although some may). What's more important is that *you* are leaving the swamp, and others may try to keep you in it.

The more organized you are—the more aware, more psychic, more spiritually supported you become—the more conscious you will be of the energy around you. Pay attention. If the energy around you is chaotic, disorganized, or negative, you will notice it now more than ever before. If you find yourself around a negative or disruptive energy, *notice* and move away! That's traveling lightly.

LIVING AT THE PROPER PACE

The final block to psychic awakening is being too much in a hurry to stop and notice what is—what is going on around you and what is going on within you. Some of the least perceptive people I know are that way because they are in such a rush. Think about it. Who will have a better idea of the road—a person flying down it at one hundred miles per hour or someone walking casually along? Who will notice more? It's a case of the tortoise and the hare. In the end, the tortoise wins.

Those who live more slowly, who take time to notice the world around them and to focus inward for guidance from the Higher Plane, will be psychically guided and more effective. This is not to suggest you become a slug, because that, too, is ineffective. What I'm talking about is *living at a proper pace.*

A proper pace is one that allows you time to take care of the necessary, a pace that allows time for work, for rest, for meditation, for recreation, and for socialization. I know this is hard to achieve, but you come much closer to it with clear goals. If you are too busy to feel, you are too busy to be aware. If you are too busy, you are narrowing your awareness, not expanding it. If you are too busy to meditate, to pace yourself through life and be aware of what is around you, you will also be too busy to notice how much support you are indeed being given from the spiritual plane.

For example, several years ago I found myself overwhelmed with sleep deprivation from my two-in-a-row babies, my house in a shambles, my clients calling for appointments, my health going straight down the drain. I was being run in circles by all the demands others placed on me and felt very detached from my intuition. I realized that, in spite of my efforts, I had lost my focus and had no clear idea of what my goals were.

After many months of this, I ended up exhausted and retreated to Hawaii to rest and rethink my goals. There I had an incredible experience. If I believed in psychic experience, I'd tell you I met an angel. Judge for yourself.

When I left Chicago it was the dead of winter. Hawaii sounded like just what I needed—a quiet, relaxing, warm, soothing beach. I slept the entire way over. Near the end of the trip the passenger next to me asked me if I was all right or if I was on drugs, because I hadn't moved in over nine hours. I was fine, I said. It was just that my daughters were babies, and this was the first uninterrupted sleep I'd had in over two years!

I checked into a beautiful beachfront hotel, and for the first two days I didn't even leave the room. I just slept or lay in the quiet dark, simply resting. I was not capable of doing more. By the third day I roused myself and decided to sit outside by the water.

It was hypnotic. I was in paradise. I never even thought of Patrick and the girls as I watched the waves. I didn't even think of me. I just thought of the water. I must have sat there alone for six hours that third day, staring into space, into the waves. It was so wonderful to be totally alone. Slowly I could feel energy and light begin to fill up my body once more. I realized that my body had been in such a dark, sad place. The sun, the sand, the ocean, the tropical flowers, all of nature began to revive my spirit.

Eventually I began, on the fourth day, to think about my life. I had two beautiful baby girls, a wonderful dear man for a husband, a sound home, work that I loved—yet though the pieces were right, the puzzle didn't fit. We were so sad, so resentful, so tired. Our lives moved so fast! And we had become so stretched among people, financial demands, and parenting that we had no time for each other, let alone for ourselves.

Patrick is a very athletic person who loves to run, ski, bicycle, and canoe, but all he had done for over two years was rehab our house day and night. I, who loved to read, to dance, to paint, didn't have the energy to watch a TV show from beginning to end. We had lost our loves, our ways of being creative, our expressions of spirit. We were merely surviving day to day. There was no joy, no fun, just work, work, work.

How did it happen? By outside appearances we seemed the epitome of success. Happily married couple, beautiful children, successful business. I had even achieved a degree of local fame, appearing on radio and television and being interviewed by some local newspaper columnists. We appeared happy, but we were so miserable. Patrick and I hardly saw each other during the week. We put in long, hard days, me at home doing readings and raising babies, and he working two jobs and rehabbing the house. We'd fall into bed exhausted by eight P.M. because we knew we'd be up all night with Sabrina.

Sabrina—my darling little child who screamed and cried all night long. I knew that this child was psychic! I knew that she screamed because she couldn't speak, and if she could, she would tell me that she couldn't sleep because there was so much tension and sadness in the vibrations of our home that she simply couldn't take it. It was keeping her from relaxing. It was Patrick and I keeping *her* from sleeping. It was our energy that felt like broken glass that kept her little hypersensitive nervous system from being able to get deep rest.

As I sat on that Hawaiian beach, detached from it all, miles away from the drama, I knew that this was true. Sabrina was the one in our family who, by screaming all night, was voicing the desperation of all of us. She was the one telling us that the energy, the vibration, in our home was very, very off balance. She with her tiny little body had a very great soul that was trying to tell us something was wrong, that it needed to be noticed and stopped. Unfortunately for all of us, she could get our attention only at night, when all was quiet.

Sitting on that beach, I knew from the voice of my own soul that Sabrina wasn't being a rotten kid. She was trying to alert us. Warn us. Save us from ourselves, from our stream of ever-increasing complications, our poor decisions, our frantic pace. She was trying to help us. I knew that was why she couldn't relax. Under the circumstances, how could she?

The next day I went for a walk. The beach was starting to get boring. I wanted to explore the area. I was still tired to the bone, so I decided to walk along the beach and take a bus back to the hotel.

I left about ten-thirty. It was another perfect day in paradise. As I strolled along the water, the sand felt great squishing between my toes. I remembered playing as a child. I rarely remember anything of my childhood, so it was very pleasant to experience these feelings. I must have strolled along for over two hours. Then I decided very spontaneously to turn and head into the city, to see what was there.

I was approaching the city when I noticed a metaphysical bookstore on the corner straight ahead, as if I had been led there. I walked in. There was one woman behind the counter. She had just received a shipment of books and seemed deeply involved in organizing them. She didn't even say hello—she was not unfriendly, just deep in concentration. I was relieved, because I just wanted to browse, not chat. My soul told me that there was something here that would be good for me, and I was looking for what it might be.

I was there for ten or fifteen minutes when out of the back room walked a very beautiful, tall black man, about six feet two. He was dressed in a beautiful white robe and white pants. The fabric was shimmery, like washed silk. It was exquisite. He had the most beautiful smile and twinkling eyes, and when he saw me, he laughed a laugh that sounded like a deep, rich chord on a harp. It made *me* laugh, it was that contagious.

"Hello," he said. "I've been waiting for you."

"Me?" I said shyly. "You're kidding."

"No, really. Come here." He motioned as he walked over to a stand that held spiritual posters. I followed, feeling suspicious and curious at the same time. The woman at the counter kept working.

"Look here," he said. "This is you." And he pulled out a poster of an angel, collapsed on a beach. It was exactly how I felt. I laughed.

"Very perceptive," I said. "That's just how I've been feeling lately."

"Look here," he said as he pulled out another poster. "This is what you must do."

The other poster was of a male angel flying with the female angel, holding each other tightly, toward heaven. I looked at it and thought of Patrick. It was true that when Patrick and I stopped working together and stopped having fun together and alone, all of this downward spiral of energy had begun. I looked at these posters and at this beautiful man, and I felt a rush of warmth, of deep relief.

"Remember to dance," he said, swaying. "I'll be back." He turned and walked into the back room.

I watched him disappear behind the curtain. I stood there holding these two posters, looking first at one, then at the other, then at the curtain. I stood there, waiting for him to come out again.

I heard the woman behind the counter ask, "May I help you?"

I turned around, startled. I guess I was in a daze. "Oh, no, thank you. The gentleman in the back room is helping me."

She looked at me funny. "Gentleman? What gentleman?"

"The black guy dressed in white who works here."

"There's no black guy working here!"

"Yes, there is," I said. "He's in the back room right now."

She got up from behind the counter and started toward the back room, all the while saying, "Who's back there? I don't have anyone here but me. Hello?" she called as she pushed aside the curtain leading to the back room. "Anyone here?"

She disappeared for a second, then came back out looking at me with a very peculiar expression. "No one's back there. No one's here but me."

I stood there in complete surprise. "Didn't you see me talking to him?" I asked.

"No," she said, looking at me even more nervously.

I stared at the posters. They were of *angels*. I remembered his shimmering white robes, his radiance. I looked at the puzzled salesclerk, and suddenly I understood. He must have been an angel. He had to have been! A real angel. And he was telling me how to get protection and restore balance in my life. He was helping me—that's what angels do.

I could still hear his laughter ringing in my head. I felt a rush of peace overcome me. I looked at the saleswoman and smiled. "Never mind. Don't worry. There's no one here."

I stood there holding the two posters, one of an angel collapsed on a beach. I laughed. It was so true. The other was of *two* angels, joined together. It carried a message. I had to rejoin Patrick. We needed to be together, to work together, to share our time together once again, like the two angels in the poster.

I could still hear this angel's beautiful voice ringing in my ears—his laughter, his words. Life had to change. Patrick and I needed to take control of our lives once again. We needed to stop the frantic wheel of more-more-more. We needed to get rid of the second job, the secretary, and the belief that we couldn't rest until our work was done.

Work is never done. The babies, the house, the clients—all were important, but so were we. We invented everything that made so much work. Now we needed to detach, watch the world go by. Focus on the necessary and give up trying to be all things to all people, meeting all demands at once. We needed to simplify. Quiet down. Find time for each other and time to enjoy our children, and above all, we needed to create the room in our very crowded lives for quiet, for calm, for the sacred to return. A time to be alone and reflect on truth, on love, on God.

It was a juggle, but we weren't juggling all the balls. We needed to add time for rest, time for fun, for love. This angel stepped in and with very few words completely changed my perspective and my priorities.

This was what I had come to Hawaii to experience. This was the beginning of real healing. It was clearly time to rethink my priorities, my goals, and my values.

As our lives calmed down I noticed an interesting element to this: that it's not so much how busy you are, but, more important, how *dramatic* you are in the way you go about the work of achieving your goals. It will be much harder for you to accomplish some required task if you do so with resentment, urgency, intensity, a sense of extreme effort, as opposed to just doing it gladly.

This easy, focused force is not hard if the goal is true! Too much emotion makes life harder. Taking time to meditate, relax, and recuperate keeps emotions clear. Then one can achieve more with less effort—and be aware enough to receive psychic guidance along the way.

PUTTING ON EARMUFFS

Another way to stop life's confusion is to stop asking people for their opinion or input on your life, unless it is absolutely necessary to have it.

You would be surprised how often you seek approval or opinions from those around you, out of habit. How many times do you find yourself saying, "What do you think of . . . my hair? my dress? my home? my work? my choice?" Or, "I don't know what I want. What do you want?" Or, "Do you like . . . my car? my boyfriend? my job? my life?"

All of this soliciting often happens in place of checking in with your own Higher Self. It is the self-approval you get from following your intuition that gives you peace of mind. Countless opinions from others only add to your confusion and make it harder to hear your own intuition.

Asking others for input as an unconscious habit has got to go. Try not asking for opinions for just one day. Stop yourself if you notice you are doing it and say to yourself, "I cancel that opinion," if you've already invited one in.

This is not to suggest that you cease being open to learning something new. Your rule should be to ask someone else only if the person you are asking is *wiser* or better informed about the question than you. Otherwise, ask your Higher Self instead.

EXPLORATIONS

Head 'Em Up, Move 'Em Out!
- Throw away the clutter on your desk, in your drawers at the office.
- Throw away all the photos you look rotten in.
- Donate to a charity ten of the books you've hung on to and will never read.
- Throw away all the makeup or ties that are *not* your color but you've felt obligated to keep.
- Throw away your ratty underwear and socks.
- Clean out your purse.
- Organize your wallet.
- Toss the magazines you keep promising yourself you'll read.
- Recycle the newspapers lying around your house.
- Weed out your closet till you can see the bottom.
- Clean your car—throw out those McDonald's bags.
- Organize your garage.
- Throw away the monster in the dark corner of your refrigerator.
- Chase out the trolls in the basement.
- Empty all your wastebaskets.
- Return all your wire hangers to the dry cleaner.
- Donate your chipped dishes to Goodwill.
- Ditto the towels, sheets, and washcloths your mother gave you when you moved out.
- Clean out your cleaning supplies—pitch out the half-used and clumped-up Comet, the dried-up and filthy sponges, the gray pieces of soap.
- Have a yard sale.

Order in Your Court: You Be the Judge

Let's see how organized you are. Ask yourself:

- Do I feel as though I accomplish what is important to me in my day?
- Do I waste time looking for things?
- Is my home in order?
- Is my workplace in order?
- Do I say yes when I mean no?
- Do I know what's important to me?
- Do I pay attention to what my body needs? When it needs it?
- Am I fulfilling my commitments to others?
- Do I keep "stuff" in my life for no reason?
- Are my closets clean? Desk organized? Bills paid?
- Do I direct my life every day, or do I find myself directed by others?
- Do I have a sense of drawing boundaries? Do I have time to do my work?

The Pot of Goals

The best way to organize your goals and intentions is to create a wish list of those things you want to experience in life and ultimately narrow down this list to uncover the most important of all your desires. I do it this way.

In your psychic journal, focus your wishes on what you want to do, to be, to experience, more than on what you want to consume or own. For example, wish for "living in the mountains in a big house" instead of "a house in the mountains." In other words, write your wishes in the active mode, with you doing what you wish for. Number a page from 1 to 20 in your psychic journal. After each number write *I wish*. For example:

1. I wish that I worked in a wonderful environment that engaged and appreciated my talents.
2. I wish that I were in a supportive, loving relationship.
3. I wish that I lived in a cheerful, safe home in the city (in the country, wherever).

4. I wish that my body was healthy, balanced, and full of vitality.
5. I wish I had the perfect party dress and the place to wear it.

It doesn't matter what you wish for. All wishes matter. This exercise is intended to help you focus on fulfilling your immediate desires.

Each day write a new wish list in your psychic journal, making sure you don't miss a day. Repeat this wish list exercise for all seven days of this week.

The first day, write twenty wishes in your journal. The second day, narrow the list down to twelve wishes. The third day, narrow it down further to nine wishes. The fourth day, bring it down to seven wishes. The fifth day, bring it down to five. The sixth day, bring it down to three remaining wishes.

On the seventh day, write down the last three remaining wishes or desires in your journal. These three remaining wishes usually reflect your truest, most important desires, your true goals for now.

1. I wish . . .
2. I wish . . .
3. I wish . . .

This focusing exercise will help you identify what is important for you to concentrate on now. This list doesn't mean these three goals are all you can hope to manifest, but it does mean that this is where you begin. Once these goals are realized, new ones will be set up. But unless you narrow your attention to your immediate goals, you will not progress toward their realization.

Mirror, Mirror
Tape your list of three written goals to a mirror, or place them on your desk or in a wallet or wherever you can see them *all* the time. This is to remind you of what it is that you are working on, what it is that you want to put time into. This list will keep you focused on what will bring you a sense of satisfaction.

"Slow Down, You Move Too Fast"

- Listen to this old Simon & Garfunkel tune or another favorite. Do not do more than one other thing at the same time!
- Take a bubble bath.
- Drive more slowly.
- Do not wear your watch for one entire day.
- Tinker with your favorite hobby for an entire evening.
- Turn off the TV for a whole day.
- Spend one hour in total silence. Unplug the phone.
- Take a half-hour walk. Don't take anyone with you, and don't do anything else while you're walking.
- The next time someone asks you to do something for them, tell them you'll get back to them about it. Then *decide* whether you want to use your time that way.
- Choose only *half* of the above to execute.

CHARTING YOUR PROGRESS

How many days this week did you meditate? Are you starting to look forward to it?_____

_____

Is your meditation becoming a pleasurable habit, or is it still hard to find the time? (Slow down and take time for yourself.)_____

_____

How many days this week did you make entries in your portable psychic journal? Have you discovered what drains you?_____

_____

_____

Which block do you think is your most pernicious? _____

_____

Which block was most satisfying to work on? _____

_____

Which block are you procrastinating on? _____

_____

Which block makes you most nervous? _____

_____

Traveling Lightly

Overcoming blocks takes a decision from you. Let it be your intention to break through! Living a life that is psychically directed and free of illusion requires a commitment on your part to let go of the negative, sabotaging, and spiritually immature feelings (which we all have!)—feelings of wanting someone else to take care of you.

In order to make the music, we have to face the music: ultimately you must accept that your well-being, your care, your progress in life, will come from you! You must learn to see your true nature and embrace the inner guidance of your Higher Self and the divine over the word and opinion of others.

As you surely sense, looking outside yourself for worth, for care, for security, puts you squarely into the world of illusion. This is what is known, metaphysically, as "the fall of man." The fall is the fall back into a dream that says unless the world loves you, coddles you, sees to your every need, then you must be unlovable and suffer. The world should do this and will do this for the lovable ones, right?

Wrong! I don't know of any case where a person's well-being is derived from being taken care of or where a person is truly secure by depending on people or things outside of himself or herself for happiness, even as a child. Happiness—and security—come from the soul and the soul's helpers.

A friend of mine recently sent me a sign that I have posted to remind myself: "The Universe Wants to Help—Let Them." What this means to me is that while no one human agent is the exclusive source of my welfare, I can trust the universe to provide for my needs.

For example, my four-year-old daughter, Sabrina, is very well cared for by Patrick and me. We see to it that all her comforts are provided. She has a warm house, nice clothes, food, love, toys—all a child could want. Is this where she derives her well-being? I don't think so. I think she's not even conscious of all of her surrounding security. She is focused instead on learning to care for herself. Her joy, her bliss, is experienced when she washes her own hair, makes her own cereal, puts her own clothes away, or makes her own work of art. That is natural, and deep down we never change.

TV and the media create in many people a sense of entitlement to happiness, love, and care—from others. It is common these days to hear, in essence, "I can't function because Mom didn't love me, or Dad wasn't around." Therefore we go on to other people, hoping they'll do for us what Mom or Dad failed to do.

The problem with this emotional, ego-based pattern is that we are stuck looking for lovability, worth, and our true place in life from other mere mortals on an ego/earth plane. If everyone is looking for it, who has a surplus of love and care to give to fill our need? Not people! People do human things, make human mistakes, and will always frustrate us and let us down. We must accept that our lovability and worth don't come from others. They come from ourselves!

If your mortal family gave you wrong information or made human errors as you were developing, forgive them. They are only mortal, suffering the same void of spirit as you. The source of love, protection, and security you seek comes from God and from your willingness to receive it. By accepting who you are—a spiritual being, a child of God—you begin to wake up out of the dream of illusion.

The more you accept who you are, the more clearly you can see others, the good as well as the bad. The more you are willing to see the truth in yourself, the more you'll see it in the world around you. We are all basically the same, looking for love and trying to stop pain. See that truth, and the truth will set you free.

If you want to develop psychic ability, if you want to receive the gift of seeing through illusion in life and start seeing truth, you must give up interpreting everything from an emotional point of view. For example, if you are around a chronically angry person, you will be "angered upon." Nothing personal! Not everything in your life happens *to* you—or even *at* you. One way to put this is, "It's not my movie!" In some circumstances you are a bit player, not the lead. In some you are just the audience—even just passing through.

A currently popular misinterpretation of metaphysical wisdom is the notion that we cause—and are responsible for—the behavior of everyone around us at all times. The truth is, we are responsible only for ourselves. We can control only our response to and interpretation of events.

You must start looking at the conditions and events in your life without emotionally charged judgment. You must study, objectively, how you got where you are right now. My favorite saying from *Alice in Wonderland* is, "Wherever you are . . . there you are."

Looking at your life neutrally allows you to see a bigger, more accurate picture. One way to break free from damaging emotional habits is to accept that certain conditions were present that affected you as a child. Recognize both the negative and positive effects of each condition. Realize that parents and other influential human beings are mortal and naturally will make mistakes. Try not to take it personally.

The explorations at the end of this chapter will help you examine each area of your life, without emotion if possible, to see how much others influenced you, how much fear influenced you, how much you manipulated the situation, how much others manipulated you in the situation, how responsible you are for your circumstances, and finally, how much intuition played a role in the outcome.

I once read for a client named Phil. Phil was short, stocky, maybe fifty. He had two failed marriages and was on his third, though it, too, was unstable, and he was beginning to have signs of heart stress and possible disease.

When he came for his reading, he had on a jogging outfit, complete with jacket, pants, shoes, sunglasses, even a watch to keep time. But I was sure he hadn't so much as even run around the block, ever. He just knew he "needed" to and was working toward it. I noticed he wore an earring in one ear. I thought to myself, He's an artistic man.

Phil, it turned out, was a doctor but over the years had become addicted to prescription drugs and allowed his practice to lapse. He was struggling to stay off drugs but couldn't bear the idea of going back into medicine. He hated medicine and felt like an utter failure at fifty-three. What could he do? He was bankrupt and about to lose a third marriage, and he knew if he went back to work, he was doomed. He took drugs to cope with the stress and contempt for himself he felt while working.

My spirits showed me an entirely different Phil from the one I was looking at, the one who was speaking. My spirits showed me that he was a man who deeply loved writing, literature, film, and screenwriting and in fact had many unfinished creative works sitting around his house, gathering dust. His marriages were failures because he married as his false self.

His true self was not a man dedicated to health, but a man dedicated to writing, production, and film. He took the drugs because they associated him with his creative side—or at least he believed they did. He pursued medicine to win his parents' approval.

My guidance clearly told me Phil was the only and adored child of truly dedicated doctor parents. He wanted to please them, but it cost him his integrity. In his soul he was a writer, a storyteller, a weaver of tales, not a man of medicine. His soul was troubled and abandoned. He still wrote but placed no value on his writing and was afraid to show it to the world. That meant, for him, taking the risk of revealing the truth and thus disappointing his parents. So he was stuck.

Writing was his love, but not his value system! His assimilated list of what was important in life didn't include being an artist or being creative. It valued being a scholar, a doctor. His soul could not operate in his own life!

While the drugs lent a temporary escape, they were a substitute for a genuine statement of truth. The only way to heal himself was to commit to his own soul, making the choice "To thine own self be true," and taking the genuine risk of being loved for what was real about himself. He had to connect with others, not through doctoring, but through writing, his legitimate creative expression.

As for medicine, I suggested he might practice a storyteller's form of healing by being a counselor and healing people with ideas, with stories and kind, loving guidance, not with drugs or surgery.

Phil laughed, a large, deep, happy laugh. "That would be perfect!" he exclaimed.

We had found a solution he could live with. He just needed to find a way to direct his background and training in the direction of his true soul path.

In the following years Phil became a rehab counselor in a detox center, helping people sort through their complicated stories. He is now working on his first screenplay. He's lost ten pounds and is still married. It's a beginning. He told me a few months after the reading that his heart felt better.

I'm sure it does.

Again and again in my practice I have seen my clients realize that where they are in life is the result of their choices. Those choices that are the consequences of damaging emotional experiences when young will probably be the most dissatisfying. They are not the result of true values. Those choices made with the help of intuition create the most satisfying conditions. Of course they do. Intuition is the voice of your inner values.

WHERE ARE YOU NOW?

No matter where you are, it is time to put out the flames of self-abuse, anger, and despair and begin the healing process with acceptance. You can move ahead toward a new place if you stop for a moment and locate where you are now. It's like finding a way out of the woods. You go in circles, continually returning to the same place unless you stop and study the place you are in now, without calling it good or bad. Only then can you begin to move out of the maze.

Just look at your life's path as the path your soul chose to walk. The more complex and difficult, the greater the opportunity for growth. All great lives are born out of great tests. Look at your life path and all that transpired as your tests. Some you passed the first time around. Others you will pass after many, many failures.

It's much more attractive to think growth is harder and more complex than this, but it isn't. Real healing begins in life, and real awakening starts to happen when we stop living through emotion and start living through love. Love is the energy of acceptance. Love is what heals. Love is not condoning of abuse. It will, as a matter of fact, alert you to possible patterns of abuse and quietly move you away from them.

Human beings make mistakes. Huge, unbelievable, horrifying mistakes. But underneath all of these errors and disruptions are souls, just like you, striving to find relief. The more capable people are of inflicting pain, the deeper, more buried they are in illusion and fear.

As you wake up and begin to hear the voice of spirit, you will be guided away from these kinds of people, or you will be able to see through their horrible crimes, find the frightened souls underneath, and release yourself from fearing them.

Once you begin to live life on the psychic pathway, everyone and everything will begin to look different. People won't be so scary, and you will feel safer. The world will still be the same crazy place, but you will be able to move toward the safe places and surround yourself with gratifying associations.

You may be thinking, Easier said than done. True! But it *can* be done.

One of my clients, Joy, was a twenty-eight-year-old woman working for a commercial interior design firm in Chicago as a researcher. It was stable but unexciting work, not at all creative—in a word, mundane. Her father had died in the past year after a long illness, and Joy was devastated. She had inherited a modest sum of money from him and came to me for some advice on a home she wanted to buy. She was single, not involved with anyone, and had convinced herself that no "prince on a white horse" would be forthcoming. Her family told her that she should buy a home and start taking care of herself instead of waiting for someone else to do it.

The problem arose because she had the money and the inclination to buy, but nothing she looked at felt like home. She had looked at over thirty different houses and condos. She wanted me to help her find a home to purchase. She "knew" that was the right thing to do—everybody told her it was!

Our reading showed me something quite different.

My guidance showed me that Joy's urge to buy a house was really influenced by her mother's emphasis on security. She herself did not really want to buy a house and settle into her life at that time. Far from it. Buying a house was a commitment she would be making out of fear, emphasizing financial security. It would mean she was resigning herself to following a pathway set up by her reasonable mind, but one she would not enjoy.

"Joy," I said, "you cannot find a house because your soul does not want to make that kind of commitment. You have lived your life under heavy influence from your mother and siblings, and you are being encouraged to make choices based on their priorities, and not your own. Your job is meaningless and repetitious. You are lonely and uninspired, and day by day you are becoming more and more depressed and anxious. You also need time to grieve your father's death.

"You need to put most of your inheritance in the bank, take a small sum of money from it, and buy a ticket around the world! Your soul wants to break out of this cautious and pessimistic frame of mind, and really do some genuine soul-seeking. Have you ever traveled?"

Joy looked as though she had been caught with her hand in the cookie jar. "I have always wanted to do something like that!" she burst out. "In fact, I read James Michener's novels all the time. He writes constantly about foreign lands, travel, faraway and exotic experiences." For a moment she flashed to another place. Wherever that was, it was obviously bliss.

"Well," I said, "it seems that your soul would like you to have some of these kinds of experiences before you draw your conclusions about what's possible for you."

"What would my family say? They would think that was so irresponsible!"

"It is, if you are living by their values. But your soul is pulling you to examine what you consider meaningful before you decide whose values are correct. Just give your natural impulses a chance before you discard them!"

Joy thought for a moment. All her life she had striven to do the right thing, but right according to whom? What I was suggesting was that she unleash her free spirit and take some risks in order to find her own priorities, really see what the world had to offer in terms of experience before she settled down.

"You'll find a true purpose and your true destiny if you do this," I told her. "Pretty romantic stuff, huh? I don't know too many people who would have the courage. Apparently, you may. Consider it! At any rate, stop looking to buy a house. You want to find your wings, not your roots. Your roots are well laid. The practical is overemphasized. It is the inspirational, the spontaneous, the spiritual, that needs a chance to express itself in you."

Joy left both excited and troubled. I told her that she needed to make a decision to listen to her soul instead of her family for a little while. Though they loved her very much, there was a part of her that was adventurous and daring. They feared that part and discouraged her expression of it. Maybe that protected her as a child, but now, as a twenty-eight-year-old woman, it was repressive.

A month later I received a call. Joy had quit her job and was going around the world! She asked that I pray for her safety and said her family was apprehensive but not negative. I periodically received postcards from Joy as her travels progressed. By the third postcard I could tell she was loving it. It was as if her world had gone from black-and-white to color! The sights, the sounds, the people. She had feared the world so much before she'd left. Now she had fallen in love with it.

When she returned after a full year away, she moved to San Francisco, where she started a freelance interior design business of her own. She was her own boss and through her world travels had developed both a great intuition with people and a truly creative design sense. She lived the life of a free bird, calling her own shots, trusting not a job, but her talents for security.

Joy was able to seize the moment and really go after a dream. The last I heard, she was studying feng shui, the Chinese art of reading the aura of a business location and changing the energy to create a favorable atmosphere. She'd first learned of it in Hong Kong, where no business-person would ever proceed without a feng shui master checking out the place. Apparently this is going to be her new vocation and beautifully complements her design talents.

Once again it was a case of someone needing to remember who she really was! She is now living in the true spirit of her name.

FORGIVING AND ACCEPTING

If we think of our life as a journey, it is easy to see that if we want to re-ally travel, we will need to practice discernment about what we take along. We don't want to move into our future lugging along the heavy baggage of our past. One way to lighten the load is to work on forgive-ness and acceptance. These allow us to let go of our heavy burdens and move forward with lighter hearts.

Forgiveness and acceptance are often difficult concepts for some be-cause they are confused with condoning abuse and past hurt or with being passive.

Forgiveness and acceptance are neither weak nor passive acts. They are acts of great courage.

Forgiveness and acceptance are the best block dissolvers. Let's talk first about forgiveness.

When you decide to forgive those who have hurt you, your ego lets go of the memory, and you can begin to see the truth. People who hurt you are only people hurting themselves. When you forgive them, you take your power back from them. You release them from your ego and place your pain into the care of your soul, where healing begins.

When you forgive those who have hurt you, you free up your awareness. You shift it out of the past and bring it fully into the moment, where it can serve you to become what your heart's desire wants you to be. Forgiveness is a great act of the soul. It allows you to become free of others—to move back to your own truth and reunite your awareness with your own pathway of growth.

If you live by the ordinary rules, forgiveness is almost impossible. The ego, ruler of the ordinary, is a very fragile and brooding entity. It doesn't like to be hurt or humiliated. Humiliation and control by others greatly pain the ego, and it has an elephant's memory!

The soul, however, doesn't like to cling to the past. It understands that all experiences are beneficial to our spiritual growth, because all experiences ultimately teach us something. When we can find the lesson, we can be free of the experience and the pain. The soul knows that no one else can control it.

Forgiveness is a natural by-product of remembering who you are. Forgiveness comes easily when you recover a sense of your soul. All attempts to find your worth through others set up the patterns that lead to pain. Once you break through the barriers to the truth and find your true worth inside yourself, you can let go of past pain and the people who have hurt you. You will be able to do this because as you find your essence and your inner voice, you feel protection and guidance, and the pain stops.

Forgiveness opens up your awareness to the soul more than anything else. When you can see those who have hurt you through the eyes of truth, you can understand how so much of the pain came from your own misperceptions about who they were and what they would or could do for you.

One day I received a call from a Polish woman who wanted me to read for her friend, a man. I scheduled the reading for 10 A.M. a few days later. That night I received a call from a client I saw once a year who wanted to schedule an appointment for her girlfriend, who was having a difficult time in her marriage. I scheduled that appointment for 11 A.M. a few days later, following the 10 A.M. appointment.

The Polish woman showed up with a distinguished-looking man with glasses, tall, fiftyish, dressed in a gray suit. He was stiff and uncomfortable, but at my door nevertheless, so I knew that he really wanted to be there in spite of his reservations. I saw that he was a doctor, an OB/GYN. He was married but involved with the woman who brought him to me, his secretary. I also could tell he wanted to stay married, but that his wife, who was caring for small children, was too tired for romance or sex, and he found himself seduced by the secretary. I could also tell he was an old-world Catholic and convinced that some horrible thing would happen to him for his transgression. In fact, he almost wished for it so he could get out of the predicament he was in. Divorce was out of the question. He enjoyed the sex and the excitement with his secretary, but he did not love the secretary. He was faced with a choice of shame-filled sex or a passionless marriage. What should he do?

He was near tears as we talked. He was convinced that his wife didn't love him, that the woman in the other room did, and that he loved his wife, not the other woman. It was quite a mess. I saw that he loved his wife and she loved him, but they didn't value their relationship, put no effort into it, and it had died from fatigue, neglect, and anger. The secretary was no solution, and that relationship no substitute for the intimacy he longed for with his wife.

The time for the reading was ending, and I advised him to tell the secretary the truth. I also encouraged him to get some counseling and work on getting things in order with his wife. They needed to forgive past hurts and work toward renewing their relationship. I saw she did love him and wanted to remain married. He shook my hand and thanked me.

Just as he was putting on his coat and they were preparing to leave, my doorbell rang. It was my next client. We were all standing at the door when I answered the intercom.

"Yes?" I said.

"Yes, it's me. I'm here with Katrinka."

I buzzed them in, turned to say good-bye, and saw that both the doctor and his secretary had such looks of horror on their faces, they had both turned white.

"You two look like you saw a ghost. What's the matter?" By now I could hear my clients walking up the stairs to my apartment on the fourth floor.

"Katrinka! That's my *wife!*" whispered the doctor, now panic-stricken. "If she finds me here with *her*"—pointing to his secretary—"I'm dead. And she will kill her, too! She suspects already. Where can we hide? Do you have a back door? A closet? Something?"

I felt so sorry for him, and his secretary, too. She saw his terror, his fright. I don't think she had seen it before, and she saw and understood in that moment just how important the doctor's wife was to him. Katrinka and her friend were turning up the last flight of stairs. I had to think quickly. This could be embarrassing for all of us.

"Quick," I said, "step into the kitchen. I'll take them both to the bedroom to take off their coats, and you two slip out the front. You'll have about twenty seconds. Shhh!"

Ding-dong! They were at the door, puffing from the climb. I let them in, smiled, and led them both to the bedroom, chatting. When we returned to the living room, the door was closed. They had succeeded in leaving undetected.

From my perspective, however, this happened because the souls of the doctor and his wife had orchestrated this scenario to bring their lives back in order. He saw she cared enough to find her way to my home. The secretary saw the doctor still loved his wife. And during Katrinka's reading, I helped her see that her marriage was something that she still wanted and needed to work on.

I said, "Don't be right! Be wise. See the truth about this man! You both are making a game out of perceiving the other as terrible. And in the end, all you really want is to feel close to each other again. That kind of intimacy is built on kindness, trust, and communication. Work on it."

She cried. She admitted that she didn't want a divorce, that she wanted her marriage to work. She needed to accept that his work was demanding and not take his absence personally, but make the most of the time they did have together. I saw that it would turn around. I suggested she and her husband go to counseling (and I knew he'd agree to go).

A year later he sent me a card from Minnesota. He and his wife had moved. He was still in practice. His wife was his secretary. They were very happy since their move.

The secretary ended up moving also, to Denver, where she met an engineer and got married. She told me that on that day at my apartment she had learned to believe in psychic energy and for the first time considered that souls arc real. The near meeting that day was too weird to be an accident. The doctor belonged with his wife, and the secretary accepted that truth.

If you truly look at your relationships with forgiving and truthful eyes, you can see just how much each and every person who has ever touched your life carried a valuable lesson. When you look at people through the eyes of the soul, it will be far clearer who will be genuinely helpful to you in your life and who is struggling more than you and could possibly hold you back.

Forgiveness activates the intuition and reveals a bigger picture. Once you remember who you are, and *believe* in your soul's complete ability to guide you in life, you will naturally start to see the past differently and in a way that allows you to become forgiving. Your work on this pathway will allow you to make a true transformation. Let me show you what one such transformation looks like.

Renata had scheduled an appointment, but twenty minutes before she was due to arrive she suddenly called and very indignantly informed us that she would not be coming after all.

Patrick, who took the call, was polite—but peeved. We always ask people to call at least twenty-four hours in advance if they want to cancel so we can accommodate other clients who are waiting for an opening.

Twenty minutes was such short notice that no one else could use her time. We explained this to her, but she wasn't concerned. She hung up brusquely.

It bothered Patrick that she was so rude, but we believe that things work out as they should. If she changed her mind, for whatever reason, then so be it. Twenty minutes passed, and Renata called again. This time she was crying and wanted to reschedule. She sounded sincere, so a new time was set for her.

When she finally arrived she was once again stiff, curt, and highly defensive. I think she expected another kind of person. There I stood in my blue jeans and sweatshirt, looking very regular and casual. As we sat down, she said incredulously, "I can't believe you are the psychic. You look so young!"

"Well, I am one just the same. Don't let appearances deceive you. I'm really much older than I look . . . lifetimes older," I joked.

She didn't laugh.

As I focused on her I could tell she was a woman in great emotional agony. "Renata," I said, "you canceled this appointment the first time, yet something in you brought you here today after all. You can leave even now if you'd like, but if you stay, it is because you want to be here, not because I asked you. I will do everything I can to the best of my ability to help you, but you have to feel comfortable before I can begin. I can tell you've been very hurt, but I won't hurt you. Okay?"

She was surprised, but after a pause she said, "I'll stay." Then she opened her purse, a big black suitcase of a purse, and pulled out a legal notepad and pen and sat poised, ready for dictation.

Part of me wanted to smile. It was obvious she was really out of her element sitting with me, and she wasn't about to relax lest she be taken advantage of. It was her fear causing her to act so defensively, and I chose to look past it. I wanted to find the real person behind the crisp and cool facade.

My reading started slowly. I saw her taking care of her parents, looking after an apartment building they owned, and working with her brother, her only sibling. Her life seemed like one long, gray rainy day to me. It was a sad, even sorrowful life, but one lived with a great deal of courage, even stoicism. She was from Yugoslavia but had no ties to Europe.

I saw a series of rather ordinary events coming up. Plumbing problems with the building. Her brother would be getting married to his girlfriend of twenty years. Her father needed minor foot surgery. But as I saw these events, I knew they were the surface ripples of her life, that the deep, profound side of her soul was shut down and the lights were out. I asked God and my guides what I could possibly do or say to help bring a little light back into her heart. She was so very sorrowful.

Suddenly I heard a very clear and beautiful voice, a young girl's voice. "My name is Eva. Tell her I'm all right. Not to be so sad. I'm all right." Then the voice totally disappeared.

"Do you know the name Eva?" I asked, feeling slightly foolish.

Her face turned white, and she gasped. "This is unbelievable! What do you see?" Her reaction startled me. Up until then she hardly even seemed to be listening.

"I only heard her voice. She said twice to tell you she is okay. Then her spirit left."

Renata sat frozen. Then she pleaded, "Please, can you see any more?"

"I'll try." I closed my eyes.

I saw a little girl about nine years old, sitting in an office. I saw her swing around on her chair as she heard a noise behind her. Then everything went white. I saw the family crying.

"She's dead," I said. "I think she was harmed, possibly unintentionally. But the soul of this child says she is okay. Was she your daughter?"

Renata started to sob. Finally she spoke. "Yes, and Eva was her name."

Gradually the story came out through her tears.

Although Renata had never married, she had borne this little girl. One day the child came to her office after school to wait for her mom. She sat in the foyer a few feet away from Renata's office and was talking to one of the other employees.

Renata had to take some reports to another part of the building before going home. It was closing time, and the building was nearly empty. When Renata came back ten or fifteen minutes later to pick up her child, she found both Eva and the employee—shot dead.

That had been twenty-five years ago. The murders were never solved. Renata had come to me to find out what happened and why.

My spirits showed me it was a case of a simple robbery and being "in the wrong place at the wrong time" for her child, but on a soul level this child never intended to live long. She had come to earth expressly for her mother, to help her find love and spirituality.

Renata did experience the love but never found a way to look past the horrible scene she'd happened upon at the murder. After Eva died, Renata's world shattered. She went black inside. She had years of therapy, then ultimately gave up. She shut off her mind, quit her job, and devoted her whole life to taking care of the small things, just waiting to die.

The family tried to help by distracting her, never talking about what had happened. After all, Eva was an illegitimate child and, to old-world European parents, hard to acknowledge in the first place. After Eva's death the child was simply not discussed, but I have never seen denial help anything, at any time, for anyone.

It was curious that I couldn't see any more details of the crime. I felt the criminal was also dead. I did tell Renata that she could simply wait to die, but it would be a long wait, as she was in good health.

"Renata, you are an old soul, and this lifetime for you is truly one of a great many intense spiritual tests. The point, the purpose of your life, is to find out the truth. Not the truth of the murder, but the truth of who you are. To reawaken to your true essence, your soul."

Renata nodded, listening.

I went on, "Having a child was your attempt to break free from your parents and live your own life. Your child came to you to help you achieve your dream: to break free of fear, to rise above the negativity you were surrounded by, and to feel love. Hidden in her death was her last great act of love. Even in its violence lies the potential of a great awakening."

Renata was still listening intently. I told her what I was being told.

"I am not given the details of her death because her soul wants you to forget the past, forgive and accept the loss, learn from it and move on."

Renata looked receptive—she had exhausted every other avenue, and this was a new one for her.

"This experience is the story of your great soul awakening. The psychiatric resources you have worked with have failed to help you heal because they have failed to recognize the spiritual aspects of this tragedy. Don't give up, but go beyond the doctors. Let go of your need to be accepted by your family. Start to accept yourself. In this lies dormant the possibility of taking your life back from those who have seemingly stolen it away."

I gave her the names of many books on spirituality, death, grief, karma, past lives, and healing, and I recommended she see my good friend Jack Miller, who is a Ph.D. psychologist specializing in healing the soul of grief.

Now Renata is healing. She is out of the coffin she lay down in with her daughter, but her work isn't over. Her life purpose is just beginning. She has taken teeny-tiny steps, brave ones, and she is allowing the healing light of God's love to slowly creep back into her heart. Every time I speak with her she tells me, "To know somehow my Eva is okay gives me the power to continue my own search for peace."

As Renata's story shows, the second part of moving out of your past is *accepting* the pathway you've walked until now. With all its pain, heartache, trauma, isolation, abuse, and sadness, it is the path your soul *chose* to walk.

Hidden in that past is honor, dignity, and growth. No matter what you've endured—you've survived! Although the wounds of your life may have left some deep scars, your acceptance that this is the road your soul chose for your growth, difficult as it may have been, is the beginning of your spiritual healing.

The more difficult your past, the more potential for your spiritual awakening. The more hurt you've encountered, the more compassionate you can be. Acceptance doesn't mean minimizing your history; acceptance means honoring it, seeing its value, seeing its integrity. Acceptance means seeing how, with each step, you learned strength, self-reliance, and creativity. Accepting that your life has unfolded as it was meant to frees your heart and attention to be here now. Acceptance means there was no lost time, no irreparable mistakes, only growth. You grew—maybe sometimes just a little, but you grew.

Forgiveness and acceptance break down the final walls between your conscious mind and your soul. Look at your life as a mosaic, a puzzle, with each episode of your life revealing another piece of the puzzle. As each piece falls into place, you'll get a closer look at the hidden truth behind the puzzle—that your path is a puzzle set up by your soul. It is the very path you have walked that will make it possible to remember *who* you are!

Both forgiveness and acceptance—in your life, about your life—will come naturally as you continue to walk the psychic pathway. As you seek to overcome your blocks and open up, you'll begin to experience more energy. You will naturally begin to understand people and events that, until now, may have both puzzled and hurt you.

As you become more aware of your Higher Self and your soul, you'll make a very important discovery—that even though your *mind* didn't know it, your *soul* has never been lost. It knows exactly where it's going, and if your ego will step out of the way and allow you to be guided, you will move *directly* toward your purpose in life. You'll also discover that it's not very far away from where you are right now. You simply couldn't see it.

Let me tell you a story about how forgiveness and acceptance transformed a human being.

One of my regular clients was a very young black man named Gregory. Gregory was a homosexual, a flight attendant who had come from a fatherless home. He was an only child but had a stepbrother fifteen years younger whom he adored, as well as a mother he cared a great deal about.

The first time he came to me, he wanted to know about the security of his job, about finding a lover because he was very lonely, about buying a home, transferring to another city, and so on. I focused on these issues. It was important and helpful for him to know that his security was stable.

But by the time he came to see me three years later, both he and I had changed. He wanted to go over basically the same issues we had talked about three years earlier, but this time I saw very different aspects and called his attention to much more serious conditions. Gregory was a sweet, caring man, but not an introspective one. He lived by his senses and found himself both drug-addicted and HIV positive. He wasn't manifesting outward signs of illness yet, but the combination was a match thrown into a barrel of gasoline.

Consciously Gregory was in deep denial about his drug addiction, his HIV, and above all, his deep, deep self-contempt for being lonely and gay. He wanted to die and was working on it. The problem I saw was that his soul wanted him to learn some degree of truth and self-love before he would be free. Even drugs and HIV were no escape from his lesson. He needed to learn about accepting who he was, see himself with truthful eyes, and learn to receive love and support from others.

Gregory's whole life was spent saving and serving others—his mom, his brother, the passengers on his flights, even lovers—but he never felt worthy of receiving love and support himself. Even though he was now moving in a lethal direction, his soul still offered the gift of healing for his heart, by experiencing support and love from others through his illness.

I suggested to Gregory that he go to a support group and see a very loving therapist. I told him he had time to look for healing, but no time to waste. I could see he was an old soul, and through his own dying process he could help others to live. He was a true server in this lifetime, and even his own death process would carry with it the gift of guiding others. I also saw he had enough time to forgive and heal his relationship with his father if he so desired. It took a death edict to give him the courage.

The last I heard, Gregory was physically weak but glowing spiritually. He was off drugs, in a wonderful support group, and at peace with his family. He was writing poetry and told me he was prepared for the future. He now had peace in his heart and had worked very hard to reach that peace. I had given him a map, marked out a few treasures, and set him on a new course. Gregory was dying, but he gave birth to his soul in a wonderful way.

Through forgiveness and acceptance, Gregory finally found his true worth and a place of peace. Even in the most bleak conditions, there is always the possibility for healing and growth. Remember, that is the point of the psychic pathway.

EASY DOES IT

As you look toward making life changes in the direction of your true self, you may feel overwhelmed. Relax for a minute. Have a little compassion. This is a process. Try looking at your blocks as the rules of the ordinary world. Once you decide you would rather live in an extraordinary world, the world of psychic awareness, creative expression, and spiritual peace, you'll experience a natural and gradual lightening as you stop living by the old rules and create a set of new rules.

We will take a balanced approach and strive to see the humor in all things. Setbacks *will* happen—they happen to us all. I ask you to expect them and have tolerance. Instead of condemning them, *study* setbacks and learn from them. Tempting as it may be to do "the big wallow," please don't indulge yourself in a self-bashing festival. It won't help your progress one bit.

As we remember who we are and start to live by our own integrity, our new rules evolve naturally. Like this:

Old Rules	*New Rules*
• I am a mortal being, full of sin, and basically not good, without worth.	• I am a spiritual being, a child of God, a divine miracle, inherently precious.
• I can't trust myself. I don't know what is good for me. Others know better.	• I can trust myself. My Higher Self always knows best, if I only listen.

- I am not psychic. These unusual experiences are coincidences, luck, "weird."

- Every moment of my day, my Higher Self directs me. Everything counts.

- I don't know where I'm going, what I'm doing. I hope it works out.

- I have clear goals. I know where I'm going. I'm in charge of my life and it is working out.

- I'm disorganized, rushed, behind schedule, too tired for it all.

- I'm organized and responsible. I say yes to what is important, no to the rest. I'm free of worry.

- People won't believe me, will think I'm weird, if I talk of my psychic ability.

- My experience is better, happier, when I trust and use my psychic ability. I don't need approval from others. My success in life will be my approval.

- I can't justify my feelings. How can I be sure?

- I operate on faith! I don't need to justify my intuition. I will be patient until it becomes clear why I am guided so.

- I'll play it safe. I'll ignore my psychic feelings.

- I'm not passive, I'm active. My psychic feelings are real. I use them for my benefit, ensuring my safety.

As you wake up, you'll begin to notice who else is awake and who isn't, and your expectations of people will change. From other wide-awake people, you can expect love, friendship, support, and integrity. From those who are still sleeping, you can expect confusion, fear, and drama. And as for those who are still sleeping, you can be more compassionate, because you will be enriched from the pleasure you experience with those who are wide awake.

EXPLORATIONS

My Toy Box

Many of us were turned from our natural pathway by being taught to adopt the values of authorities outside ourselves—parents, teachers, peers, even television! This exercise will help you recover your childhood loves. Fill in the blanks.

When I was a kid, I loved _to watch movies_ .

When I was a kid, I loved _to sit w/ my Dad_ .

When I was a kid, I loved _to play w/ my brothers_ .

When I was a kid, I loved _to talk to Gil_ .

When I was a kid, I loved _to go to Manor Park_ .

When I was a kid, I loved _read_ .

When I was a kid, I loved _write poetry_ .

When I was a kid, I loved _to listen to music_ .

When I was a kid, I loved _bicycle / rollerskate_ .

When I was a kid, I loved _play w/ friends_ .

"Somewhere, Over the Rainbow"

Now let's look at what you imagined you would be when you grew up. Fill in the blanks.

When I grow up, I want to be __Marine biologist__.

When I grow up, I want to be __film critic__.

When I grow up, I want to be __Married__.

When I grow up, I want to be __a mom__.

When I grow up, I want to be __living by the water__.

When I grow up, I want to be __in a caring community__.

When I grow up, I want to be _____.

When I grow up, I want to be _____.

When I grow up, I want to be _____.

When I grow up, I want to be _____.

"You May Ask Yourself, How Did I Get Here?"

Write a brief description of where you find yourself in life today. Be neutral. Don't define it emotionally, just define it. Stick to the facts.

Where do you live? __Arlington, MA__

What is your work? __Sp Ed teacher, reading__

What is your emotional/relationship status? _____

__Married__

How is your health? _so so_

Do you have family? Children? Pets? _2 children, 1 dog_

Do you have enough money to pay your bills? _yes_

_____

Ooh, That Hurt
Make a list from your past and present.

_____ hurt me by _____ .

_____ hurt me by _____ :

_____ hurt me by _____ :

_____ hurt me by _____ .

_____ hurt me by _____ .

_____ hurt me by _____ .

_____ hurt me by _____ .

_____ hurt me by _____ .

_____ hurt me by _____ .

_____ hurt me by _____ .

_____ hurt me by _____ .

_____ hurt me by _____ .

_____ hurt me by _____ .

_____ hurt me by _____ .

_____ hurt me by _____ .

_____ hurt me by _____ .

_____ hurt me by _____ .

_____ hurt me by _____ .

_____ hurt me by _____ .

_____ hurt me by _____ .

That Feels Better

After listing all the people and hurts, sit down on a comfortable chair and, with your list in hand, say out loud, to one person at a time:

_____, I forgive you for _____ .

Thank you for teaching me _____ .

_____, I forgive you for _____ .

Thank you for teaching me _____ .

_____, I forgive you for _____ .

Thank you for teaching me _____ .

_____, I forgive you for_____.

Thank you for teaching me_____.

_____, I forgive you for_____.

Thank you for teaching me_____.

_____, I forgive you for_____.

Thank you for teaching me_____.

_____, I forgive you for_____.

Thank you for teaching me_____.

_____, I forgive you for_____.

Thank you for teaching me_____.

_____, I forgive you for_____.

Thank you for teaching me_____.

_____, I forgive you for_____.

Thank you for teaching me_____.

_____, I forgive you for_____.

Thank you for teaching me_____.

_____, I forgive you for_____.

Thank you for teaching me_____.

_____, I forgive you for_____.

Thank you for teaching me_____.

_____, I forgive you for_____.

Thank you for teaching me_____.

_____, I forgive you for_____.

Thank you for teaching me_____.

_____, I forgive you for_____.

Thank you for teaching me_____.

_____, I forgive you for_____.

Thank you for teaching me_____.

_____, I forgive you for_____.

Thank you for teaching me_____.

_____, I forgive you for_____.

Thank you for teaching me_____.

_____, I forgive you for_____.

Thank you for teaching me_____.

That Feels Great!

Now let's look at some of the great things that you've experienced in your life. Ask yourself:

What's your favorite memory of your mother? _____

_____

What's your favorite memory of your father? _sitting w/_

him in the den watching movies

What's your favorite memory of your siblings? _____

Girl - little red tape recorder

What's your favorite memory of the house you grew up in? _____

lots + lots of memories -

What is your favorite memory of your grandparents? _____

_____

Who were your favorite friends? _Lili, Fran,_

(Eileen (Carolyn -)

What fun things did you do together? _____

_____

When was the first time you fell in love? _____

Billy -

Who gave you your first kiss? _____

Billy _____

What was the funniest thing that happened to you in high school? _____

_____

Who was your best friend after high school? _Carolyn_ ___

What was your first vacation on your own? _____

_____

What was your first really *great* car like? _Plymouth Colt_ _____

_____

What was your greatest triumph at work? _____

_____

What are you best at? How did you learn? _Teaching –_ _____

_____

What did you like best about your childhood? _My brothers –_ _____

+ Dad _____

What did you like best about your teens? _Billy –_ _____

_____

What did you like best about your twenties?_____

_____

What did you like best about your thirties?_____

_____

What did you like best about your forties?_____

_____

What do you like best about your life now?_____

_____

CHARTING YOUR PROGRESS

How many days this week did you meditate? Any new perspectives?_____

_____

How many days this week did you make an entry in your psychic journal? (Any old memories resurface?)_____

_____

Which exercise did you find most powerful?_____

_____

Which exercise did you find most painful?_____

_____

Which exercise did you find most joyful?_____

_____

How did you feel physically after you did these exercises?_____

_____

_____

What forgotten piece of yourself did you find in these exercises?_____

_____

_____

Discovering New Territory

Start practicing this week being more aware of the world around you. You will notice that this is possible only if you slow down, breathe, and pay attention. When you drive or travel to work, pay attention to the scenery around you—really look and notice what is there.

Half of psychic awareness is awareness, period! If you go through life tuned out, it is very hard to tune in. Make a point this week of actually being where you are: not in a book, not in the past, not in the future—right where you are.

Notice. Use all of your senses. What do you see? What do you hear? What do you smell? What do you feel? Where are you? This information alone is a revelation for many.

As I tell my students, this is like beginning an exercise program. At first, your muscles resist. Eventually, through gentle repetition, they become more flexible and strong. We are doing the same thing with your awareness.

As you set yourself up to be more sensitive to psychic energy, you must first set yourself up to be aware of energy, period.

BECOMING AWARE OF OTHERS' ENERGY

When dealing with people, look at them. Study them. Hear what they are saying. This will be easier to do if you have been meditating to shut down mind chatter. Allow yourself to notice and sense the energy of people, places, and things.

We all have distinct vibrational patterns and tones. Some people's patterns are tense and static and their tone high-pitched. Other people's patterns of energy are slow and thick and their tone low and dull. Practice noticing the various types of energy, or "vibes," people give off.

Whenever you encounter someone—friend or stranger, whether or not you know or like them—take a deep, slow breath when you are interacting, and as you exhale concentrate on how their energy feels to you. For the sake of helping you identify their energy pattern, see if you can classify it as:

1. fast	2. moderate	3. slow
1. tense	2. relaxed	3. dull
1. warm	2. lukewarm	3. cool
1. vibrant	2. calm	3. lethargic

Emotionally, how does this person feel to you?

1. happy	2. neutral	3. sad
1. healthy	2. neutral	3. sick
1. calm	2. neutral	3. nervous
1. honest	2. neutral	3. lying

Don't rely on the conversation you may have with someone to identify a person's energy. As we all know, many times what a person says is not at all an indication of how he or she really is.

Also during this exercise, notice your own energy pattern and vibration. How do different people affect you? Again, ask yourself, am I:

1. calm	2. neutral	3. nervous
1. content	2. neutral	3. angry
1. happy	2. neutral	3. sad
1. comfortable	2. neutral	3. uncomfortable
1. honest and open	2. neutral	3. lying or covering up

You may also find it fun to ask yourself, What color is this person on the emotional rainbow? Do they have red, warm, zoomy energy, full of heat? Do they have orange, glowing, bouncy energy, full of vitality? Do they have golden-yellow energy, full of radiance, optimism, and strength? Do they have green, calming, nurturing energy, responsive and accepting?

Maybe their energy is light blue—serene, open-minded, reflective, and cerebral. Perhaps it is indigo—intense, mysterious, profound. Is it violet—powerful, inspiring, regal, and uplifting? It could even be white—clear, safe, quiet, and high. Maybe they are none of these colors. Some people are gray. Some brown. Some, a very rare few, will feel black.

What color are you?

You are training yourself with this activity to notice how a person's vibrational pattern affects you. The fact is, we are constantly being influenced by people on an energy plane all the time. I believe it is *more* influential in how it affects us than what we say to one another.

We need to stop our mind chatter and notice these energy patterns, study their influence on us if we want to develop our psychic ability. The hardest part of learning to do this is to stop your own mind chatter long enough to really *pay attention* to the interaction of energy actually taking place in front of you. Simply noticing people, noticing their energy and its influence on you, is a great breakthrough in psychic development.

Up until this point you have been no less influenced by others' energy, but you were far less conscious of it. This often left you confused about what you felt and why.

Try to notice how people affect you, but try not to fall into a habit of interpreting it simplistically as "good" or "bad." People who make you feel "good" may be giving you energy, whereas people who make you feel "bad" may be draining your energy.

It isn't that one type is a good person, another bad. It's that one type has a beneficial energy and the other a detrimental energy to you. By studying the effects neutrally, you can adjust yourself to the person's energy and act accordingly.

For example, if you are around a draining force, you can:

- move away,
- cut the conversation short, or
- redirect that person's attention.

By being aware, you give yourself choices and can act appropriately. When you are unaware, you may not notice you are being drained, and you may become cranky or upset with the next person down the line, just to vent your pent-up frustration. Then, of course, that person will consider you the negative one.

GROUNDING

Once you are alert to how people's energy affects you, you have to train yourself to keep them from affecting you. People's energy patterns are real. If you could see these energy patterns, you would notice that they look like swirling cocoons of energy surrounding each individual.

When a person's energy intermixes with your own, it is literally a commingling of two bands of energy. Sometimes it's nice, but usually it's cumbersome and draining. Ideally you want to learn to observe these energy patterns mentally but not absorb them emotionally.

Let me give you an example. Let's say you are in a relationship with someone. Imagine that you have a dinner date, one that you have been looking forward to for several days. Now imagine that when your friend meets you, even though he or she is smiling, the energy is tense, static, and disturbing.

If you notice *emotionally,* chances are that you'll feel disappointed, angry, or defensive, even though the conversation may be superficially pleasant and cordial. If this occurs, your energy will change and start to set up defensive barriers.

When two energies intermingle at this intensity long enough, an explosion will undoubtedly occur, usually resulting in an argument or fight. Another possible outcome is that one person's energy can completely drain the other's. Have you ever been locked into a conversation with someone and it feels like the blood is draining right out of your body? Or, after disengaging from the person, did you feel an overwhelming urge to lie down?

Another type of commingling of energy occurs when you are around people who are very energetic, and you are down in the dumps. You may unwittingly tap into their vitality, leaving you energized, but leaving them depleted. If you are sensitive to energy but unaware of it, this sort of thing may happen to you frequently.

If you are aware of energy patterns, you will notice that the energy pattern of your companion is dissonant to your own, and if you choose not to engage it emotionally, you can respond in a better way. You won't take it personally and won't get defensive.

If you continue to observe, you will probably be able to locate the source of your companion's tension. At that point, depending on your social skills, you can ignore it, humor your companion into a different mode, or offer to listen to your companion's problem causing the tension. At any rate, all three choices are better than fighting or getting hurt and frustrated.

This is easier said than done, however, unless you learn a skill called "grounding."

Consider that we all are huge electrical energy stations, sending out, picking up, and holding in energy all the time. We have multiple layers of physical, emotional, mental, and psychic energy flowing into, around, and out of our bodies at all times. Grounding is a technique that calmly drains your self of excess energy, thus keeping your perceptions clear, your emotions balanced, and your body relaxed and so preventing emotional explosions.

The best method of grounding is so obvious you will not believe it: touch the ground. That's right, simply put your hands onto or into the earth. We are as much an energy station as an electrical station on earth, and we are as dangerous to ourselves and others when not grounded.

Grounding means channeling your energy into the *ground*. If you are lucky enough to have a yard, go into it and dig up the earth. Plant a garden if possible, and tend to it every day. Literally put your hands and feet in dirt. Potting soil will also work. Plant herbs or flowers in small pots if you live in the city. By playing with dirt, your excess emotional energy will drain. It's healing and effective and a lot of fun!

Working with clay is another way to get grounded. A simple bag of children's clay, the kind that won't dry out, is very grounding. Play with it for an hour.

Any activity that uses your hands in a creative way is very grounding. Clean a closet, paint your walls, organize books. Cooking and baking in particular are grounding. Baking bread both grounds your energy and nurtures your self. All these activities are grounding, drain you of excess energy overload, and restore balance.

City dwellers may need to touch a tree. If possible, lay on the grass. If not, in the dead of winter in Manhattan, you may want to buy that bag of potting soil and keep a bowl of it available to play in. (Remember how much fun it was as a little kid to make mud pies? It's still fun.)

Exercising, going for a walk, or playing sports can also be grounding, and is especially helpful if your energy is really sluggish or overcharged.

You may realize that you do these things naturally. That's how smart you really are. Your soul does know what it needs, always. Now you just know why.

CRYSTALS AND OTHER GROUNDING MATERIALS

In addition to these exercises, there are other ways to get grounded. For example, crystals are very grounding, and specific crystals help you in different ways.

Obsidian is volcanic rock. It is black and opaque and is excellent for blocking energy. This is a good crystal for hypersensitive types, people who pick up too much energy and are too concerned about other people.

Fluorite, especially green fluorite, is especially good for grounding and balance and is calming to the nervous system.

Hematite is also grounding and helps people with addiction problems, because it stabilizes emotions.

Carry these crystals, wear them as jewelry, or sleep with them by your bedside. Crystals are an especially practical tool to hide in a desk drawer if you have a tense work environment. Whenever you feel too charged up with other people's energy, simply reach for your crystals, hold them in both hands, and imagine this unwanted energy flowing out of you and into the crystals. Occasionally, put your crystals in the ground to drain and clear them of their negative charge.

Keeping yourself clear of other people's energy and staying grounded enhance your awareness a hundred percent. Try it. The clearing exercises above are similar to cleaning windows and looking at life in clear weather. When you are not grounded and clear, it's like looking at life through dirty windows during an electrical storm.

When you notice people around you, when you look for and study their energy from a clear, grounded frame of consciousness, you will see and know so much more about them than before. Not only will you have a clearer point of reference, but your awareness will also be more connected to the voice of your Higher Self.

How often should you ground your energy? Let's put it this way: as often as necessary—all the time, every hour, every day. Do it until it becomes second nature. Do it so often that you become used to having grounded awareness. Do it until it becomes automatic. Do it until being clear is the most comfortable and natural way for you to be. That sounds like another big assignment, but if you do it as little as five times, you will experience the changes I am talking about. You will be more aware, more informed, more relaxed, more in control. Let your experience argue for the effort.

As I said, being psychic is being in the world differently. It is being aware of energy *before* it sets up conditions. It is noticing everything and *responding* rather than reacting. It is teaching your awareness to work harder, until it opens up and operates on a grander level.

Again, the best way to go about this is to play games. Grounding and clearing should be integrated into your morning shower. Do it after you brush your teeth, eat your lunch, take a bath, go to the bathroom, comb your hair. Be creative. Do it all the time!

Your awareness exercises are more interesting if you record your results in your psychic journal. You don't have to write a lot. Just a note or two. For example:

> Today boss's energy was relaxed, her vitality up, calm. Mom's energy was tense, nervous, tired. Daughter—energy scattered, all over, excited.

Just *notice*. Notice your own, too, before grounding and after. Psychic development is the direct result of paying attention to everything. It all counts! You must live in the world by a new sense—awareness—if you want to develop your intuitive gifts. Until now, you may have shut down your awareness or dulled it by being too busy, too disorganized, too unconscious. Meditation and grounding put you into a wide-awake, alert state. It may feel as though you are coming out of a fog! It may shock you, and you will have to adjust. Being more aware means being more honest and more responsible. It also means being more effective and satisfied in the end. Enjoy all of this. It's very exciting!

JUST IMAGINE

The *best* and most direct way I know to expand your awareness and to access the psychic arena is through the imagination. By using your imagination, you shift your focus off the five-sensory world of appearances and place it onto the extrasensory world of possibility, solutions, and answers. You cannot experience psychic energy without your imagination, because psychic energy comes *through* the imagination! That is why most people dismiss their intuition as simple imagining. It is!

More exactly, it is the imagination that receives your intuitive messages and makes them intelligible to your conscious mind. How else would you receive psychic impulses?

You cannot become psychic, at least consistently psychic, without imagining it possible. If you can't imagine it, you won't experience it. Imagination is the magic wand that, once waved, will change your experience from one of reacting to your world into one of creating your world. The ability to be psychic, to use all your senses fully, lies with you giving yourself permission to do so. If you want to be psychic, start imagining that you are! If you do this, an extraordinary shift occurs. Your imagination is set free to access the psychic support systems that will guide you toward a better experience.

With your permission, you expand your realm of input from one that depends largely on your five senses and your ego to one that draws from your sixth and highest sense, and your soul. With this decision alone, your psychic awareness will "turn on." It is like pushing a button and seeing the show light up.

When you use your imagination to ask for psychic guidance, where do you think your imagination will look for answers? First, it will check with your *subconscious*. Next, it will focus on *telepathic rapport*, and finally it will shift and zero in on *superconscious guidance*. The imagination directly accesses your psychic support systems when it is given a problem. It is the front door to your intuition. Let's try opening that door through a few psychic games.

All of these games enhance your awareness, focus your attention on the moment, teach you to see, hear, and feel what is real, and once again, return to you the power of the imagination. There is no greater power, as it is the imagination that creates experience.

EXPLORATIONS

Grounding

This exercise should be done whenever you feel your vibration is over-active or out of balance or you feel you are being excessively influenced emotionally by someone else's—or your own—energy. Remember to pay attention to your energy. If you are anxious, nervous, short-tempered, volatile, or emotional, you need to get grounded.

You may sit or stand, but you must place both feet flat on the ground. If you are sitting, sit up straight, hands on lap. If standing, place your hands at your sides, palms inward. Then exhale, forcing all the air out of your lungs, before *slowly* inhaling to the count of eight. Now exhale once again, and imagine all the excess energy in your being draining down from the top of your head, down the spinal column, splitting, and continuing to move down your legs, out the soles of your feet, and into the ground.

Repeat this until you feel calm. It takes about five minutes.

Now that you are grounded and balanced, we'll do some psychic calisthenics.

The "I Wonder" Game

One of the best psychic ways I know to engage your imagination is to play a game called "I Wonder." Every time you say to yourself "I wonder . . ." you summon your imagination and turn on the intuitive flow. Use this game every chance you get. Here's how: Introduce this query into the flow of your daily life.

I wonder . . .

- who's on the phone?
- which elevator will arrive first?
- what will be on sale at the grocery store?
- where my keys are?
- whom I'll meet today?

- what's the best way to get downtown and avoid traffic?
- who will win the basketball game?

The idea is to present as many "I wonder" questions to the Higher Self as possible, then allow yourself to imagine the answers. Don't make the questions complex, and avoid asking emotionally charged questions at this time. If a question is emotionally charged, the ego reenters. Until you are comfortable with introducing your psychic voice to your conscious mind, you want to avoid setting up a conflict with your ego! At this time you simply want to play.

When your psychic choice is right, say, "Hurray!" Celebrate! Write it down. Tell a sympathetic friend. When you are not, shrug it off and say, "Oh, well," and try again. This is not a test or measure of your worth. It is an opportunity to let yourself loosen up and play and let your imagination reenter your experience.

No matter what the results of your I Wonder game, your life will be greatly stimulated by working your imagination so actively. Do you realize that every invention in the world today reflects someone's imagination? Imagination creates the world! It is not only the source of your psychic ability, it is the source of *all* your ability. By playing I Wonder, you stimulate your awareness, you focus your attention, and you bring your full attention to the here and now. You pay attention and enhance awareness.

Being psychic means seeing what *is*—not what *isn't*. Paying attention is a fundamental part of awakening intuition. Here's how.

Bursting the Bubble

Most people live in a bubble. They see what they want to see, hear what they want to hear, notice what they want to notice, rearrange the truth to fit their perceptions, and then call this jumbled concoction "reality." The amusing part is that no two people's reality is the same, because no two people record the world the same way.

Learning to be psychic requires an honest willingness to see what is real without modifying it to meet our desires or preconceived notions.

Learning to see what *is* means learning to look closely and objectively. Set up games that require you to look and record experiences accurately, so that your subconscious mind is given correct information for storage and so that you learn to see the truth, free from emotional coloration.

How do I do that? you ask. Start by playing attention games. The following are children's games redone with a psychic slant. Let yourself enjoy playing. Remember: These are games, not tests!

Hide-and-Seek

One good way is to get children's books (surprised?) that have you search for hidden pictures. There are whole series of books out there, such as the *I Spy* series, with exactly these types of scenes to study. They help you develop a keen eye, teach you to look and notice subtle or hidden objects, and train your eye to register what is on the page.

Finders Peepers

In your journal write down from memory what each family member or office worker was wearing—today? yesterday? Relax and try to see in your mind's eye every detail. Recall as much as you can! It is exercise, so don't give up after one day. Make it a habit.

Telephone

Play this one by having a friend say a sentence to you. *Listen.* Breathe. Repeat the sentence, word for word.

Psychic ability is the art of listening to your intuition. This begins by learning the art of listening, first to others, then to your Higher Self. The better a listener you are, the more psychic you'll become.

Repeat after Me

Listen to every word that someone says in a conversation with you— *really* listen to each word. Before you come back with an answer or response, repeat to yourself each word the person said to you, exactly as it was said, until you *hear* the message. It helps to breathe when listening. This one takes effort!

CHARTING YOUR PROGRESS

How is the meditation going? Is your meditation experience changing? Did your imagination inspire anything new in your meditation?_____

_____

_____

How many days this week did you make entries in your psychic journal?_____

Are you remembering to check your energy?_____

_____

Are you checking other people's energy?_____

_____

Have you grounded your energy? How? How often? Do you have a favorite way of grounding yourself?_____

_____

_____

How do you feel after you are grounded?_____

_____

Does it help you notice more of your surroundings?_____

_____

Checking the Weather

Psychic ability is expanded awareness. This heightened awareness is received (perceived) through your physical body. The more you understand how your body receives energy from others and from higher planes of consciousness, the more energy you will be able to receive and use to your benefit.

Last week you noticed energy. This week you will notice how this energy is psychic and how it affects you physically. Pay attention to how it comes into your field of awareness. Start by reflecting on how you feel when you get an intuitive feeling.

It may seem odd to try to define how psychic energy feels, but it does feel *some* way. . . . To the best of your ability, try to notice how a psychic or intuitive feeling is different from your normal flow of thoughts. Do all your intuitions feel the same? Can you describe a "good" psychic feeling versus a "negative" psychic feeling? Do these different types of feelings affect different parts of your body? Remember, the first step in psychic development is to *notice* more subtle energy, energy that usually escapes your awareness.

This week, whenever you get a psychic feeling, examine your experience and try to answer as many of these questions as possible. Now, let's talk about how your body is designed to be psychic.

THE AURA

When you begin to develop your psychic ability, you will notice that there's far more to the world than you noticed before. As you begin to train your senses to work harder, you will start to perceive energy you never knew existed.

The very first new discovery you'll make is your aura, which is the field of energy flowing closely around your body and extending up to twelve inches from it in all directions—above your head, in front of you, behind you, and under your feet. The aura is like a protective force field surrounding your body. (An exercise to help you see your aura is included in the explorations at the end of this chapter.)

This field is composed of your *consciousness,* your level of awareness. When your consciousness is fearful, angry, sick, sorrowful, resentful, aggressive, or vindictive, the aura becomes dark, and the nature of this field of energy becomes sticky, like an oily sludge. It will hold negative thoughts in its field, making a person feel physically and emotionally depressed. A negative aura also attracts other people's negativity, which can congest it further, weighing on both your emotions and your health.

The higher the state of your consciousness, the lighter and more clear your aura will be. The flow of energy will also be faster. If you are happy, optimistic, forgiving, and loving, your aura will be light, clear, and moving quickly. You will feel "up" and energetic and will attract positive energy to you from others.

The reason for this attractive quality is that like attracts like, and your state of consciousness will automatically attract to you other people of like mind. In many ways we are aware of the energy around us, energy from the people we focus our attention on.

But what you may not know is that you are even more affected by people's energy in their thoughts and emotions than you are by their words. For example, a person may be overtly agreeable but may really resent you, sending you very negative energy without your even being aware of it. You will recognize this happening to you if you experience a sudden change in mood, feeling suddenly nervous or irritable for no apparent reason. This is called *psychic attack*. Psychic attack occurs when someone willfully or consciously is sending you negative energy.

For instance, I once read for a client named Jeanine. She was a very charismatic woman and ran a successful public relations firm, employing about seventy people. She came to me because even though she loved her work and felt it was the right thing to do in her life, she was cranky, impatient, and irritable, especially with the person she depended on most—her secretary, Catherine.

Jeanine felt guilty and ashamed of her lack of self-control, yet every time she spent more than ten minutes with Catherine, she would sink into a bad mood that she couldn't shake. Outwardly Catherine was very accommodating and helpful, so there was no apparent reason for Jeanine's irritation. Nevertheless, it was there. She asked me if I had any clues on the matter, as it was taking up too much of her time mentally.

One look at Jeanine's aura showed me she was experiencing psychic attack. The energy in her aura was very negative and full of jealousy. It was muddy brown and red and looked like sludge. Her efficient secretary, who *was* very hardworking, was also very ambitious and coveted Jeanine's job. Even though Catherine was outwardly pleasant, she secretly resented not being the boss herself and was extremely jealous of Jeanine.

Negative, draining, and damaging as it was, this consciousness attached itself to Jeanine's aura every time she was in Catherine's presence long enough for this to happen—about ten minutes. This psychic energy of resentment began to attack Jeanine's aura, causing a reaction in her mood. She became irritable, thus further antagonizing the already jealous secretary, who in turn sent out more hostile energy. It became a vicious, though subtle, cycle.

When I told Jeanine what I saw, she didn't believe it. Yet four months later she called back to tell me that this same woman had started her own company, taking several of Jeanine's employees and clients with her. Jeanine was shocked, but she remembered our discussion. Now she's far more alert to how people affect her mood and her aura.

A milder form of psychic attack is called *psychic pollution.* Psychic pollution occurs when you are exposed to someone's negative energy, and this energy attaches itself to your aura, affecting how you feel. The result is a milder form of the irritation, nervousness, or anxiety you experience under psychic attack. It can even make you sick.

I once read for another client named Lisa. Lisa was a very sweet, gentle woman who had a difficult time believing she was lovable. She was quite beautiful and had married a very successful man and for all the world looked very happy. But Lisa never felt quite right physically. She suffered from mild depression, stomach and intestinal problems, and fatigue, which prevented her from working. Fortunately her husband was very successful in business, and there was plenty of money. She came to me with questions about her health.

One look at her aura showed me she was suffering from psychic pollution. There were no rips or tears in her aura, but it looked like a smoggy day in Los Angeles. I asked her whom she was spending time with, because wherever she was the negativity was harming her health.

She told me that she spent quite a bit of time at a battered women's shelter as a volunteer. She felt guilty for having such a good life, both emotionally and monetarily, and felt she should do something for less fortunate women or she would be selfish.

The idea was noble, but the reality of the situation was that all the negativity, abuse, and anger she was working with was infiltrating her aura and clinging to her like smog. It entered gradually, but before she knew it, her aura was full of this negative, depressing energy. It was compounded by her own guilt over being well supported. She wasn't comfortable receiving love from her husband, so she tried to pass along the energy rather than use it as protection for herself.

I told Lisa that to energize her drained physical state, she needed to clear her aura of all the negativity she was surrounded by, as well as that which was generated by her own guilt. She also needed to use her husband's love and support as protection and raise her self-esteem enough to receive love. Finally, because her vibration was so easily influenced, I told her she should consider working in a preschool with children, where the energy was lighter, more loving. She didn't have the temperament or the ability to protect herself from negative energy.

I showed her how to clear her aura and protect herself through grounding and aura-clearing exercises. It was like washing windows and letting in the sunshine. With concentration and a few new decisions, Lisa cleared her aura and regained her vitality.

If you find yourself drawn to the important work of assisting in a shelter or the like, use the protective energies of grounding and aura-clearing exercises before, during, and after your work. You should also meditate afterward to clear your mind of troubling vibrations. My teacher Charlie taught me to *observe*, not *absorb*, energy when doing service for others.

I know being affected by auras sounds farfetched, but it really isn't. People's moods affect others all the time. We constantly react to people, often unwittingly. Think about it. The tense boss. The volatile wife. The depressed friend. The joyful child. The more sensitive you are, the more easily you will be affected by the vibrations people carry in their auras. Yet people are not in the habit of noticing how another's energy affects them.

Once you embark on the psychic pathway, you must begin to notice everything. The simple act of paying attention will alert you to many new levels of energy influencing you.

STORMY WEATHER

When people experience frequent arguments, fights, or a severe trauma, the energy that accompanies this consciousness can actually rip or tear the aura, leaving holes or weak spots. This causes their equilibrium to shift off balance, and they may become vulnerable to random violence, further attack, sickness, or depression. This is because the tear or rip allows random consciousness floating in the universe to seep into their personal space, wreaking havoc on their mind and emotions. Drug abuse, alcoholic states, sexual assault, and extreme fear or anger also tear the aura due to the intense imbalances in energy flow.

For example, a woman named Shelly once came to me for a reading. She was an artistic woman and devoted her life to singing in a band, doing performance art, and writing music. When she arrived, she was severely depressed and physically debilitated. Her aura looked as if a cat had been let loose in a paper bag. Every part of it was ripped, torn, shaggy, and ragged. There was no flow of vitality or protection around her. She was in grave danger.

Shelly's problem was multiple. She had a drug-addicted husband, and she herself was an alcoholic. The two of them waged war against each other relentlessly. They were both usually either high or angry. Shelly also took many lovers as a way of retaliating against her husband's aggressive attempts to control her. She and her husband were in the same band, and it was very successful locally, so they had a hard time separating since they depended on each other for money.

The toll this craziness took on Shelly was destroying her psychic body as well as her mental health. Her aura gave her no protection at all, and she was exposed to all sorts of psychic debris. For her soul it was the equivalent of being homeless. Shelly needed much care and love over a long period of time to recover.

She was so weakened by the time I met her that she rejected the work of self-care her healing involved. Later she had a nervous breakdown, a condition where the aura erodes completely. After that she began to receive treatment, but by then the damage was so great that it will take a long time to heal herself completely. She is working on it.

A torn aura requires healing. If you are exposed to abuse, fighting, anger, intense emotions, or substance abuse, chances are your aura is torn. If it is, you will feel weak, emotionally volatile, unstable, and even physically drained. To heal the aura, you may need to see a professional body worker who is trained in massage therapy, rolfing, or aura realignment treatment. If you feel this is your problem, seek a professional on the recommendation of someone you trust, as you may be very vulnerable. You also may need the care and guidance of a counselor.

Healing the aura is achieved when a person is helped by a loving and wise support person. Healing the aura involves learning to receive love and forgiving and releasing grudges against antagonists. Support people can be found in therapy, Twelve Step groups, support groups, spiritual and religious groups, and sometimes within your family.

Learning to love yourself is the antidote to most relationship battles. It heals both the aura and the emotions.

EXPLORATIONS

Feel the Energy

Ask yourself exactly how you feel when you get a psychic or intuitive feeling.

- Do you get a tingling in your stomach?
- Do you feel an unusual tension in your chest? Or your heart? Around your ears?
- Do words pop into your mind?
- Do images flash across your mental screen?
- Do you sense pressure or a change of sensation anywhere in your body?
- Do you get a "gut" feeling?
- Do you get a "lump" in your heart?
- Do psychic energy or impulses make you nervous? Restless? Antsy?

Aura Awareness

Becoming aware of your aura is easy. Simply rub your palms together, then shake out your hands. Rub them together again, then face your palms inward toward each other, five inches apart. Close your eyes and notice the pull of energy between your palms. This space between your palms is part of your aura. It feels like sticky or thick air. For some the temperature of the aura is cool. For others it is warmer. It may send tingles up your arms.

This energy is like a spider's web. It catches and holds vibrations in it. Therefore there will be various textures and tones to the aura. In some places, like around the head, the aura will be one color and flow, and in another place, often around the heart, the aura will be a different color and flow. The aura is like your personal weather pattern, and like the weather, it changes—from sunny to overcast to stormy, from cool to warm, from muggy to crystal clear.

When you are unconscious of the aura and of the different effects the energy of others has on you, you can be easily manipulated and influenced by vibrations you cannot control. When you become aware of the aura, you can begin to control whether someone will affect you or not, simply by noticing.

Seeing Your Aura

The aura reveals a lot about the state of mind, body, and soul a person is in. If you practice relaxing your eyes, you can see the aura emanating from a person's body. This exercise takes a little practice, but you can succeed with patience.

Stand in front of a mirror with only soft light behind you. Let your eyes relax. Imagine seeing the haze of your aura as it emanates from your body. Look for the wavy lines flowing like a force field. If you could imagine seeing a color in the aura, what color would it be? Remember the chapter on imagination? Let your imagination direct this exercise. Relax into it, don't force it. Imagine seeing the color of your aura. What color is this? Do you see any shapes or dark spots? Any weak places? How far does your aura extend outward from your body? Make it up—imagine you are psychic.

Let your eyes close and relax after two or three minutes. You can repeat this exercise once or twice, then try again at another time.

Aura Hygiene

It's important to keep on your toes and notice the tone and feel of your aura. Is it loaded with psychic garbage? Does it need to be cleared out? The best thing to do is to clear your aura daily, as a part of your hygiene routine. Brush your teeth, comb your hair, clear your aura.

It is also beneficial to check your aura throughout the day to see if it feels clear and free of psychic debris and pollution. If it is becoming congested, clear it by meditating or grounding yourself, or by doing the following clearing exercises.

Rain, Rain, Go Away

If someone's energy is unappealing to you, stand away from them and imagine a silvery-white energy shield surrounding your own aura, standing between you and the person with bad vibes. Intend for this shield to shut out all energy that comes from a place or person other than yourself. (Energy tends to hang in the air, and even places have vibrations that you may not want attached to your aura.) Imagine this silvery-white shield blocking all unwanted vibrations, be they from places, people, or atmospheric psychic debris.

A Breath of Fresh Air

Another way of removing and clearing negative energy from your aura is to stand up, feet apart, solidly on the ground, and close your eyes. Imagine your aura in your mind's eye. See all the floating debris and particles hanging in your aura. Now, as you breathe in, imagine all this energy coming to a standstill. As you breathe out, imagine pushing all negative energy other than your own out of your force field and back into the atmosphere. Finally, fill your aura with clear, loving energy and seal it with the silvery-white shield. Try this and you will feel a great difference in your mood. You will feel lighter, freer, and more refreshed.

If you feel you are psychically polluted or under attack, do the following exercise.

Ozone Alert

Stand with your feet twelve inches apart. Close your eyes and imagine standing inside a beautiful pink bubble. Fill this bubble with golden-white light and ask your guides and angels to remove from your aura all negativity directed toward you or left behind by someone else. Ask your angels and guides to replace all such energy with a golden-white light and vibrations of God's love.

If you know the source of psychic attack, tell that person's soul that it must leave your vibration and imagine yourself unplugging from your aura an attachment that it has made to you. If you feel the energy of psychic attack and don't know the source, then imagine your guides and angels simply unplugging all attachments of any sort to your aura, regardless of their source. See your aura filled with white light and love.

Now envision unplugging yourself from any attachment you may have made to others. Release all attachments and return your consciousness to your own energy and aura. Breathe in and see your aura in a crystal clear light. Slowly open your eyes.

Auras affect people more than words. Auras bring the sum total of one person's consciousness into contact with the sum total of another person's consciousness. It's like intermingling two different radio frequencies—leaving a confusing end result.

CHARTING YOUR PROGRESS

Remember, meditation is a very thorough way of clearing the aura. How are your meditation periods going?_____

_____

How many days this week did you make entries in your psychic journal? Were you more aware of the energy from others?_____

_____

How many days this week have you remembered to ground yourself? Were there any changes in your experience after doing this?_____

_____

_____

Have you been aware of your aura? _____

_____

Have you cleared it? Feel better? _____

_____

Have you felt a psychic attack? _____

_____

Have you repaired any tears? _____

_____

Are you remembering your aura hygiene? _____

_____

Wheel Alignment

THE CHAKRAS

The concept of the aura is *not* a metaphor—the aura is real. It exists, and so do the magical, powerful, whirling energy centers you will learn about now. These seven energy centers are known as *chakras,* a Sanskrit word meaning "wheel."

You may have heard about chakras before, and you may even have thought, Yeah, right. They may have struck you as an obscure, complicated, *possible* concept—but something only an adroit could actually experience.

No. Chakras are not complicated. They are both real and well within your realm of experience. In fact, you experience them all the time—although you may call these experiences "a gut feeling," "a sense," "a funny vibe," "a mood." The chakras are like internal radio satellites, going from punk rock to classical. Each chakra picks up a different band of energy, from dense to very fine.

There are seven of these psychic relay stations in your body and extending outward into your aura (see illustrations on pages 142-143), each designed to send out and pick up psychic energy. Classically they are described as wheels of energy, located approximately along the spine from the tip of the tailbone to the top of the head.

Chakras work as communication satellites. They control the degree and quality of conscious awareness we possess. The chakra satellites relay information three ways:

- From person to person
- From the subconscious to the conscious mind
- From the conscious mind to the plane of the Higher Self, guides, and divine guidance.

The three lower chakras (called the "first three") govern self-consciousness, survival, and will. The middle chakra is the center of love and connects physical awareness to spiritual awareness. The top three chakras direct the psychic activity of clairaudience, clairsentience, clairvoyance, and enlightenment.

Each chakra vibrates at a certain speed and emanates a different color in the aura. These chakras work together, and when balanced in your body, they create a very grounded and receptive psychic awareness level.

FIRST CHAKRA (BASE)

The *base chakra* is located at the base of the spine, near the tailbone and extending outward into the aura. This chakra vibrates slowly and emanates a vibrant red hue in the aura. The base chakra primarily controls the consciousness of survival. It stimulates the urge for a person to take care of him- or herself in order to stay alive. It is the vortex of energy that urges a person to eat, to sleep, to protect him- or herself, and to be aware of danger. This consciousness is important to keep a person alive and moving in life.

If this chakra is overactive, it causes a person to be paranoid, self-centered and selfish, aggressive, manic, overactive, nervous, and self-

THE SEVEN CHAKRAS

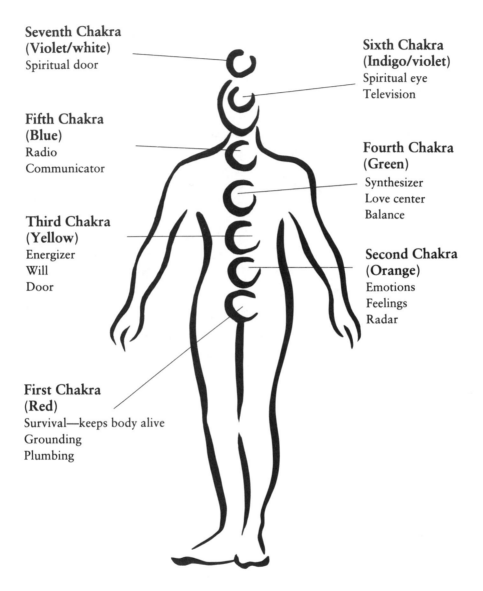

**Seventh Chakra
(Violet/white)**
Spiritual door

**Sixth Chakra
(Indigo/violet)**
Spiritual eye
Television

**Fifth Chakra
(Blue)**
Radio
Communicator

**Fourth Chakra
(Green)**
Synthesizer
Love center
Balance

**Third Chakra
(Yellow)**
Energizer
Will
Door

**Second Chakra
(Orange)**
Emotions
Feelings
Radar

**First Chakra
(Red)**
Survival—keeps body alive
Grounding
Plumbing

indulgent. If this chakra is underfunctioning, a person may be passive, depressed, deny him- or herself basic care and survival needs, and be out of touch with the body's physicality.

THE SEVEN CHAKRAS
Side View

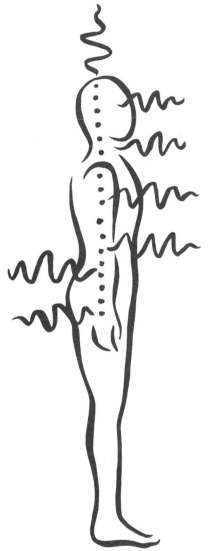

Nola came for her reading both angry and exhausted. She and her husband fought constantly. Neither would give in. He attacked her verbally, she attacked him physically, yet neither one really wanted to leave the other. The problem was that they were in a battle of first chakra "survival" energy. Each thought giving in was capitulation, that they were putting themselves in danger of being oppressed or being controlled by their partner. They were engaged in a power struggle on the psychic plane. They fought to win, and neither spouse was willing to lose.

I tried to encourage Nola to work from love instead of her first chakra of survival. She thought her husband should do this, not her. I explained that most likely he would never change first, as his survival chakra was more expanded than hers.

As far as I know, neither of them ever redirected their energy. Sadly, their battle rages on.

To balance and calm your first chakra, you must close your eyes and place your attention directly on this satellite. In your mind's eye, see the satellite of energy spinning around evenly, about the size of a large orange, maybe four inches in diameter. Imagine this satellite spinning around like a perfectly balanced orb, resting about three inches behind your body at the place of your tailbone.

Envision the satellite drawing in consciousness energy to keep the body strong, healthy, self-accepting, and with a balanced appetite for sustenance. Imagine this red-colored chakra sending waves of vitality to every cell in your body. If you are insecure or fearful, see this vitality bring along with it a feeling of protection, establishing comfortable boundaries around you.

An overactive or underactive base chakra contributes to patterns of addiction that can harm the physical body. An imbalanced base chakra can't do the job it is designed to do, of balancing, protecting, and maintaining the physical body.

If the chakra is overactive, a person may overeat, as the need to feel safe and nurtured becomes distorted. Or the person may crave certain foods, like fats and sugars, in an attempt to gain relief from consciousness of danger, survival, nervousness, or anxiety. A person may also drink alcohol excessively or take drugs in an attempt to diminish feelings of insecurity, paranoia, or vulnerability.

In the underfunctioning base chakra, a person will choose to "abandon ship" and withdraw from the body altogether instead of fighting. Some common consequences of this retreat are depression, chronic fatigue, daydreaming, delusions, anorexia, chain-smoking, and mental illness.

If you have an overactive chakra, especially an addiction problem, it helps to work on visualization techniques to calm the base chakra and bring its energy into a more balanced state. It also helps to use affirmations, such as:

> I am in a balanced state. My body is balanced, safe, secure. I see my base chakra functioning properly. I am grounded.

Meditation, prayer, and acts of service, kindness, and generosity toward others will quickly stabilize an overactive first chakra.

The method of stimulating this chakra is also a visualization technique. See the balanced red orb swirling in motion, ushering into the physical vehicle vitality, energy, and vigor—only this time emphasize the color red. Imagine it to be as intensely red as possible and four inches in diameter. To stimulate this chakra, your affirmation should be:

> I have a beautiful physical body to use as my vehicle of creative expression. I assume responsibility for my body. I recognize it as a gift from God. It is my vehicle to work through. I am safe inside my vehicle. My base chakra is open, balanced, and bringing me energy of renewal.

Diet influences the chakras and consciousness because food, like everything else, breaks down into energy. All foods vibrate and influence the different chakras. Some foods that influence the red chakra are:

- red meat
- animal fats
- coffee and colas
- peppers and hot spices
- spinach (because of its iron content)

Of course, if your base chakra is overly stimulated, you should avoid these types of food and drink. You are emphasizing the function of survival too much. On the other hand, if your chakra is understimulated, adding these foods to your diet will be stimulating to your consciousness, connecting your soul more solidly with your body and increasing vitality.

SECOND CHAKRA (SPLEEN)

The second chakra, sometimes called the *emotional chakra,* is located next to the spleen, halfway between the base chakra and your navel and slightly to your left, extending outward into the aura. This chakra controls and determines the consciousness of emotion and pleasure. This chakra vibrates at a slightly faster rate than the base chakra because as consciousness rises to a higher level, the vibrational rate increases. The color of this chakra is orange.

The consciousness this chakra influences is the emotional sphere. It is the consciousness of sensation and sensuality. This chakra allows us to experience the joy of feeling, both emotionally and physically. It influences our ability to experience pleasure, to enjoy sensuality and sexuality on the earthly plane.

As you might guess, it is this chakra that controls our appetite for sensation, be it through sound, smell, taste, touch, or sight. It is the center where our consciousness can experience the wonder of being in a body—the human experience.

A balanced orange second chakra allows us to have balanced emotions and enjoy our sensuality, our ability to sense. It encourages us to discover life through feeling. This chakra is the center of self-care and gives us the urge to make choices that bring pleasure. This is good! Believe it or not, God wants us to enjoy ourselves, our bodies, and our earth. This physical plane is beautiful, and we are here to enjoy it.

Diane was beautiful, but extremely overweight. She cried when she came for her reading, saying she was sick of having "such a pretty face, but . . ." Diane ate and ate and ate. Diane was stuck on her second chakra, confusing pleasure and sensation with love. She loved the pleasure of food but couldn't get enough to fill the void. She needed to concentrate on moving her energy toward love, where she could become self-caring.

I suggested several self-care rituals such as massage therapy, as well as giving her second chakra balancing exercises. Diane listened. She was open. With concentration and patience, she changed her energy. She lost eighty pounds and entered a healthy relationship after a year of personal work.

An overstimulated second chakra pushes one's pursuit of pleasure to the point of greediness. This, too, influences tendencies toward addiction. Often people confuse the experience of sensual pleasure with love. Their addictions are substitutes for love. People like the temporary impression a pleasant sensual experience or feeling may give them but become frustrated by its fleeting aspect. They continue to pursue more and more sensual stimulations to maintain these emotions of pleasure.

To balance your second chakra, begin by doing the same visualization technique you did with the base chakra. Close your eyes and locate the second chakra on your mental screen, just at the place of your spleen. Envision this wheel swirling around, about four inches in diameter in a perfectly balanced state and emitting the color orange—deep, rich, and warm, like an orange in a sunset.

When focusing on this chakra, imagine a feeling of comfortable pleasure filling your body, but attach no anxiety to this feeling. It is good, spiritual, and healthy. Breathe in deeply and enjoy this pleasant feeling. Give yourself permission to experience sensation and pleasure in your life. It is one of the reasons we are physically incarnate. Spend five to seven minutes on this exercise. Then breathe in, relax, and open your eyes.

If you are greedy or addictive about pleasure, or are controlled by your physical senses instead of your higher consciousness, then your second chakra is overstimulated. To tone it down, imagine again this same orange orb, spinning perfectly balanced. But this time imagine any sense of attachment to your senses, or any anxiety or tension in your body, easing up. Use this affirmation:

> It is okay to feel. God gave me a body to experience pleasure. I allow my body to experience pleasure, but I realize it does not take the place of the enduring energy of love. I imagine this chakra is calm, bringing in the proper influences of emotion, leaving me peaceful and content.

Breathe in and relax. Open your eyes. This exercise should take about five to seven minutes.

If you have an underdeveloped orange chakra, experiences of scarcity in love may have caused you to repress your urge to feel. If this is your problem, you may limit the amount of sensation you experience. Often people with this chakra problem become overly intellectual and may advocate the denial of bodily pleasure, denigrating sensuality as unspiritual. There is no spiritual benefit to denying you have a body. Your body is not the problem—balance is.

People with this problem become overly analytical and lose touch with their feeling perceptions. The way to balance an underactive second chakra is through the same visualization exercise you did before, but followed with this affirmation:

> My body is a divine creation. Part of the miracle of being alive is my capacity to feel, to learn and experience the world through my senses. I do not confuse this wonder with the greater wonder of love. I can allow myself to feel without fear. I am controlled by the voice of my Higher Self, not by my body. My body seeks only pleasure that is healthy and balanced.

Foods that affect the second chakra are:

- chocolate
- fruits such as bananas, watermelon, pears

- honey
- bread and butter
- milk and dairy products
- ice cream
- pastas

If you are overly sense oriented, go easy on these foods. If you are under sense oriented and have trouble feeling, eat more of these foods.

The second chakra also responds well to classical music, art, gardening, flowers, cooking, and dancing. All these activities are naturally sense balancing. Sex with someone who is loving toward you is a great sense balancer. If you engage in sex with someone who has no love for you, the exchange of energy is very disturbing to both your first and second chakras and is weakening to your soul. Avoid this!

THIRD CHAKRA (SOLAR PLEXUS)

The third chakra, sometimes called the *will chakra,* is located in the aura in the region of the solar plexus, above the navel. This chakra, spinning even faster than the second, is a bright yellow color. This chakra stimulates the consciousness of decision, willpower, and creative expression.

This chakra gives a person the ability to make decisions and choices, to follow through, to assume responsibility, and to express the creative impulses that God gives. When this chakra is balanced and opened correctly, we become aware of divine guidance flowing into our lives. This imbues us with natural charisma.

Stephen had just gotten out of the hospital and was recovering from back surgery. After being housebound for two weeks, he decided to venture out and walk to a friend's home four blocks away. After staying several hours, he headed home at 9:30 P.M., walking tentatively so as not to aggravate his back injury.

A block and a half from his friend's house, Stephen caught a glimpse out of the corner of his eye of a man following him on the other side of the street. Grounding himself in his third chakra, Stephen continued to walk, but was conscious of the other man's footsteps. Sure enough, the man following Stephen crossed the street and was now behind him. After a moment, the footsteps behind Stephen quickened, and he knew he was about to be mugged.

Before the man reached Stephen, however, Stephen turned around and confronted him, using the energy from his third chakra. Stephen put out his hand, almost touching the man's chest, and stopped him cold, yelling, "Stop! Go away!" Startled, the man stopped, and Stephen noticed he had a gun but seemed very disoriented. Continuing to exert his will through the third chakra, Stephen repeated, "Go away, you're going to get into trouble!" The man hesitated for a moment, then ran. Stephen, his heart pounding violently, continued his walk home to safety.

This is a beautiful example of the will chakra in action. The third chakra's energy is formidable and can inspire others to follow your intentions easily.

This chakra also opens up a person to the astral planes—which are simply higher levels of awareness or finer energy bands than normally experienced. It is the gateway to simple psychic impulses and out-of-body experiences. Unlike the first two chakras, this is the first of the chakras that connects you to others.

The more open and balanced the third chakra is, the more you will be aware of auras, other people's vibrations, and divine spiritual forces. This is the point of consciousness in the body where you become receptive to divine energy. If it is opened, you are able to experience the help of the higher planes. If it is closed, you depend on your ego alone for guidance.

If this chakra is understimulated or closed down, a person will be tired and tiring. Life will be very draining, and the person may be overcome by sleepiness. If the chakra is shut down, a person will not perceive the subtle planes of psychic energy all around. When this chakra is underfunctioning, a person will be very egocentric and unable to receive psychic energy from the soul or higher planes.

If this chakra is off balance, it also makes a person wishy-washy, unable to say no, or unable to stand confrontation. You may be a day-dreamer, lack concentration, or have to be policed by other people. You may live constantly in an anxious state, dwelling on past events or fearing future ones. You may also be unable to control your appetite, be lazy or manipulative, and be passive-aggressive with people in your life. Your ego will override the voice of your Higher Self.

To balance your third chakra, close your eyes and locate this chakra in your body just above the navel and extending outward into the aura. Imagine this chakra is a spinning orb, perfectly balanced and glowing in a brilliant yellow light.

With each breath, imagine this chakra is bringing with it the energy to be alive, responsible, and confident. See your chakra opened just enough to fill your body with courage, creativity, and follow-through. Tell yourself you will be receptive and open to divine energy flowing into your body, guiding you moment by moment. Hold this image in your mind for five to seven minutes, then open your eyes.

The affirmation to use for your third chakra is:

I am receptive to divine energy moving into every cell of my body. I am committed to expressing my creativity, to accepting my responsibilities, and to making decisions that are balanced and helpful to my spiritual growth. I am guided by and receptive to divine will at all times.

Third chakra foods are:

- fish
- chicken
- eggs
- apricots
- oranges
- carrots
- sweet potatoes
- cranberry juice

- papaya
- squash

Eat these foods to balance your third chakra. Stay away from fish and chicken if you are too ego based and having a difficult time picking up any psychic energy.

FOURTH CHAKRA (HEART)

Located in the aura at the level of your heart is your fourth chakra. This is known as your *heart chakra*. Vibrating faster than the first three, emitting a vibrant green color, this chakra is the center of *love* in your consciousness. You will notice this center of consciousness is different and higher in the body than the center of consciousness for emotion. A lot of us forget that love is a totally different vibration from emotion. Love is balanced, calm, giving, and accepting of one's self and others.

This chakra also connects the lower ego/physical self to the higher soul/spiritual self. It is the midpoint vibration of consciousness in the body.

This chakra controls the consciousness of self-acceptance, acceptance of others, trust, well-being, a sense of having what you need, abundance, prosperity, and good health. It is also the point of consciousness where a person can feel the pain and joy and struggle of another person or of the world. It is the empathic center. This chakra point is the beginning of perceiving another person's experience. It is also the gateway for any type of psychic reading. For example, I use my fourth chakra when I do psychometry readings, which means perceiving another's energy by holding an object that belongs to that person, such as a key, watch, or photograph.

Let me tell you about when I first began to use the energy from my fourth chakra.

One night when I was in high school, I walked in the middle of a huge snowstorm to the pizza parlor where I worked. The snow was just dumping on the streets. When I got to the restaurant, I took quite a few delivery orders on the phone, but absolutely no one came in to eat. Angelo, my boss, had been in the back office that night for a while, but at seven-thirty he walked out and said, "Sonia, do a reading for me. I've got things going, and I want to know what you see."

I was caught completely by surprise. I had never done a psychic reading before, although I had been trained to. I felt the way you do when, as a child, you are asked to perform by a parent but you don't really have your act perfected. I wanted to do it but didn't want to at the same time.

"When?" I asked.

"Now. No one's here, and no one is coming on a night like this. How about right now?"

I cleared off the tables, cleared away the salt and pepper shakers, and tried to move myself into the frame of mind to do a reading. I experienced a sudden flood of insecurity. I was approaching this reading as "Sonia, fifteen-year-old waitress," and from that perspective, that self-image, I couldn't see or feel or intuit anything.

I started to panic, but before the feeling took over completely, I brought my awareness to the area of my heart and imagined waves of green, balanced energy flowing through my entire being, opening my awareness. Soon everything slowed down, and suddenly I was totally confident that I could do this reading.

I sat down at the table and took Angelo's pen from him. I decided to use his pen to do a psychometry reading because he always used the same one. I closed my eyes and looked around in my mind's eye. I saw Angelo standing at the door of his restaurant. Then I saw him standing next to a new building, putting up an "Angelo's" sign on it. Then I saw the restaurant full of people, but everyone went home early.

"Angelo, I think you are going to have two restaurants. I see your name on another one. It's called Angelo's as well, but everyone goes home early. I'm not sure what that means," I said. I didn't see images—I simply felt it.

Angelo listened very closely. "Do you see me in trouble?" he asked.

"No, not really. I just see two restaurants."

He said, "That's it?"

"Yes, that's it," I answered. "Give me a break. You're my first client!"

"You did okay," Angelo said. "I have to decide if I want to buy another restaurant in northwest Denver. I told the guy I'd let him know tonight. Looks like I'm going to. You didn't see any trouble, huh?"

"Not really. Just people going home early."

He laughed. "I think your psychic sense is confused with you going home early. Thanks. I guess I just needed some feedback before I go ahead with this."

That night Angelo bought a restaurant on the west side of Denver. He did name it "Angelo's 2." He wanted to make it into a fine Italian restaurant and nightclub, not a pizzeria, but after a year of trying, he didn't get the right liquor license to stay open past midnight. The nightclub part didn't happen, so everyone went home early.

My ability to read for Angelo came from my focus on the fourth chakra. It was that center of energy that allowed me to tune in to *his* vibration.

If your fourth chakra is understimulated or off balance, you may act loving but really feel resentful. You may give to others out of obligation rather than out of a genuine sense of goodwill. You may also have a hard time receiving from others. You may struggle with receiving because they fear being resented, as you have resented others. You may not feel the energy of others, leaving you isolated.

I don't know of a case where a person has had an overstimulated heart chakra. Genuine love is self-balancing and naturally healing. Occasionally, however, people can resonate too strongly with others' vibrations, causing them to obsess or worry unnecessarily, throwing the chakra out of balance. Some people also call this codependency.

For example, Toni had finally achieved her dream of having a son after much struggle and disappointment with infertility. But her overzealous enthusiasm for baby Jake threw her into a protective frenzy, causing her to obsess over his every move. Her heart chakra had become totally connected to her son's life force. This played out in her being controlling and anxiety-ridden rather than joyful, as she had expected. Her heart chakra was unbalanced. I helped her rebalance her chakra to allow an easier, more natural flow of love to pass between them.

To balance and stimulate the fourth chakra, close your eyes and locate this chakra at the place of your heart and extending outward into the aura. Imagine this chakra is a perfectly balanced spinning orb, five inches in diameter, and the green color of freshly mown grass. Breathe in and imagine this wheel of energy is pulling in waves of healing energy, washing over each cell in your body, healing all wounds and hurts, and filling you with a sense of love. Imagine this loving energy coming from God, pulling into your consciousness the feeling of being loved and cared for by God.

The fourth chakra affirmation is:

I am loved, and loving God provides all I need. Everything I
do, I do with love. I am receptive and open to receiving love.
My heart is healing, my needs fulfilled. I let go of all resent-
ments. I forgive others and ask forgiveness and lovingly let go
of the past. I allow the abundance of the universe to pour into
my heart. I feel others, but do not attach to their lives.

Breathe and relax. Hold this image for five to seven minutes.

Remember that all chakras both give and receive energy. In working with the loving feelings of the heart energy, be sure to focus this energy inward as well as outward, allowing yourself the experience of loving *yourself*. This will also open the way to your being able to receive love from others.

Heart chakra foods are:

- plums
- cherries
- strawberries
- whole-grain brown rice

- couscous and other grains
- miso, soy, and bean proteins
- greens, except spinach

FIFTH CHAKRA (THROAT)

Located in the aura at the level of your throat is the fifth chakra, called your *throat chakra*. This chakra controls the consciousness of psychic *hearing*. It is sometimes referred to as the "radio." It allows a person to be telepathic, which means hearing the thoughts of other people. It also allows you to hear the voice of your Higher Self and, when fully opened, to develop the psychic ability of clairaudience, which means hearing guides.

Let me tell you about my first experience with the fifth chakra.

I had success with psychometry, but clairaudience was harder. Charlie, my teacher, advised me to concentrate on my fifth chakra and be patient. I would sit and listen and wait, but I would hear absolutely *nothing*. We would meditate, and Charlie would say, "The guides are here. Can you hear them?"

No, I couldn't. It was discouraging, frustrating, annoying. It was boring, and I was restless. I was fifteen years old. I had come to study with Charlie every week for over 2½ years, and I felt that I had learned all I could. I didn't believe I was going to hear voices, spirit voices. I simply didn't believe it . . . but yet . . . maybe? I was struggling.

I left that day, troubled, still annoyed, and a little angry at Charlie, but he had shown me so much, and I couldn't be sure it was impossible, so I prayed about it and meditated all week, focusing on my fifth chakra. I remember pleading with my guides, "Can you speak a little louder, *please?* I can't hear you," half sarcastically, half desperately. Once again I found myself *trying*—and trying never works.

Then one day I sat down at my mother's sewing machine and started to sew a pantsuit. I hadn't sewn a lot, but the style was a simple two-piece, with midriff top and hip-hugger bell-bottoms, in a bright floral print. I needed a new outfit. I got busy cutting out the pattern, pinning it together, and threading the needle to my mom's machine, and I was lost in concentration.

I whipped together the top in no time and was beginning to stitch together the bottoms when, from just behind my right ear, a man yelled, "Stop! Not that way!" I absolutely flew out of my chair, almost out of my skin. I whipped around, but no one was there.

Then I heard a very lighthearted laugh. An amused laugh. It stopped but kept ringing in my head. I looked back at what I was doing and realized I had been just about to sew together the insides of my pant legs instead of front to back. This voice, this clear loud voice, had stopped me.

I had goose bumps all over. I remember Charlie telling me always to make sure the voice of a spirit gives you good, helpful information. Otherwise it's not a high-vibration spirit. Well, this spirit had just stopped me from ruining my sewing project. That was good information. I said out loud, "Thank you!"

A moment or two later, once I resumed sewing, again I heard, "Better!"

I jumped three feet into the air again. This was going to take some getting used to. I didn't like being surprised like that.

I called Charlie and told him what happened. I remember him saying, "Did you really hear it, or was it in your mind?"

All I could answer was, "Yes, I heard it!" It was a clear voice. This was my first of many experiences in hearing spiritual guidance.

In addition to clairaudience, the fifth chakra also connects your consciousness to your subconscious storehouse and to the subconscious records of all time, known as the Akashic records. Sometimes, through this chakra, a person will also hear spiritual music.

If this chakra is off balance or shut down, you will have all sorts of problems with self-talk and inner voices. You may repress your ability to express yourself, to be honest, or to listen to what you hear. You may tune out others, or partially tune them out, to manipulate what you hear.

If your fifth chakra is off balance, you may also hear "voices" that confuse, coerce, or upset you. You may tune in to negative astral planes, attracting confusion or distorting your focus and concentration. You may struggle with intense negative self-dialogue, telling yourself mean and harmful things. You may have too many voices in your head at one time—those of yourself, others, and spirits all mixed up together. This is what many people call mental illness.

To balance the throat chakra, close your eyes and locate it at the place of your throat, extending outward into the aura. Place your full attention on this chakra and imagine it is spinning at an even faster rate than the fourth chakra.

This chakra emits the color of a blue sky at noon into the aura. As you concentrate on this chakra, imagine you are programming your chakra to focus only on the channels of:

- your conscious mind to your Higher Self
- helpful guides and divine guidance
- telepathy (but *only* if it comes from a source that is both loving and wiser than yourself)

Imagine this spinning sky blue orb opening like a twirling flower, to a size of five inches in diameter. See the light and energy of God's divine guidance pouring into your mind, enlightening every cell of your being. Hold this concentration for five to seven minutes.

If you have a blocked or off-balance fifth chakra, finish the visualization with this affirmation:

The only voice influencing my life is the voice of my Higher Self and God's divine wisdom. All other voices I lovingly ask to leave. *I am a clear receiver.*

As with the other chakras, there are certain foods that aid and balance this function. Some fifth chakra foods are:

- ginseng
- *Ginkgo biloba*
- reishi mushrooms

- barley
- wheat grass
- bananas
- supplements like KM
  (a natural mineral supplement derived from plants)
- echinacea
- kelp

SIXTH CHAKRA (FOREHEAD)

Located at the level of your forehead, between your eyes and just above your eyebrows, and extending outward into the aura, is the sixth chakra, usually called the *third eye*. This chakra is connected to the pineal gland in your head and acts like a mental screen that picks up images. When this chakra is open and stimulated, a person possesses the ability to see clairvoyantly—which means to see people and places at a distance in the future, as well as probable events beginning to form. Such a person will have the ability to see auras, chakras, and spirit guide images. The sixth chakra also allows one to see the soul.

Mary came to me for a reading after she had an unexpected experience involving her sixth chakra. She was riding home from work one day on the bus, feeling extremely tired and irritable, as usual. While she sat in a daze, a face suddenly appeared floating in front of her and told her she had a tumor in her stomach. It also said she needed to get over her anger. Then, in an instant, it was gone.

She blinked. She rubbed her eyes. She believed she had imagined it, and yet . . . ?

The next day she made an appointment with her doctor. She had, indeed, felt terrible for a while and thought her "hallucination" was simply a reaction to her low energy. Much to her horror, but not surprise, the tests ordered by the doctor revealed that Mary had stomach cancer.

Mary never did overcome the cancer, but she did have time to turn her life around and heal her relationships before she succumbed to her illness. We had several conversations about the floating face during this time. Her sixth chakra had opened up, allowing her to see one of her guides and help herself spiritually before it was too late.

The sixth chakra is wide open all the time in only a very few people, but as in Mary's case, it can open spontaneously in a crisis. To open this chakra voluntarily takes much more than visualization and focusing imagery. It takes meditation, which we have all been working on. By following this exercise, you can begin gently to open it farther and farther.

Breathe in deeply, then out, and gently close your eyes. Imagine placing your full attention onto your sixth chakra, located in the middle of your forehead and extending outward. Imagine this chakra whirling in space, the color of indigo blue, almost a black blue then fading into violet. Imagine that as you watch this satellite swirling round and round it begins to expand, growing larger and larger until it becomes a very large sphere.

Now, imagine that this sphere begins to turn into a large screen, and upon this screen you notice a beam of white light entering into the center. As you concentrate on this light, it begins to expand, lighting up the screen.

As it expands, imagine seeing your own reflection—not as your mortal image, but your soul image. Imagine that your soul is looking back at you on this mental screen. Don't force the image. Just let your imagination create this image for you. Be patient. . . . Look at this image in wonder, without judgment. As the image emerges, make note of all the details, even if they are vague.

After doing this exercise for a few minutes, let yourself relax. Breathe in and very slowly watch the image fade. See the light go out on the screen, and watch it return to a deep indigo blue fading into violet. Watch this screen slowly reduce back into a swirling round orb, resting in the middle of your forehead. Breathe in, relax, and open your eyes. Recall your soul image.

If this chakra is completely shut down, you will have difficulty imagining. You will be overly intellectual, seeing only concrete aspects and missing the energy that flows before, behind, and beyond the concrete world. You may be blind to the essence of things, often missing the soul of what's around you. Your life will be linear, rational, and flat.

If this is your problem, you may want to try to stimulate the sixth chakra with imagination exercises such as drawing, coloring, and painting. You may also try to imagine, daydream, or make up pictures in your mind. You may try to see into situations instead of just taking things at face value, and of course, the sixth chakra imagery exercise will help you. You should practice it often.

Some sixth chakra foods are:

- lecithin
- wheat germ
- barley
- vitamin E
- alfalfa
- chamomile
- water
- water
- water

SEVENTH CHAKRA (CROWN)

Located at the top of your head, the highest point of your body, and extending outward into the aura is your *crown chakra*. This chakra is connected to your pituitary gland and governs the consciousness of spiritual awakening, enlightenment, and spiritual wisdom.

When this chakra is open, a person can see and understand the deepest mysteries of life. At this crown point, divine energy flows into our being, allowing us to look into past lives and see our soul's history. When this chakra is open, a person knows things without having a reason, tapping into universal mind and finding the information there.

Opening the crown chakra takes years of learning, meditation, prayer, and training with a spiritual helper. It requires a pure heart and profound integrity and is a gift that your soul earns.

* * *

Cookie was a serious student of psychic awareness, having studied and practiced walking the psychic pathway for over fifteen years. By day she was a flight attendant, but her avocation was taking care of souls. Whether she was working on a flight or doing psychic readings, she was continually nurturing, assuring, and guiding people on their own spiritual journeys.

One day Cookie called me and excitedly reported what had happened to her. While she was closing her eyes and meditating, preparing to start a reading for a client, she slipped into a trance. She said she found herself talking, but someone else's voice was coming through.

She told her client that the reason she was unable to leave her marriage to her drug-addicted husband, in spite of three tries, was that in a past life she'd been her husband's mother. In their past life she had died when her son was entering adolescence. She'd married the son in this life in order to finish "raising" him and complete the job she had not been able to do before. This was one of her soul goals, and she couldn't leave until she had achieved this.

The strangest thing about this reading was that up until that point, Cookie hadn't really been sure she believed in past lives. When this information came out of her, she was as surprised as her client. She said she felt very far away when the words came to her. She could hear people talking, but she couldn't see them. Then, suddenly, she found herself blinking, then staring at her client as if she were waking from a dream.

In fact, she was coming out of a trance. She had slipped into seventh chakra consciousness spontaneously, and the reading followed. Apparently it helped her client to stop mentally beating herself up for being so weak and to try a more loving approach with herself.

To open your crown chakra, you must meditate carefully so as not to raise your consciousness too abruptly. Prayer is a wonderful way to slowly open this center up to God's love and guidance. Take your time, and as you meditate or pray, imagine seeing God's energy pouring into your crown chakra, which is a violet-white orb spinning at a very fast rate at the top of your head.

Imagine a golden-white light pouring into your chakra and filling up your soul with love and divine wisdom. Let this awareness sink into your body slowly, bringing the golden-white light of love and awakened enlightenment into your understanding. Pray for God's protection. Breathe in, relax, and slowly open your eyes.

The highest degree of psychic ability comes with successfully opening the crown chakra. (Highly developed mystics experience chakras even higher than this, but they do not concern us for now.)

There are no special foods for the seventh chakra. Its food is simply energy.

RULES OF THE ROAD

In order to become safely psychic, guided in the right way, and not intruded upon by negative or undesirable energy, it is important that you start working with the first chakra, moving upward. Some people try to "start at the top," but this is not desirable or safe unless you first open and balance all the other chakras, one at a time. Working in this way provides you with physical grounding and allows you to adjust to an increase in the flow of energy into your body. If done properly, you control energy rather than having energy control you.

Remember, the first, second, and third chakras control the body, the emotions, and the will. Ideally you will want these three aspects of your nature to be grounded, cared for, balanced, and directed. In fact, it is essential! These chakras take care of you, which is important. This is self-love. No one else will take care of you. It's your job. If you are taken care of correctly, the energy of those around you won't harm you.

Bear in mind that the fourth chakra introduces to your consciousness the awareness of others and the beginning of psychic connections to others, the center of love. The fifth, sixth, and seventh chakras all concentrate on psychic energy and ability. Each center introduces more powerful vibrational energy into your body. This increased energy courses through your body and affects you physically. That is why it is so important to have a balanced and grounded physical body, so this heightened psychic energy doesn't overload the physical circuits to your mind, the way an ungrounded electrical wire can cause damage to electrical circuits.

These seven chakras show you how you are *designed* to be psychic. The seven centers of consciousness graduate from the dense physical level to the highest, most ethereal level. They build on each other like steps. Climb them in order—the experience of this energy is powerful!

Claire had been a serious meditator for many years, and concepts like the chakras were very familiar to her. Claire knew, for example, that many practitioners talked about *kundalini,* the Indian name for the energy rising out of the base chakra and climbing to the crown. She had heard it described as a sort of sacred snake that climbed the spine like a tree. What an interesting metaphor, she thought. Then it happened to her.

"It was incredible!" Claire said, laughing. "I could feel this . . . *snake* climbing right up my spine inside my body. I swear to you, I could have held it!" Despite all her reading, Claire was astonished by the *experience* of her psychic energy moving.

"It traveled in waves!" She gestured with her hands. "It went up, up, and up, slowly, steadily . . . powerfully. I was startled and a little scared. Then I remembered: This is what I have been working toward. I was very, very excited. The experience gave me great hope and faith."

As Claire's story illustrates, psychic energy is *physically* felt. And as we work with our chakras, we become more and more sensitive to this energy. As we work, our sensitivity and consciousness of energy will continue to expand.

A last word: The chakras can fluctuate, opening and closing at different times, but with imagery and meditation you can keep your chakras open and balanced and working beautifully together.

EXPLORATIONS

Balancing the Seven Chakras

• Breathe, relax, and close your eyes. Bring your full awareness to the base of your spine. At this level, resting in the aura just outside your body, is the first chakra. Notice it spinning gently, emitting a clear red color into the aura. See this orb four inches in diameter, balanced and glowing.

• Now move your attention to your aura at the level of your spleen, where you will find your second chakra, spinning slightly faster, emitting an orange hue, four inches in diameter, perfectly balanced.

• Now focus on your aura at the level of your navel. See there the bright yellow orb of the third chakra, spinning in space, four inches in diameter, perfectly balanced.

• Now move to your heart chakra in the aura at the level of your chest, centered and balanced. You see the green orb spinning faster yet, sending out the color of green grass.

• Let your attention center next on your throat chakra. There you see, spinning faster yet, a perfectly balanced orb the color of a summer sky at noon, spinning faster and faster, brilliant blue rays flowing out.

• Let your awareness shift next to the level of your forehead. There you will see a perfectly balanced spinning orb the color of the sky at midnight, black blue or indigo, fading into violet, five inches in diameter.

• Finally, let the brilliance of the final chakra, the crown chakra, pull your eyes up to it. See it there above your head, spinning so fast as to appear motionless, a brilliant violet-white orb, surrounded by a golden halo lighting up the top of your head. Allow yourself to marvel at its glory.

• Now, very carefully, connect these centers, moving downward from the top chakra to the base chakra: violet . . . to indigo . . . to sky blue . . . to green . . . to yellow . . . to orange . . . to red . . . and finally down into your feet and into the ground.

• Breathe in, relax, and open your eyes.

This imagery exercise balances *all* your chakras and lets psychic energy flow easily.

Listening to the Radio

Using a small tape recorder, go back through this chapter and tape your own voice reading the exercises. The use of *your own voice* is extremely powerful. Use these do-it-yourself tapes to work with your chakra system.

Practice listening to these tapes as your meditation technique for this week.

Color Your World
Take a box of Crayolas or pastels. Draw the outline of a body. Now, draw a circle for each chakra and color it in with that chakra's color. Next, write down what each chakra governs, and mark which chakra you think you work from most. Post this near your meditation area.

Repeat this exercise, and mark any changes in your chakra activity.

CHARTING YOUR PROGRESS
Reflect on your experiences this week when answering these questions.

How many days this week did you meditate? (I hope by now it is a valuable experience.) _____

Have you grounded yourself this week? _____

_____

Have you cleared your aura this week? _____

_____

Which chakra did you focus on most easily? _____

_____

How many days this week did you make an entry in your psychic journal? Has knowing about chakras changed your perspective? _____

_____

What chakra feels like your favorite?_____

_____

What chakra feels like your least favorite?_____

_____

What color is easiest for you to imagine?_____

_____

What color is hardest for you to imagine?_____

_____

What foods do you tend to eat most?_____

_____

What foods do you tend to avoid?_____

_____

Which chakra felt like your strongest?_____

_____

Which chakra felt like your weakest?_____

_____

Which chakra are you working from most of the time? _____

_____

Have you recognized which chakras feel "home" and which could use a little attention? _____

_____

_____

Expanding Your Horizons

From the time I was twelve years old until I was fifteen, I apprenticed in psychic development with a gifted teacher named Charlie Goodman. And Goodman was a perfect name for him. He taught me to meditate, to remove my blocks, to become aware of auras and chakras, to receive energy from objects, to receive telepathic messages from others, and to open up my third eye. Even after practicing all these lessons, however, I kept waiting for the day when I would know enough to consider myself officially "psychic."

One day when I went to class, Charlie asked me to do a psychic reading! It was something I'd never done before, and I froze. I couldn't do a reading. I was still a student! I wasn't yet a psychic.

Charlie asked, "Why not? What are you waiting for?"

"I don't know," I answered. "Permission from you?"

He laughed. "The secret to being psychic, Sonia, is that the *permission* to be officially psychic comes from you!"

"Me?" I asked incredulously.

"Yes, you!" he said.

Then I remembered the games I used to play with my mom when I was little. She and I would play a game called "Let's Be Psychic." In this game I would pretend I was a psychic and she was my client. I would lay out a deck of cards in various patterns that I would invent, and then, while looking at them, I'd predict the future. When playing this game, if what I predicted did not come true, my mother taught me to say to myself, "Oh well." After all, this was a game to teach me to allow my impressions to be expressed. It wasn't a test. I said, "Oh well" all the time, but we were having fun.

Once I told her that my oldest brother, Stefan, who was away for the summer on a work-study program, would be coming home to surprise her. How did I know? I just made it up. After all, it was only a game. It wasn't serious, so I was free to make up whatever I wanted. This prediction about my brother just popped into my mind. My mother wrote down everything I said when we played this game, and then she would just wait for my predictions to happen. I remember that nothing much of what I would say came true, or at least none of it impressed me, until that day.

Three hours after I told my mother that Stefan would surprise us with a visit, he walked through the door! I was shocked. He and a friend had hitched a ride to Denver with another guy in the program. They could only spend one night before the friend would drive them back to Utah. My mother was delighted—and not only by Stefan. She was delighted by me, that my prediction had come true!

"We've been expecting you," she told Stefan.

That experience changed me. It showed me what I was capable of. It showed me that if you *believe* you are psychic, you will be. That's what Charlie had been talking about! The permission really did come from me.

Once you understand what the psychic voice is, that it is the voice of your soul, it is up to you to give yourself permission to use this voice. No one else can give you permission. No one else has the power or authority to allow you to use the voice of your Higher Self. This voice is yours, a gift from God. It belongs to you. It is your God-given right to use it— you, and you alone, are in charge of whether or not you do.

There is no special skill or power you must possess. There is no special "veil" you must be born with. You don't need visions, apparitions, séances, or bizarre episodes to prove you are psychic. You just need to believe it.

Skeptics and nonbelievers will laugh at this and call you crazy. Some people will scoff and say it can't possibly be that simple. Yet I ask you only to try it, and you'll see for yourself.

Psychic ability is the natural voice of your Higher Self, your soul. It is not the voice of your ego (or anyone else's). Anyone who scoffs does not know the truth about who they are. They are still blocked, and they still live from the fearful voice of the ego, so don't let such people discourage or stop your return to truth. Anyone who really is psychic will agree with me.

I repeat: The greatest catalyst to your being able to hear your inner voice and see the truth about yourself and the world you live in is to simply believe you can. Belief pulls back the curtain of illusion and allows you to see the truth.

In my classes I tell my students what my mother taught me—if they want to be psychic, make it up! In other words, *pretend* you are psychic. *Imagine* what your Higher Self would say to you if you were psychic. Whatever you make up comes from the soul; any time you give your soul a chance, even if you are only *pretending* to be psychic, the soul becomes available to guide you.

My student Kathy believed me in her usual way: what I said was interesting, but somehow a metaphor for what I really meant. I urged her just to pretend and see what happened. Kathy was to do a reading for another student in my class, Arnie. Feeling pretty nervous but reassuring herself it was all just pretend, Kathy gave Arnie her reading.

She told Arnie that she saw wood and bricks all around him. She also told him that he loved places more than people and that he would be working as a carpenter all over town in a few months. All of this Kathy thought pretty unlikely as she looked at this man in a three-piece suit.

But Arnie told her the reading was amazing. He had just quit his job as a mortgage broker to become a home renovator. His classes were to start the following month. He wondered how Kathy had known.

"I didn't know," Kathy said. "I just *pretended* I was psychic."

As Kathy discovered for herself, the reason I suggest to my students that they pretend they are psychic is that when you pretend, you play—and when you play, you overcome the blocks your ego has set up for you. When you tell your ego that you are only playing, the ego stands back and relaxes. After all, the ego can't be bothered with such a trivial matter as *play!*

I love the ego. It's like a cartoon character of the king from Antoine de St. Exupery's *The Little Prince.* So important! So silly. Play? It has more important things to do, like seek for worth, or focus on worry, or puff itself up to feel important. Face it: The ego doesn't like to play. So by playing, you creatively sneak past the ego and open yourself up to the wonderful world of the soul. Try it—it works!

THE "I AM PSYCHIC" GAME

The words *I am* are two very powerful metaphysical words. Whenever you say "I am," you are making a statement about who you are, your *self,* to the world around you and to your subconscious mind. When you say "I am . . ." followed by a statement, you set up the experience that follows. That's why it's very important to be aware of what follows the words *I am.* Whatever follows in words will follow in your experience.

Think about it. What kinds of statements do you place after the powerful words *I am?*

I am . . .   happy
                             sad
                             beautiful
                             unattractive
                             rich
                             poor
                             healthy
                             sick
                             loved
                             lonely

The words *I am* release to the subconscious mind a powerful instruction that the subconscious mind obeys. Therefore, one of the most powerful and exciting games you can play is I Am Psychic! When you play the I Am Psychic game, you give yourself permission to be your true self. You tell your subconscious mind to pull back the curtain blocking your awareness of higher energy, and you put yourself in the most receptive frame of mind to be conscious of spiritual guidance. And by making it a game, you tiptoe around your ego and all its potential ambushes.

Here's how you play I Am Psychic.

First, choose a day in advance in which to play the game.

You may want to start with a day when you will not be under a lot of pressure. If you work a Monday through Friday job, start on a Saturday or Sunday. Then, in your psychic journal, create a psychic persona you will assume when you play your game.

Some people's psychic persona is a queen or king. Some people adopt a hermit. Or Merlin. Or a fairy. A priestess. A guru. A monk in orange robes. For some it's an animal. A little bird. A big bear. A frog. A cricket. For others it's a spirit, an angel, a voice. It can be whatever you want—anything goes.

This is just like a child's "let's pretend" game, so allow yourself to enter the game without reservation. Write in your journal what your psychic self will look like, sound like, act like. Imagine how your psychic self will feel about things, how much it will know about things. Will your psychic self get feelings? Pictures? Vibes? Telepathic messages? Let your mind simply contemplate what your psychic persona will be like. Then write down all the details. Change them if you wish. This isn't a test, it's play—creative play that opens the door to your intuitive playground.

When the day you've chosen arrives, slip mentally into your creative costume. Leave your ordinary self at home that day. Every time you must make a decision, let the psychic make it for you, from what direction to take to work to what will be available for lunch in the cafeteria. Start with neutral decisions and eventually work up into more important ones. Playing this game doesn't mean that you disregard information you may have concerning something. Psychic ability works best with a well-informed mind. What this game asks of you is that you integrate what your senses convey and then move beyond, using *all* your awareness, including intuition.

All throughout your I Am Psychic day, *act* as if you are psychic. Be open to your intuition. Expect it, trust it, and just for today, *act on it!* Don't hold back. Don't let yourself stop playing the game.

Just for one day really allow your inner psychic, the voice of your soul, to come out and play. Let the psychic make the decisions. Experience the energy! Let the psychic inside direct you, lead you, guide you. Surrender completely to the game, just for one day. Let your psychic advise and guide you *all* day long.

When your psychic is accurate, say, "Hurray!" and celebrate. Focus especially on how you *feel* when your psychic is accurate. It's a very specific type of feeling. When I teach my students the I Am Psychic game, I tell them to look for that very special feeling that you have when you really tap into intuitive experience. It's very distinct.

A fairy tale about feeling this subtle energy is the story "The Princess and the Pea." If you remember, a prince was looking for a wife, but she had to be a *true* princess. The way to determine if she was indeed the real thing was that she had to pass a test. She had to sleep on 150 mattresses, and under the very bottom mattress was placed a pea. A true princess would be able to feel this little pea, thus revealing her authenticity.

One by one, princesses filed to the palace to try and win the prince's hand in marriage, and one by one they failed the test. One day, however, a princess came to the palace, and upon waking the next morning she had a terrible aching back. "I don't know what was under the mattress," she said, "but it *felt* so lumpy I couldn't sleep a wink!"

Hurray—a true princess had been found. This princess had the gift of feeling the subtle, of noticing what most overlooked and acknowledging it. The prince married his true princess and together they inherited the kingdom.

The prince in this story is reason. Reason is seeking its other half, its princess, intuition. When you wed reason with intuition, you inherit the kingdom of fully informed awareness and indeed at this point do have a genuine opportunity to live happily ever after. So look for how you feel in any given situation. What, through subtle feelings, is your soul trying to convey? Pay attention. One student who played this game described the feeling as "satisfied, right in the area of my heart."

When your inner psychic is off—remember, you're just starting— shrug your shoulders and say to yourself, "Oh, well," *not* "Oh, no!" Remember, it's just a game, not a test. When you are off, reflect on how it felt. Did you have the same feeling of "satisfaction in the heart area"? Or did you just feel as though you were guessing? Simply study and observe the different sensations between accurate psychic feelings and those that prove to be false or misleading.

A word of caution here. Don't discard a psychic feeling just because it can't be instantly proven accurate. You may be picking up some future activity or experience. Acknowledge everything. Be psychic about everything on your I Am Psychic day—absolutely everything.

At first you may want to try playing the game just on weekends. Every day you play this game, write down the results in your psychic journal.

Focus on how it *felt* to play I Am Psychic. Did you feel psychic? Did you successfully pretend to be psychic all day? If yes, what experiences did you have that were different from when you are not being psychic? If no, what prevented you from playing the game successfully? This may be an overlooked or stubborn block surfacing. If you uncover an old block, be happy you can now go back to the block section of this book and seek to dismantle it or remove it from your path.

Once you are in the habit of playing I Am Psychic one day a week, add a day and play the game twice a week. Again, when you do play it, see and feel the inner transformation from your ordinary self into your extraordinary soul—like Clark Kent turning into Superman. The costume is necessary for the transformation, and it's fun! But remember, even though you are having fun, the play is serious creative work, carving direct pathways into your inner kingdom, where all you need exists.

Notice the difference in the tone of your life on the days that you play I Am Psychic. Notice the way events and experiences unfold. Notice any synchronicity. Notice any spontaneous manifestations. Notice any coincidences. Notice any and all connections unfolding. Did you see more when you were "psychic"? Did you feel more? Did you know more? Pay attention to how much more your subconscious mind will make you aware of when you are playing I Am Psychic.

I describe the experience you have when playing this game as like going from a life in black-and-white to one in color, or like the difference between listening to the radio and listening to a live orchestra. The difference in perception when you play this game is explosive! Your sensory awareness will burst wide open, but in a safe and beneficial way.

You may say, "That's all well and good, but you can't play every day. You have to be realistic!"

The paradox is, when you play this game you are being more completely real than ever before. By setting up as many nonthreatening opportunities as possible for your soul to express itself through games, you will naturally integrate your intuition into your life. It is the real you, the soul you, that is the psychic.

When you play, you allow the most real part of you to participate in your life. Why can't you play it every day? The you that you have been playing out, the ego you, is no more real than the psychic you. In fact, it's less real.

Aren't you discovering that the ego you is a hodgepodge of misperceptions, half-truths, pains, and traumas, all compacted into a dense, tight, fearful ball? Aren't you beginning to sense that the psychic you, on the other hand, is open, creative, flowing, spontaneous, loving, inspired, and visionary? (Not to mention . . . fun?)

Of course it is. It is a more evolved, higher you. It is the truthful essence of you. It's hard to accept, but your soul really is as wonderful and wise, capable and competent, as you can possibly imagine. Your imagination pulls directly from your soul essence—the genuine you, the real McCoy, your true self.

When you play I Am Psychic, you release the grip you have on your false self, and for a while you get to experience the safety, security, inspiration, and protection of your real self. It's liberating! There's no feeling that matches this!

Bit by bit, more and more, introduce this game into your life and watch what happens to you. You will see a transformation take place inside you. The ugly duckling you may feel you've always been will transform into a beautiful and graceful swan. Your inner beauty will come forth with this game.

The magic wand of permission to be psychic is waved by you, and it can be waved only in the spirit of creative expression. The transformation from ordinary to extraordinary is subtle. Each step you've taken so far has turned the wheels of your personal evolution just a little more. By now, with the I Am Psychic game, you will start to experience your true self emerging and expressing itself in your daily life, changing it from one of drudgery to one that is exciting, wonderful, and ripe with possibility.

The I Am Psychic game allows you a safe way to experience yourself at your most conscious, most aware, most grounded, and most creative. The game pulls your soul essence out of hiding and puts you fully in command of all your senses.

By now you must realize that the more you play, the better you'll become at playing; the more psychic you will be; the more conscious, aware, and capable you will feel; the more alive and inspired you will experience yourself to be; and the more intensely you will know that the soul is real—that it is your essence. You will remember who you are.

If you feel I have gone on and on and on about this—I have! This is a breakthrough game. It will bring all kinds of wonderful discoveries to your attention.

You will not only notice and see the truth about little things, but you will also begin to notice and understand the truth about big things—answers to questions like, Why am I here? Why did I have these parents? This family? These relationships? This kind of work path? This health problem? This creative path?

The I Am Psychic game is the way into wonderland. The more you allow yourself to creatively express who you are, the more will be revealed to you about the mysteries and dilemmas of your life.

A last word (really): It is important to pursue this game in the spirit of creative play and wonder. The minute you *try* to be psychic, the minute you get serious about it, you put your ego back in charge and send your soul back into the background, into the shadows.

By now you know that "psychic" means "of the soul," not "of the ego." So even though it is a paradox, the way to the soul is through play, creative play, and not effort!

EXPLORATIONS

Psychic Dress-Up

The idea of this exercise is to play dress-up. By this we mean creating a costume that represents your psychic persona. It may seem a little odd to have a Merlin outfit in your closet, but it is a lot of fun!

My personal dress-up costume as a child was a Gypsy getup. Of course, that's the Romanian in me! I would wear long scarf skirts, big hoop earrings, and bracelets up and down both arms, clear to the elbow. I also wore bandanas around my head and huge amulet necklaces. Maybe I had to get this out of my system before I became a professional, but I'm still prone to bracelets and swooping skirts.

Let yourself enjoy being a psychic child. Go to a thrift shop, the five-and-dime, Goodwill, your mother's closets. Design, devise, and invent. *Trust your imagination*—it knows best.

I'm not asking you to wear this costume to your next dinner party or to the office—although feel free! I'm not asking you to wear it at all. Just own it. (It's irresistible to put it on. Like your psychic gifts, it's a part of you.)

Image Collection

Assemble a stack of old magazines. Leaf through the magazines and tear out *any* image that appeals to your psychic child. Put these images in a folder.

Visit a card shop. Select one each of any image that appeals to you or reflects your psychic child persona. One of my students has a collection of Merlin images. One has a collection of St. Theresa cards. Another collects angels. One collects pictures of wolves. For another, it's owls.

The amazing thing is that once you start to collect your psychic images, they'll come hurtling toward you from the universe. They will find you. This is an amazing and amusing psychic game.

Psychic Closet

Many of us have been in the closet for years with our psychic abilities, so we might as well make it cozy in there.

Select a closet or corner in your home. Imagine that this is your psychic closet. If you pick a real closet, decorate the inside of the door, the walls, ceiling—floor, if you want to—with all your psychic images. Use stars, rainbows, and, above all, images of your psychic persona. If you are using a corner, decorate this space the same way.

It also helps to put incense in this closet or corner (not left burning if you leave, of course), to infuse an aroma indicating that this is a sacred space. As you may have discovered, scent is an often overlooked highway to the psychic self. Many of my students find that lighting a ceremonial stick of incense gives them "permission" to access their psychic self—a tiny but highly effective magic wand.

You may want to store your psychic costume in this corner, and you might feel an impulse to construct a psychic altar where you place your psychic toys. This can be a real altar or a shoebox. Use your imagination.

Don't be surprised if you decide to meditate in this psychic space. You will not be the first student who has claimed this space for yourself.

When I was growing up, it was my favorite place. You could always find me there. Even today I maintain a sacred space in my home, where I meditate, pray, and ask for spiritual guidance. And by virtue of it being a special place, I always receive spiritual guidance when I'm there.

CHARTING YOUR PROGRESS

Reflect on your experiences this week when answering these questions.

How many days this week did you meditate? By now it should be a pleasure. Any new images of yourself during this meditation? _____

_____

Have you remembered to ground yourself? _____

_____

Have you remembered to clear your aura? _____

_____

How many days this week did you make entries in your psychic journal?

_____

Any psychic images show up? If yes, glue pictures of them into the space below.

What does your psychic persona look like?_____

_____

Does your psychic persona have a name?_____

_____

Did you enjoy putting together your costume?_____

_____

Have images of your psychic persona found you?_____ _____

_____

Traveling
Companions

As you've discovered, life changes when you play I Am Psychic. It is about to change again—perhaps in a way you have always been skeptical about yet yearned for.

As you saw, the minute you allow yourself to be psychic, you open the door to being psychic—naturally. Much of this book has been spent undoing the damage done to these natural gifts. Now let me share a few stories about what happens when psychic gifts are regarded as natural.

My own little girls speak freely of their angels and guides and of feeling loved and guided by God. From the time they were babies I've talked to them about God, heaven, and knowing that God's helpers are all around us, guiding us on the path back to heaven. And to my great joy these little girls, who are now four and five, are already displaying significant psychic awareness.

Sonia, my older daughter, is a gentle old soul. She is sensitive, perceptive, artistic, poetic, and loving. She cares deeply about the earth. Some of her favorite possessions are rocks that she has noticed and brought home along the way in her life. Sonia also loves plants and animals and is sensitive to their needs. She waters the flowers, feeds the birds, and talks to any animal that will listen. She experiences great pleasure in the love and beauty they emote. Sonia is friendly and easy, and she possesses a natural patience and understanding of people that reveals what an old soul she really is.

Once Patrick and I, Sabrina, and Sonia were driving in the car when suddenly a driver cut right in front of us, almost causing an accident. Patrick lost his temper and yelled, "You idiot, where did you learn how to drive?" Sabrina immediately started parroting him, saying, "That's right. You idiot!" Sonia, however, waited a moment and said, "Dad, she wasn't an idiot. She just drives differently. I think she was in a hurry." Patrick and I exchanged glances. Sonia at the time was not yet four.

Every day Sonia and I have a "private chat." I ask her how school is, how her friends are, and what she learned. Sometimes she displays a profound insight for her age. She'll say things like, "Ana was naughty to Michael, but she didn't have good dreams last night, so it made her cranky." Or she'll say, "The kids called me snotty-face and gross and disgusting, but I forgive them because they don't know who I am. I'm really an angel from heaven."

I'm always amazed and charmed by her tolerance. My own weakness is impatience, and I find myself frequently telling Sonia to hurry up. She takes her time, moving at her own natural and more balanced pace, and suggests that I try to "breathe" if she makes me irritable.

Sonia's first psychic display occurred just before Christmas when she was three and a half. We had our Christmas tree set up, and a few presents were sitting under it, given to the girls by our friends Ann and Leon. When it was time for the girls' bedtime story, Sonia said, "I want to read *Where the Wild Things Are,*" a book we had checked out from the library.

"Sorry, Sonia," I said, "but we returned that book to the library yesterday, remember? Why don't you choose another storybook to read?"

She replied, "Uh-uh! We have *Where the Wild Things Are*—I'll show you," and she flew out of bed and grabbed one of the wrapped packages from under the tree.

I laughed and said, "Honey, I believe you are right in thinking this is a book." It was obvious that it was. "But I don't think it's *Where the Wild Things Are.*"

She insisted it was. "Yes, it is. My spirit told me it is."

I had taught the girls that it is our spirit that guides us and to always ask their spirit for guidance. I also tell them to listen to God speak in their hearts, so she was quite sincere when she said this.

I relented. "Well, why don't we open it and see," I said.

She tore off the paper in three seconds, and much to my surprise, and to her utter delight, it was *Where the Wild Things Are.* We both squealed with joy.

It was a profound moment for me. In that experience I was so joyous to see the legacy of psychic consciousness passed from my mother to me continuing to pass to my little Sonia.

"Sonia, that's terrific. Be sure you say thank you to your spirit for sharing that little secret with you."

Just a few days later Patrick and I received a call from an old colleague of Patrick's who worked in the gift business. He called to say that a toy company he worked for was selling its Christmas floor samples and there was a beautiful life-size clown for sale for $50. It retailed for over $500 and was a bargain. He wanted to know whether we wanted it.

We both love a bargain. We said we did and went together to look at it. It turned out to be a beautiful harlequin about three and a half feet tall. I love harlequins and have collected them all my life. I think it's from my many past lives in France. I had to have it. We put it in the trunk of our car and decided to leave it there until Christmas morning, three days away.

We went home, and as I was dressing Sonia for bed, she looked up at her shelf where there was a little six-inch harlequin I had given her. She said, "Mommy, see that clown? Let's get a big one like that, okay? I know you would love it. Would that make you happy?" I couldn't believe she'd picked up on exactly what I was concentrating on in my mind. What a little telepath!

Not wanting to ruin the Christmas surprise, I just smiled and said, "I believe you are right, sweetheart. I would love that."

Then she said, now dressed in her pajamas and sitting on my lap,

"Don't worry, Mommy. God told me that Santa Claus will bring us one."
I had to laugh and give her a hug. This was the best Christmas present of all. Another psychic soul!

Sabrina started to display her ability when she too was around three years old. I was in the kitchen making breakfast one morning and was mentally planning my itinerary for the day. I wanted to go to Marshall Field's to buy new sheets for the beds while their annual linen sale was on. I was thinking about asking Patrick to watch the girls while I took off for a few hours to shop.

All of a sudden, Sabrina, who was at the table eating toast, said spontaneously, "I want to go shopping with you."

I turned my head toward her in complete surprise, because at just that moment I was concentrating on leaving her at home. "How do you know I'm going shopping?" I asked, feeling I had been busted.

"My spirit told me," she said rather nonchalantly. "You are going to buy a new bed."

I was thrilled. She had both surprised me and exposed me. Again I had to laugh. After all, she was absolutely right. I was so proud of her psychic display, I thought she should be rewarded, so I took her along with me. She had earned it.

We frequently talk about God and spirits and angels, and I encourage the girls to trust their feelings even if other people tell them not to. And I listen to them and take everything they say seriously. Once Sonia told me that her new preschool teacher, Jan, didn't like children, and that she was a liar. This alerted me, because Sonia never says a mean thing about anyone. Jan seemed like a sweet woman on the surface and appeared to be a devoted teacher.

I alerted Patrick, and we began to watch her carefully. Two days later Patrick caught Jan sneaking out of the preschool, leaving an unqualified teenager to care for the children in her place. We took the girls out of the preschool that day. A month later a neighbor told us that the school was closed because Jan frequently abandoned her post to unqualified caretakers, and that all Jan had to say about it was, "Fine with me. I hated those brats anyway."

I was relieved to have taken Sonia and Sabrina out of the school shortly after Sonia alerted us. In our family framework, if someone has a feeling or intuition, we act on it.

One day Sabrina woke up and announced to us at breakfast, "My nana is coming to see me. She told me in my dream."

I said, "Is that right? I don't know about it, but we'll wait and see."

Sure enough, at two o'clock my mom called and said she and my father were thinking of visiting us. I laughed and said, "I know. Sabrina told us this morning. She dreamt about it."

My mom was excited. "Yes, that's *my* grandbaby," she said. We laughed, and we were both happy to know that these little girls were already showing us that they walked in the awareness of spirit.

As a mother, this was a great thing to know. For me it all started with these same kinds of feelings. It's reassuring to me that through their development of psychic awareness, their paths in life may be a little easier and a lot more fun than if they weren't aware of the love and support of the universe.

Which brings us back to you.

Now you are aware of the love and support of the universe. Now you, too, will start to experience all kinds of wonderful psychic events. Please allow yourself a child's wonder. You will notice what you didn't notice before. You will hear what you didn't hear before. You will become aware of what you missed before. In short, you will experience being guided. You always have been guided but may have called it coincidence.

At this point you may begin to become consciously aware of the help you have in your life, help that you weren't acknowledging before. This help is your spiritual guidance. Although you may not, at first, be able to pick out each of the voices in this chorus, it is the help given to you by your angels, runners, helpers, teachers, masters, and joy guides, collectively called your "guides."

Each soul has guides. Consider all your guides as your spiritual support system, assigned to your life by God at various times to help you along your path.

Even though all guides guide, the help you receive from them is varied, and you'll recognize it more readily if you know the differences among the types of guides, how each type helps you, and how they work in your life.

ANGELS

The first spiritual guide you receive is an angel (sometimes plural). Angels connect to you at the time of your birth. Your angels are with you to see you safely through your life, until the point where you complete your purpose or goal for this lifetime. You do have one!

Although we may not remember making this itinerary, each soul decides in advance on its spiritual agenda of growth before coming into the physical body. A young soul may want only to learn a few basic survival skills. A more ambitious soul may want to uncover far greater spiritual understanding and develop the capacity to love and forgive. The more ambitious soul will have a more complex life path, with greater potential to grow. No matter which course you have set for yourself, angels are with you to keep you from harm until you accomplish what you want to accomplish on a soul level.

Countless reports of angels all indicate the same basic experience. An angel saves a person from danger—physical and spiritual.

I have had two extraordinary experiences with angels. I have already described the angel who saved me from spiritual jeopardy in Hawaii. That angel told me to go back to working with my husband *for my protection,* and that guidance saved my life.

But my first experience was 15 years ago.

In the winter of 1979 I had decided to move back to my hometown of Denver from Chicago, where I had been living for a year. I asked my best friend and fellow psychic Lu Ann to come to Chicago and help me drive my 1968 lime-green VW Bug full of my belongings back to Denver. She graciously agreed.

It became apparent that packing all my stuff into the backseat of the VW was going to take the first miracle of our journey. We crammed, shoved, jostled, jockeyed, and eventually made everything fit. It was so tight there wasn't a free inch of space anywhere. It was almost noon when we piled in, revved up the engine, and took off. We didn't have a map, but we were confident in our psychic abilities and decided to let our guides lead us to Colorado. An hour and fifteen minutes later we were in Milwaukee, 90 miles *north* of Chicago. Some psychics we were! It was now almost two in the afternoon, and we had actually *regressed* from our starting point.

We filled up the tank, purchased a map, and turned around. It was our intention to drive straight through, and since Denver was twenty hours from Chicago—twenty-two hours from Milwaukee—we decided it was better to follow directions if we hoped to make it without stopping.

So we turned around and, map in hand, were on our way to Denver.

The skies were turning very dark, and in a few short hours we headed into the most incredible snowstorm I had ever experienced in my life. The visibility was less than two feet, and the snow was swirling all around, dumping piles and piles of it on the road. It was almost surreal.

Cars were sliding off the highway left and right as we drove, but we kept going, plowing through, hugging the road. We kept losing track of time and distance because there was only a sea of white, and no way to mark the miles. We had no idea how far we had gone. There was nothing to see but the glow of highway lights in the wet snow.

The drive was getting tedious. At one point I looked at my watch. It was 2 A.M. I figured that with any luck at all we would arrive by 10 the next morning and began to worry about staying awake. We had driven well into Nebraska, but the night was desolate and the highway lights few and far between. Lu and I had stopped talking. Fatigue was setting in, and we were both fighting sleep.

We were also starting to feel anxious. We began to sing the Pointer Sisters' version of "Fire," and we were really bellowing along at the top of our lungs when suddenly, as if out of nowhere, a young woman in a white dress stood ahead in the road waving her arms frantically.

"Oh, my God!" we both screamed.

I was driving, and I slammed on the brakes. I braced myself to hit the woman because we had come up on her so fast. The car went into a spin and we slid off the road into a snowbank. For a moment neither one of us moved.

Lu and I looked up, and no one was there. We jumped out of the car and looked around but, apart from the area lit by our headlights, it was pitch black. We took a few steps to make sure someone wasn't lying in the snow. The adrenaline was pumping hard through my veins. We stood staring at each other. All we could manage to say was *"Wow!"* with eyes as big as saucers.

We slowly got in the car, backed up and onto the road.

"Did you see that woman, Lu?" I asked.

"Of course I did," she said. "I thought you were going to hit her."

"Do you think we could both hallucinate the same person?" I mused.

"I guess so. . . . We both did."

We were still in shock. We just kept saying over and over, "How bizarre!"

After driving for maybe 20 more minutes, we saw the glow of a town ahead. That must be Lincoln, we decided. We agreed to stop and get something to eat. We drove a couple more minutes and saw a sign that said DENVER, 47 MILES.

Denver! How could we be in Denver? We were only in the middle of Nebraska. We couldn't possibly be in Denver.

Lu looked at her watch. It was 3:50 A.M. We had been traveling for only fourteen hours from Milwaukee in the middle of one of the worst snowstorms of the century, in a 1968 loaded-to-the-gills VW, traveling at best sixty to sixty-five miles an hour, with four stops. The earliest we had expected to arrive in Denver was six hours from now, and yet we were almost home!

It was physically impossible. The odometer registered the miles, but the time didn't make sense. The only thing we could conclude was that the woman we saw was an angel. She appeared when I was in the dangerous situation of falling asleep at the wheel on a desolate highway in a major snowstorm. Hard as it was to believe, she had somehow saved us from a potential disaster and transported us safely near our destination.

Once again, when I really needed assistance, help had appeared from the realm of spirit. Just how *much* help there was, and how it worked for us mere mortals, kept me thinking for a long time!

Angels may show up as people, but they appear out of nowhere and disappear just as fast. They are always beautiful, even glowing, but they are not always blond haired, white skinned, and blue eyed, as they are so often portrayed in pictures. My Hawaiian angel had skin as black as human skin can be, but he was radiant and dressed in shimmering white robes.

How do you know if you've encountered an angel? You realize an angel has just helped you the moment the angel disappears. They leave their essence in your aura for a while, like a calling card. After you experience an angel, you are energized. You have been obviously helped and spiritually touched. Their essence is pure love. It's serene—out of this world, really!

RUNNERS

The next type of guide you have is known as a runner. The runner's purpose is to help you find things, notice things, or to connect you to things or people you need. (In many traditions, runners are known as earth spirits, fairies, or souls who once lived in great harmony with nature.) You maintain the same two or three runners all your life.

For example, my baby-sitter bought herself a beautiful gold bracelet last year, which she wore to work every day. We all admired it, but one day when I returned from work, she was beside herself because the bracelet was missing and she couldn't find it anywhere. She had combed through the house for over an hour, to no avail. It was gone! When I arrived, she was near tears.

As I heard her tell me the story of her lost bracelet, I asked my runner to take me to it. Instantly I had an overwhelming urge to look at the bottom of a very deep basket in the toy room. I walked directly to the basket, emptied it out, and there was the bracelet! It was my runner who took me to the place where it was. My baby-sitter was both relieved and surprised that I had found it so quickly.

"No problem," I said. "Don't thank me. Thank my runner!"

HELPERS

The next type of guide you may receive help from is called a helper. Helpers do exactly that—they help on *specific* problems. You will attract different helpers depending on what it is that you need help with.

For example, if you are having difficulty with your health, or you are not feeling well, you will attract a spirit doctor or healer to work with you. This type of guide may make you stop and notice behavior or habits that may be harming your health or bring your attention to a new way to help yourself.

I have struggled a great deal with sciatica, a low back pain disorder that's very difficult to treat. Even while I walked through the maze of conventional treatments of ultrasound, heat packs, and muscle relaxers, I had an overwhelming urge to seek the treatment of a massage therapist instead of what I was doing.

At the time, I didn't even know how to find a massage therapist, and the pain was almost crippling. I tried the conventional treatments for over two years, and every time I asked my doctors about massage therapy, they dismissed it as nonsense. But my pain didn't subside. My life was becoming more and more complicated by the pain.

One day a friend of mine began telling me about a naprapath who helped her with fertility problems. I asked her what a naprapath was.

"Sort of a massage therapist," she answered.

A light went on inside me. That's it! I thought. This was the "massage therapist" I had been feeling an urge to see for over a year.

I made an appointment with this naprapath and had him work on my back the following week. For the first time in over two years, I felt some genuine relief after the treatment. After three sessions my pain disappeared completely. The naprapath manipulated my spine in a very gentle way that relieved the trauma and the source of my pain. Where conventional treatment failed to help me, this alternative healer eliminated the problem completely.

It was a spiritual helper who encouraged me to be receptive to this type of treatment. Without this helper putting the idea into my head and keeping it there for some time, I would never have been receptive even to trying massage treatment.

Your spirit helpers change, depending on what it is you're working on. When I was looking for a house with my husband, we were driving up and down streets in various Chicago neighborhoods, trying to find what we wanted. Patrick, my husband, grew up in Iowa and has better "land" helpers than I do, so we put him in charge of the search. He turned the job of finding the house over to his helper. As we drove, we spotted a two-flat house that we liked on a pleasant street. However, it did not have a FOR SALE sign on it.

My husband said, "I want a building just like that. Let's find a realtor in the neighborhood to work with."

There was a real estate office at the corner, a block and a half away from the building we liked.

"Let's go there," I suggested.

"No," he said. "I don't want to. Let's just keep driving."

We drove around for another twenty minutes and finally came across another real estate office, in a different neighborhood entirely. We walked in and met with a salesman. We told him we were interested in buying a two-flat house, possibly on the street we liked.

He said, "Hold on. I took a listing on that street this morning. Let's see . . . yes, here it is." He told us the address.

I couldn't believe it. That was the exact building that we had in mind! It was Patrick's helper that got us to that realtor, the very one in the whole city who had listed the building that morning. We liked it as much inside as outside. We put in an offer and had a contract the next day.

* * *

Whatever you are doing or trying to accomplish, you have attracted spiritual helpers to aid your progress. They inspire you, give you bright ideas, offer solutions to problems, attract your attention to where there is help, and work with you toward your success.

The number of helper guides you have working with you changes, depending on what you are doing and how spiritually relevant it is. For example, a scientist working on developing an AIDS vaccine is going to have more help from the spiritual plane, as he seeks to uncover a secret that would benefit all mankind, than someone having to assemble a bicycle for the first time.

One of the most important things a helper guide can do is attract you to helpful people and information that you otherwise wouldn't be aware of. Your spirit guide may compel a friend to mention something, for example, that is exactly what you need to know!

TEACHERS

The next type of spiritual guide is called a teacher. Spiritual teachers come to you to help you remember who you are. This type of guide influences your conscious spiritual development and awareness level.

The teacher is the guide that will assist a soul to go to an AA meeting or to seek therapy. A teacher will create an urge in a person to delve past the appearances in life and probe to find greater meaning. A teacher will influence your inclination to forgive others, accept yourself and others, and recognize the more profound aspects of life. Your teachers stay with you, and as you grow, you may attract more teachers.

The purpose of teachers is to work to channel understanding into the planet, bringing about greater balance and harmony. Teachers raise consciousness. That is the true meaning behind the statement "When the student is ready, the teacher appears." The teacher does appear.

This type of guidance is often called *synchronicity*. A person being influenced by a teacher might say, "I just started to study metaphysics, and I received these metaphysical books as gifts. Isn't that something?"

Yes, that's something: that's a teacher guide. They are always connected with bringing to you what will aid your soul's learning.

I've had many spiritual teachers in my life. I very frequently dream of a church in Reims, France, a huge cathedral where I am being instructed by two priests. They speak to me in each dream of the importance of prayer and ritual. They are always the same two priests. The dream is always at the cathedral, and I *know* that these two souls are my spiritual teachers, working day and night to guide my spiritual path.

One of the most significant tasks of a spiritual teacher is to introduce you to teachers on earth who can help you grow. They often borrow people for a moment to say to you, through someone, Go to this therapist . . . or that counselor . . . or take this class . . . or that workshop.

Your spiritual teachers will influence your awareness in such a way as to help you notice where to go for the instruction you need, as you need it, when you are ready. It is the spiritual teacher that stirs in your heart a spiritual restlessness and a thirst to seek to understand more about the true nature of things. The more urgent your need to grow spiritually is, the more frequently your spirit guides will bring your attention to the need.

MASTERS

Your master guide is a very compassionate and loving soul, totally devoted to overseeing your spiritual evolution as you move from one level of consciousness into another. You know a master is touching your soul when, for example, you feel compelled to meditate after years of avoiding or ignoring it.

The guidance of a master brings a love and light into the dark, wounded places of your soul. This spiritual influence stimulates the ability to love and accept yourself and others and enables you to find the insight to forgive and let go of any attachment to patterns that hurt or impede your growth.

You may have only one master or you may attract several, depending on what you want to do in this incarnation. Master guides lead you past understanding and into healing and enlightenment.

The energy of a master is profoundly reassuring. This energy compels one to let go and be done with attachments to illusions or patterns of behavior that are contrary to truth. A master's guidance urges one to be compassionate, nonjudgmental, unattached to the ego plane, and above all, peaceful.

JOY GUIDES

Joy guides are child essences whose purpose is to make you laugh and to let you play and feel free to express yourself without self-consciousness. They twinkle past you all the time, trying to engage the child in you. They lighten you up, free your spirit, and amuse you.

A joy guide is always present at funerals, to usher out the pain. They show up at somber moments and make you burst out laughing. Joy guides are here to remind you to enjoy the walk.

I met my first joy guide at my uncle Rudy's funeral. Uncle Rudy was like my grandfather. He was really my great-uncle, my dad's uncle, and did all that grandfathers do as I grew up. My brothers and sisters visited Uncle Rudy and Aunt Emma every Easter break. He was a big guy and moved slowly. He smoked cigarettes, read *National Geographic,* and called us all "pickle puss." He liked to tell us long-winded tales of my dad as a child, and he was very patient.

When he died, I was devastated. The sadness at the funeral was almost overwhelming. We all had to file past his coffin at the wake. All I kept thinking was, Poor Uncle Rudy.

When I got right up to him, much to my surprise, I was overcome with an urge to laugh, and I did—I burst right out. It started my sister laughing, then my brother, and spread like fire through the entire family. We couldn't stop.

I know that psychologists have an explanation for this, but I have an explanation of my own: A joy guide breezed by. Uncle Rudy was eighty-three. He was happy to go! A joy guide made us laugh because we should have been happy—for Uncle Rudy.

Joy guides show up at the darnedest times. When the pain and drama are too great to bear, they break the vibration, release the tension, and remind us that there *is* no death. They are funny, silly, irreverent, tricky, and sly, and they like to shake up the drama and bring in the joy.

BEING AWARE OF YOUR GUIDES

As you develop and open the chakras, the ability to be conscious of your guides' help begins to develop. Angels surround you at all times and are connected to your second and third chakras. Joy guides and helpers are connected to your third and fourth chakras. Teachers are connected to your fourth, fifth, and sixth chakras, and your master is connected to your seventh chakra.

The best way to be aware of spiritual guidance is to be *aware*—of your body, of your aura, of your feelings, and of your chakras. Most of all, accept that these are the pathways and doors to spiritual guidance. If you learn the pathway, the door opens naturally.

Let's pause just for a second and review the work we have done! Together, we have walked through these various steps. I have taught them to you, and you can teach them to others:

- Recognize you are a soul.
- Identify your blocks.
- Work on strategies to overcome your blocks.
- Start to notice the world around you—pay attention.
- Meditate—turn inward and learn to quiet your mind.
- Notice your aura—learn about its purpose and be aware of it.
- Notice the chakras—learn about their purpose and be aware of them.
- Play I Am Psychic. Give it a try!
- Discover your support group of guides from a higher plane.

As you continue to follow this pathway, you will realize that you are becoming a different kind of person, an *extra*ordinary person. You are slowly shifting your emphasis in life off your ego mind and allowing it to move into the seat of your soul—your heart.

Life will begin to get easier as you discover that when your ego lets go, you don't fall flat on your face. Instead you are lifted up to a higher plane, to a higher vantage point, a place where things come more easily—and the possibility for happiness begins to creep back into your heart.

EXPLORATIONS

Asking Your Guides for Help

This week, practice being receptive to your guides. Follow these simple suggestions to allow your guides to work for you. The best way is always the direct way. As Jesus said, "Ask and you shall receive. Knock and the door shall be opened."

If you want your guides to help you, *ask* them to help you! They can't help you unless you allow them to. When you ask, you give them permission to go to work, guiding you in every possible way to your spiritual awakening.

Things to Ask Your Angels

Protect me from . . .
- negativity
- violence
- danger
- accidents
- psychic attack
- psychic pollution
- unstable vibrations
- unhealthy people
- angry people
- guilt- or shame-based people
- my own negative patterns of self-destruction
- depression
- weakness
- my own mistakes

Protect me . . .
- when sick
- when in surgery
- when sleeping
- when in an argument

Things to Ask Your Runners

Where can I find . . .   my keys?
a parking space?
a needed piece of information?
the perfect dress/shoes for an occasion?
the best bargain on travel, hotel, car
rental?

Connect me to the   baby-sitter
right . . .   secretary
job
friendships
apartment
house
relationship
travel agent

Things to Ask Your Helpers

Help and guide me   doing the best job
in . . .   saying the right thing
getting the right health diagnosis and
treatment
taking care of my animals
working on my job tasks
planting my garden
uncovering my creativity
healing my creativity
discovering my right emphasis
keeping to my self-improvement plan
choosing the correct foods and activities
using my time correctly
getting the best possible support people
making a decision

Things to Ask Your Teachers

Guide me to find the lessons . . .	in my friendships
	with my family, parents, siblings, children

Also help me . . .	in my love affairs
	with my body
	with my sexuality
	with my money
	with the path of the soul
	with intuition and psychic awakening
	with releasing old patterns
	with learning self-care
	with how to have fun

Help me to . . .	meditate
	slow down
	get organized
	ground myself
	become aware of my aura
	become aware of my chakras
	awaken telepathically
	awaken to spiritual hearing
	trust the truth
	live the truth
	feel loved

Things to Ask Your Master

Help me . . . feel my spirit
recognize my true purpose in life
release the past in the spirit of love and
forgiveness
feel the acceptance of who I am
remember my soul path
recall my past life connections to others
heal my emotional wounds
love unconditionally
find the power of my soul
laugh

Things to Ask Your Joy Guides

Make me laugh when . . . I'm feeling depressed
I'm feeling grief
I'm feeling afraid
I'm feeling rejected
I'm feeling blocked
I'm feeling drained
I'm feeling overwhelmed
I'm missing the point
I'm causing trouble
I need to be stopped
I need some air

Help me recover and creativity
express my . . . playfulness
humor
silliness
joy

This week, ask your guides to help you with everything you need, big or small, profound or trivial. If the help requires a runner, ask a runner. If it requires an expert, ask a helper. If you require insight or knowledge, ask a teacher. If you want to be released from old patterns, ask your master. And if you're just plain in need of reassurance or protection, ask your angels.

The biggest task this week is to take the chance of asking for and letting yourself receive the love, support, and guidance being channeled to you from your guides. Your guides love you. Your guides are there specifically to help you. And when they help you, they in turn are evolving ever upward into the light of divine oneness.

By agreeing to be helped, you help your guides. You help the planet, too; as you achieve more balance, you contribute more balance to the earth plane. And you help your relationships. If you are spiritually peaceful, you can touch other people's lives in a good way, and the domino effect goes on and on. The more you receive light from the spiritual plane, the more light you throw out. At this point you begin to shift toward those who heal and away from those who hurt.

When you open yourself up to the influx of psychic support, every life you touch will also be helped. It doesn't stop with you. The energy flowing into you ripples outward from you like ripples on a lake, on and on and on. That is the continuance of love.

Write in your journal this week all experiences you have of being helped. Get ready—you're in for a wonderful surprise!

CHARTING YOUR PROGRESS

Reflect on your experiences this week when answering these questions.

How many days this week did you meditate? Were you aware of any guides? _____

_____

How many days this week did you make an entry in your psychic journal? Talk to anyone new? _____

_____

Have you remembered to ground yourself?_____

_____

Have you remembered to clear your aura?_____

_____

Did you meet an angel?_____

_____

Did you employ your runner?_____

_____

Did you feel a helper's hand?_____

_____

Did you learn from a teacher?_____

_____

Did a joy guide make you laugh?_____

_____

Did your master whisper new directions?_____

_____

Asking for Directions

What you need to know is that your Higher Self and guides are ready and available to help you with everything and anything, at all times. Nothing is too small or too great. Anything you are willing to receive and be responsible for, anything you are willing to put time into and honestly work to make happen, your soul will help you with, whether it is a new recipe or a Ph.D. dissertation.

Know: Anything that expresses your creativity is important. All of it! And you will be helped on anything, *anything*, that you ask for guidance on. You are never, ever, really alone! Simply allow yourself to be aware of it. It is your birthright. It is the spiritual truth. It is the process of God's love pouring into your life.

By knowing this, get in the habit of asking, all the time, for guidance. Every morning, upon awakening, thank God for a new day and say:

> Divine Mother, Father, Higher Self, guides, and angels, lead me this day to the highest degree of awareness, the highest degree of creativity, and to my best possible good. Surprise me! I am open to miracles.

After doing this, ask for and listen to all your psychic impulses, on all matters. Ask for guidance, from where to park the car to how best to do your job. Learn to invite your Higher Self into every choice and decision you make—every single one. If you do this over the next few weeks, you will slowly reveal to yourself what you really want help with, your deepest, most profound desires. The little triumphs will set up the security to ask for help with bigger ones. Be patient and record in your journal all your experiences with asking for guidance.

Once you begin to liberate yourself from the blocks to your Higher Self, and begin to focus on what's important, you can move toward a more direct communication with the Higher Self.

Now that you've primed yourself to receive psychic guidance, now that you've noticed the guidance you do receive, you need to ask yourself, In what areas do I *want* psychic guidance?

The next step on the psychic pathway is to get in touch with what you really want Higher Forces to help you with. What is it that you would like to do, to be, to experience in your life at this time? In what area would you like your Higher Self to guide you?

Psychic ability follows your heart's desires.

Your Higher Self and your guides are always available to help you proceed in life toward experience and creative expression that will bring you a sense of peace, of gratification, of security. Your part in all of this is to discover what it is you really want, what you *long* to experience in your life. As soon as you know, your Higher Self can get to work to help bring it about.

Some people have no problem. They know exactly what they want in life, clearly, specifically, and without any hesitation. Consider them lucky. But for the rest of us, getting in touch with our heart's desires and having the courage to express them is often a difficult, frustrating, and scary process. This is because many of us have been taught along the way that asking for something is selfish. We believe we have no right to feel that what matters to us is important.

You may have been raised with a harsh religious point of view that emphasized self-denial, or you may have been trained to put others' wishes ahead of your own. If you are a woman, you have probably been given the message that it is impolite, unfeminine, or unattractive to focus on your desires. Women have been raised to nurture others, often at our own expense.

Man or woman, you may carry the belief that to suffer or struggle is spiritually profound, or you may have been handed the news that life stinks, it's a dog-eat-dog world, and survival is the only real thing you should focus on.

Many of us don't bother to think about what we want because we believe it doesn't matter. We don't believe we could possibly experience what we really want, so why think about it?

This belief system is the ordinary way of looking at life. Most people focus only on the appearances and opinions of the world around them. They miss the powerful and intuitive world of consciousness and creativity within them. Of course they do! This world is hidden. On the psychic pathway, you break through to discover the truth of the extraordinary world.

The truth is that you are a child of God, a co-creator with God. Furthermore, you are surrounded by loving spiritual support at all times, lovingly helping you succeed in realizing who you are, who you want to be.

God wants you to succeed. God gave you the power to create, and everything in your life at present is your creation. You have already demonstrated your creativity in every choice you've made. Can you imagine what kinds of choices you would make if you had unlimited spiritual assistance to help you manifest your wishes? Would you still be settling for second best? An "okay" life, "better than a lot of people's"?

Probably not.

The truth is that you do have this kind of spiritual support available to you, and the more focused you become on what you want to do and be, the more you will experience this loving support from your Higher Self.

Ask. Expect. Accept. Experience.

That is the formula. Use it and it will work for you. Remember: I am not asking you to believe this. I am asking you to experiment and *ex-*

perience this. That is the key to embarking on an extraordinary life.

The more focused you are in your life, the more you have a clear idea of what you are trying to do, the more psychic guidance you'll receive. Conversely, the more aware you are of the fact that you have an infinite source of love, support, and guidance available to you from God, the easier it will be to find your true and genuine desires and intentions.

Let's face facts: It's a lot easier to acknowledge what you really want if you know you will have help—lots of help—in creating it. The more specific you are, the more help you'll receive.

Imagine you have available to you an expert on every possible undertaking you commit to, to advise you, guide you, and show you the best way to go about your mission. Imagine that you also have available "gofers" to find anything you could possibly need in your life; counselors to advise you on whether to speed up, slow down, or redirect your efforts; and protectors to keep you from dangers and harm.

Imagine, too, that you have comforters when you are anxious and guides to show you how much farther you need to go before you reach your chosen goal, in *any* area of your life.

If you had all that support available to you, do you think it would be any easier to go for the real wish, the true desire, the highest goal? Of course it would! This is the truth, yet most people have no idea of it. You do have this much loving support, and more, available. You may still feel all alone—but you aren't.

Ellen was a lovely, thirty-four-year-old waitress. She had come to me for a reading because she felt her life was so empty, so lonely, so ordinary, and she simply couldn't accept that this would be all she could look forward to. She was struggling. How could she change her life? She was open to helping herself, but "clueless."

Worse still, she denigrated herself for being, as she put it, "just a waitress." She felt there was something inadequate about it, even though it made her a fine living and she loved the people. Further, she believed she must do something more important to raise her self-esteem. Why? She felt her low self-esteem was the cause of her nonexistent love life.

I saw things differently. I saw that she was a very old soul, which meant that her life was driven by love and not ego. Waitressing didn't really bother her. She'd been told that it "should." I didn't really believe that, and neither did she.

I also saw that she, on a soul level, had decided to commit a huge part of her life to serving people, to being kind and caring, and wouldn't seek a lot of attention for it. The work was its own reward. I saw her restlessness at this juncture in her life not as a result of her having settled for a less than appropriate career, but rather as a stirring from her soul to take up art as a form of expression.

I said, "You are being reminded from your soul that you have a creative urge to express, and that service is only half of what you are here to do. The other half is to invent beautiful things. Perhaps in fabric. You have unexpressed talent that is birthing itself."

Ellen's eyes lightened. I had her attention.

"As for your life, you are and have been alone because you wanted to spend a huge part of your life working on you. Until recently you haven't been honestly available. To say, 'I'm this or that, I have low self-esteem, I'm just a waitress,' and so on is an erroneous interpretation of what is in fact happening. You are doing exactly the right thing for yourself. Can you sew?"

"Yes!"

Indeed, she had just started again after having dropped it as a teenager. She really loved it. The vest she was wearing was her own work, and it was lovely.

"Ellen, relax. You are on schedule. Your life is shifting focus. But don't devalue your work up until now as a way to inspire movement ahead. It's unhealthy. Now is a time to learn, grow, take risks. Travel. Take classes to challenge yourself. Try to shed an outgrown identity."

As for her love life, I said, "Ellen, don't worry about living an old maid's life, doing the same old thing. I see you meeting your soulmate and moving halfway around the world. To Australia or something!"

She laughed. "Sounds good, Sonia. How do I begin?"

"Just follow your *true* impulses, *focus in on them,* and don't let your work define your spirit or your possibilities. Look up and out. Surprises are coming!"

She saw her situation in a different way and left uplifted. Focusing on her own true desires, she let go of her concerns with being "only" a waitress. Freed to be as creative as she truly was, she dove deeply into sewing . . . and literally began selling the vests off her back. Her new career was unfolding a stitch at a time.

A few months later, needing a break, she followed a "strong urge" and enrolled in a Stuart Wilde seminar in Taos, New Mexico. The seminar was one where students challenge themselves to face their fears, even walk on fire. While dancing on coals, another spark ignited: she met a man from Texas there, and they eloped!

As she said, "I *knew,* and so did he, that we went there to intercept one another."

What next? They moved to Hawaii, where he just landed a job. It wasn't Australia, but it was close enough for me!

As Ellen's story shows, our souls are never confused, only our minds. At our soul level, each one of us has a point, a plan, a purpose for being here. Sometimes we forget and fall into the dream of setting up the wrong life. As a psychic, my point, my purpose, is to remind people of who they are and to urge that they go for the fullest expression of it.

Recently Ellen sent me a vest, now my favorite. Wearing it, I often reflect that like the lilies of the field, we are clothed by the universe—with just a little help from our own hands.

If you are on the psychic pathway, you are declared receptive to all the love, support, and guidance available to you from your Higher Self. You know—even if you can't always practice it—that life no longer has to be lived from your ego's point of view, a point of view that says, "I must do this alone . . . and it's hard!"

My point is, it isn't necessary to continue to feel it's you against the world, although it sometimes appears that way. As you grow in your psychic awareness, you will increasingly see the truth behind appearances. That vision *through* appearances is the difference between the ordinary person and a person walking on the psychic pathway.

But it doesn't happen overnight.

The psychic life, lived from the soul's point of view—the truthful point of view—says, "I am infinitely loved and supported by God, by my Higher Self, and by my guides, who all want me to succeed in being who I really want to be! I no longer have to worry about my survival, my security. I only have to focus on what I must do *today* toward my goals, and I await with joy guidance and miracles!"

I have had many miracles in my life. I believe the only difference between my life full of miracles versus the life of someone who struggles is that I know I'm helped, and I joyfully expect miracles. I place myself in the direction of my Higher Self and leave it to God to show me which way to go. I allow the universe to surprise me as to how it will unfold. And God has surprised me many times.

The rule you must adopt at this point is, Tell the universe what you want, but don't tell it how. In other words, you don't have to play God and take care of you. Let God play God and take care of you. God takes care of you as much as you allow. Your greatest gift is free will. You use this free will to choose what you believe is possible for you. Let me share a very personal example.

Once upon a time (twelve years ago, to be exact), I decided to believe it was possible for me to find true love. I realized that I really wanted love, commitment, and stability, but with someone who was also adventurous, romantic, and fun. I had met the extreme of both types. I wanted someone who had all these qualities blended into one personality.

I decided to visualize this person coming into my life. I believe we all have soul kin on the earth, people who, though not necessarily family, are deeply connected to us. I believed that somewhere out there, there must be a true partner for me. I couldn't accept that God would have me do this much psychic work and remain lonely. If I was willing to be committed to a partnership, then maybe my soul partner would show up.

Inventing my soulmate became my hobby.

I saw him as tall, slim, handsome. Every day I would add new traits.

He could sing. He could dance. He was romantic. He liked to ski. He had a large family. He loved to travel. Every day I would write down the qualities of this ideal partner I longed for. I was calling him from out of the universe. I really wanted him to show up. He would be single, never married, ready for commitment, know a lot about spiritual and psychic awareness, and be interested in it. He would be artistic. He could cook. He was generous to people. Also he was sophisticated, well read, and, yes, sexy.

On and on.

I wrote and visualized him for four months. Every day I would wake up wondering if Mr. Perfection himself would arrive that day. I was in a state of constant anticipation. Then, one night, I had a dream.

I dreamed I was working on a large sheet of paper, making very intricate calculations. I kept walking over to a large window and looking at the sky. Then I'd return to the table to write some more.

Standing across the table from me was another person, his back to me. We were both wearing gold-and-green robes. We didn't speak, but we were both aware of the other. I never saw this person's face.

Suddenly the windows I kept looking out of disappeared as if they were never there. My calculations weren't finished, and I had to continue working. I was afraid to bother this person, but I needed to look out of *his* window. I knew if that person stopped me and wouldn't share his view, I couldn't continue my work. I was quiet for a moment, then decided to just go ahead and look out his window without asking.

I slipped past him and stared out his window. Suddenly I could see masses and masses of people below. I hadn't seen those people before, when I was looking out of my window. Then the man's hand touched my shoulder, and I jumped. It was time for me to stop looking out the window and look at him. I was frightened, but I turned. . . . His face was very beautiful. I started to greet him, but he put his finger up to his lips to silence me.

"Ssh! Come here." He motioned to me. I started toward him, and then . . .

I woke up.

I lay there a long while, thinking about that dream. It seemed like another place, another time. I felt it was a past-life dream. I could almost feel a mood, a tone, a vibration, affecting me from another plane of experience. It felt more like a memory than a dream.

With the morning hours, the images began to fade, but not the mood. Whoever that was in my dream, he was protecting me somehow. And then the image slipped away into the day.

A few days passed. I was busy with clients during the day, but my evenings were spent quietly, alone and lonely. One night, quite impulsively, I picked up the phone and called an old friend, Jimmy, whom I hadn't seen or talked to in a while.

We were very good friends and used to have long conversations about spiritual subjects, but he had moved to a new neighborhood across the city. I called and invited him to meet me for dinner later in the week. He said Friday night was his night off from work. How about then? So Friday night it was.

On Friday about five, Jimmy called. He said he and his new roommate had been painting their loft all day, and they were both hungry. Did I mind if this guy joined us?

Actually, I did mind. I had looked forward to having a heart-to-heart talk with Jim, which wouldn't be possible with a stranger along, but I didn't want to be rude, so I said sure. Moments later another friend of mine, Terry, called and asked me if I had any plans for dinner. Since three of us were already getting together, I invited him to join us, too. Terry lived only a few blocks away, and he said he would walk over.

After I hung up, it started to rain—hard. Twenty minutes passed, and the intercom buzzed. It was Terry. He had been caught in the downpour. He came in soaking wet and upset. I told him not to worry, that he could take his wet shirt and pants and socks and throw them into my dryer for a few minutes. He could wear my robe while they were drying. He took off his clothes, put on my robe, and waited for his clothes to dry.

A few minutes more passed, and the doorbell rang. It was Jimmy and his roommate.

"Come on up," I said. "I'll leave the door open. I'm getting ready."

Terry was in my bedroom, waiting for his clothes. I was in the bathroom, combing my hair and putting on my lipstick. I heard Jimmy walk in. I came out of the bathroom. Terry came out of the bedroom in my robe. We both walked into the living room together to greet Jim and his roommate . . .

. . . and there with Jim stood the guy from my dream.

I immediately started to explain that Terry was my *friend,* that his clothes were wet from the rain, hoping the guy wouldn't jump to the wrong conclusions. All the while I kept staring.

He was the guy I had been visualizing for months and months! This guy was *the guy,* the one in my mind, the one I had visualized, the one I had asked the universe for. I could hardly believe it.

Despite my much practiced psychic skills, I was taken completely by surprise. As for him, he looked a little embarrassed seeing Terry standing there in his underwear and my robe.

I kept talking and explaining about why Terry was undressed. I was so nervous.

He stood there listening for a minute, then put his finger up to his lip and said, "Ssh! Come on!"

His name was Patrick Tully. I couldn't believe he even had the same last name as my great teacher, Dr. Tully—yet here he was. My *dream* man! . . .

THE *YEAH, BUT* . . . SYNDROME

Working with guides opens your awareness to a whole new level of support. Your days will become adventures. Every moment will provide another opportunity to be reminded that you are helped. Loneliness will start to fade as you realize that you are surrounded by love. The invisible barriers of your ego will begin to fall down, and your life will now start to become lighter and easier. You will no longer feel as though you are floundering in the dark by yourself. Magical moments, one after another, start to occur at this point and will finally convince you that you are safe. The pathway of your life will begin to brighten up with the light of higher consciousness. The fearful questions that darkened your heart will now begin to evolve into confident knowing, from moment to moment, as you are guided.

What happens at this point for many people is that they can't believe life is so much easier and makes so much more sense than before. The change is radical and even unsettling. Even though your experiences are now exploding with synchronicity, and you are attracting to your life exactly what you need before you even fully ask, don't be surprised if you go into denial or start to panic. When this happens (and it will), I call it the "Yeah, but . . ." syndrome.

Jane was a nurse in her late thirties, who had come for readings and attended my psychic development and creativity classes. Her heart's desire was to meet and marry a genuine partner and have a family while she still could. In class she demonstrated great intuition and even did psychic readings for other members of the group that were insightful and accurate. The psychic awareness was really working well, so I was surprised when she called a month after the workshop and asked for a reading.

"Jane," I said, "are you sure you want a reading from me? I think your own soul was making itself *very* apparent to you."

"Please," she said, "I'm really confused."

So we set up an appointment for a few days later. When Jane came to my house, I looked at her aura and could tell she had been introduced to a wonderful and loving vibration. Indeed, as I held her watch, I could see it was true.

"Jane, I see you've met the partner you've been waiting for. You are loved!"

"Yeah, but this guy is very shy, and that makes me worried,"
she said.

"My guides tell me that he is reserved, and serious about love, but not necessarily shy."

"Yeah, maybe that's true, but he's forty years old and never been married, so maybe he has a problem with women."

"No, he doesn't. He just never found the right person—until you."

"Yeah, I think you're right. But he lives in another state."

"Well, my guides say he lives in Utah, where you've been wanting to move for years."

"Yeah, but I'm afraid my parents won't like him because he's an artist."

"My guides tell me that your parents only want you safe and loved by the right person, which he is."

"Yeah, but—"

"What does your *soul* tell you about this man, Jane?"

She was quiet. "My soul is very happy when I think of him. I know he's the right one."

"Do you feel loved by him?"

"Completely," she answered.

"Well, it's clear to me that what you have is the 'Yeah, but' syndrome."

The "Yeah, but . . ." syndrome is your mind making a final stab at regaining control of your awareness. When this happens, your mind tries to diminish your awareness and seduce you back into seeing things on the surface. What follows is confusion. Your soul has shown you the truth of a situation, but your mind doesn't want you to believe it, because if you do accept what your soul tells you, you finally let go once and for all of the ordinary life, the life your ego controls! This is the last hurdle you must overcome before you really integrate your psychic awareness fully into your life.

"Yeah, but . . ." is a test—a test of commitment on your part to see the truth. Everyone goes through this, but once you get past it, you'll be home free, living completely and consciously with the insight and the vision of the soul.

Philip was a sales rep who hated his job. In the psychic development class, his soul told him that he really wanted to be an actor. This revelation took a huge burden off his heart. In front of the group he said, "I'm going for it! I'm ready!"

Philip was very psychic and very aware, and when he used his intuition, the whole world lit up. A few months later Philip called for an appointment. "Man, I really need to talk to you!"

He showed up energetic and antsy. I started his reading.

"Philip, my guides say you are on your true path, but you are attached to the false security of the money you made in your old job. You have a chance to move to New York and work, but you'll have to quit your job here in order to go."

"Yeah, you're right. I've been offered a great role in New York on a soap. But it's three weeks of taping, and there's no guarantee I'll have more work."

"My guides tell me that ever since you've started this path, doors have flown open, and that this job in New York is a gift."

"Yeah, some of my actor friends can't believe it. They've been trying to get a break like this for years. But what if I blow it and they don't like me? You can't trust agents, you know."

"My guides tell me you are perfect, and being in New York will open doors to the stage that will never happen for you here."

"Yeah, but New York is scary and expensive, and I don't know if I'll like it."

Then I posed my question. "Philip, what does your *soul* say about this?"

Philip was quiet. "My soul says *yes!* This is the beginning of exactly what I want."

"Are you going?" I asked.

"Yeah, I am . . . but—"

"Philip, you have a case of the 'Yeah, but . . .' syndrome. You know the truth, but it's scary. You have to take a real chance, with no outward guarantee that this will work. It requires a leap of faith, and you need support to take the leap." Philip was listening. "Letting go of the illusion of control you have when you live from the ego/mind point of view is a big release, a huge surrender. It's like letting go of a trapeze bar to do a somersault. It all depends on someone else being there to catch you. But it's that very release, that letting go and gracefully tumbling into that somersault, that you have been preparing for and praying for your whole life. Your soul is there to catch you! Your guides are completely around you to direct your leap, and because you really are ready to leap, you will land victoriously on your feet! 'Yeah, but . . .' is fear. You have to pray for courage, and honor the truth that you feel in your soul. Go for it!"

Philip's "Yeah, but . . ." attack was alleviated by support and encouragement. Letting go of the familiar, even if it's been an illusion, is frightening. Taking the final step toward trusting yourself is a bold, courageous act, but if you have been following the steps along the path, and doing the work as it's been laid out before you, you will at this point feel absolutely compelled to push forward. Let me tell you about one of my own "Yeah, but . . ." attacks.

Meeting Patrick Tully for the first time took me by surprise. I had visualized a car. I had visualized jobs. I had visualized trips to France. And one day, standing in my apartment, was the living, breathing soulmate I had been visualizing into my life.

Did Patrick, on a soul level, pick up on my visualization? Did I tune in to his visualization of me? Or were we past life partners meeting again? All I know is that when I met him, I recognized him instantly as the person in my dream and the person I had seen in my mind for four months . . . except for one thing. The person in both my mind and my dream had an old, wise look. This man standing in front of me had a youthful, boyish look. And he was *very* cute!

Terry, my robed friend, was getting dressed. My robe was a green-and-gold kimono. I suddenly remembered that in my dream we were dressed in green-and-gold robes. Now, upon meeting, we were discussing one. It was another aspect crossing over from my dream into my experience.

I kept looking at Patrick and smiling broadly, almost laughing, because of my secret, but I couldn't tell him why. We'd just met . . . at least in *this* lifetime!

We went to dinner. It was embarrassing to admit, but I totally ignored both Jimmy and Terry. All I wanted to do was talk to Patrick. It was not something I could control. No one understood why I was acting so peculiarly.

At my (semiravenous) urging, Patrick told me all about himself.

He had been traveling around the world for a year and had just come back. He was a mental health counselor and had worked with the chronically mentally ill for over ten years. He had spent a year abroad: in India for three months, in Southeast Asia, and across Europe, studying alternative healing for mental illness. This included various styles of meditation and spiritual practice. He was currently working at the University of Illinois Hospital in the mental health ward.

In short, he was very well traveled, spiritually conscious, and had devoted a huge part of his life to helping the extremely sick—just as I'd requested. He showed a profound compassion for the kinds of illnesses most people shun. Another special request.

"Do you ski?" he asked.

"Sure," I said. Not well, I thought to myself, but a minor detail.

I found out all I could about him.

Patrick was from Iowa. My dad was from Iowa. Patrick was the oldest of nine children, six boys and three girls. He said he loved his family a lot. He loved to ski and seemed very happy to know I was from Colorado.

The more he talked, the more convinced I was that this was *it,* my soulmate. Jimmy and Terry tried to join the conversation, but it was hopeless. Patrick and I were locked into a very private dialogue.

We eventually floated back to the room and started to talk with the others. We had been focused on each other for only about twenty minutes, but it seemed like a time warp to me. I felt as though I knew him. I wondered if he felt the same way.

And the best part was that when I told Patrick I was psychic, his reply was, "Jimmy told me. I imagine that's very draining. What do you do for fun *after* you work?"

It was the first time ever that someone I met acknowledged the *work* part. He focused on how my work affected *me,* not others. I appreciated that. In fact, I adored that. The entire evening was blissfully pleasurable.

When it was time to go, Jim and Patrick, Terry, and I stood outside the restaurant, saying good-bye. We were not far from their loft, and it was a crisp fall night, so Jim said, "We live close. We'll walk home."

Patrick didn't ask me for my phone number or in any way indicate that he had any desire to see me again. He just smiled and said, "Good night! Nice meeting you!" And that was it.

I was so disappointed. I tried to hide it, but I was really let down. All my fears and insecurities rode home with me in the car. My friend Terry noticed right away.

"You sure lit up like a Christmas tree tonight. I haven't seen you this enthusiastic ever. Like Patrick, did you?"

"Yeah. . . ."

I would have readily admitted it, screamed it off the Sears Tower, even, if he had so much as said, "Let's get together sometime."

But he hadn't.

My dream person, my soulmate, and he didn't show a flicker of interest in pursuing me.

What a bummer.

I had to go home and think. This was yet another curveball for me. I had to adjust, meditate, and calm my emotions. In the last four hours I had projected myself as his long-lost lover, his other self, his soulmate. He, on the other hand, had said good-bye to me as warmly as he'd said good-bye to the waitress. It didn't make sense. I went home and tried to tune in to what had gone wrong.

Have I mentioned that a surefire way to knock your intuition out of operation is to get your emotions stirred up? It's impossible to be truly psychic when you are invested in the outcome. Which didn't mean I didn't try. For hours. Every time I tuned in to him, I picked up . . . nothing.

Miserable, I concentrated on him for several days, telepathically asking him to call . . . and nothing. Miserable, I astral-projected to his West Side loft . . . and he wasn't home. Miserable, I tried to tune in and seduce him psychically . . . no takers!

Days passed. No contact. Absolutely none.

I went back to my notebooks and journals and reread my visualization notes.

Tall—Patrick was six feet three.

Good-looking—I knew it was subjective, but he was subjectively good-looking to me.

Single—yes, he was. Never married.

Large family—nine children.

Caring—took care of very sick people.

Traveler—just returned from around the world.

Could sing—he sang with a chorus that went to India with Jimmy Carter.

Understood my vocation—I didn't know if he understood it, but he did seem to be comfortable with it.

And I had dreamed about him! It was *his* face! He even used the same gesture in my apartment as in my dream: "Ssh!" Finger to lip. "Come on!"

I was completely smitten and befuddled and exhausted. I'd tried every psychic skill I possessed to influence him to contact me.

I was struggling with an incredible paradox. On one hand, there was my gut-level recognition and conviction that this man was my destined partner. That was my psychic and spiritual knowing, my never-argue-with-this-kind-of-feeling feeling.

Then there was my mind. It said, "He was just attractive. You are lonely. You read more into it than existed. He's not available. He's not stable. Even your friend Jimmy said he's a wanderer, a womanizer, and to forget it. And he didn't even seem to take an interest in pursuing you at the end of the evening together. Spare yourself the humiliation. Forget it. You want a commitment. You want a meaningful partnership. Patrick doesn't seem the type."

This dialogue went on for a week, my ego and my intuition arguing with each other. Two weeks went by, and it was starting to make me feel a little obsessive. Finally I decided to take a very drastic step and do something I had never before done in my life: I called him on the telephone and asked him out!

As I was dialing, I realized I had taken risks in going to France, in learning to become a psychic, in getting accepted into a study abroad program—indeed, every time I did a psychic reading. But I had never before risked looking like a fool and revealing my interest in love. In my past relationships I was very much the pursued one. In the years since, no one had even sparked my interest. Here I was, having found a truly exciting person in my path, and I was waiting for him to land on my doorstep with a ring.

No. The way my life worked, had always worked in every aspect of my growth, was the result of my following my instinct and going after it with my whole heart and soul. I realized that this would be no different.

I felt strong, full of conviction, as I dialed. The phone was ringing. One time. Two times. Three.

"Hello," a voice said. It was Patrick! My heart stopped. This was my big chance! I took a breath.

"Hello," I said, barely audible. My voice had disappeared completely. I couldn't believe it. "Is Jimmy there?"

I'd asked for Jimmy! What a chicken. I'd completely lost all courage. What a wimp.

"Jimmy, no. He's at work. . . . Is this Sonia?"

"Yes," I said calmly, but screaming inside. "Is this Patrick?" Of course it was. Who else would it be?

"Yes, it is. How are you?"

"Fine. I was calling to invite Jimmy out for a bite to eat. Too bad he's not home." Pause. "How about you? Are you doing anything?"

I was so scared. This was harder than wandering around Marseilles at midnight. I was completely ready for him to reject me. I thought everything I had felt intuitively a minute before was nonsense. I felt like a complete fool. I held my breath.

"Sure. I'd love to go out with you. I'd been thinking about calling you, too, but I've been so darn busy between painting the loft and my job. I'm working the night shift, eleven to seven A.M. I literally haven't stopped for a minute. Dinner sounds great! Can you pick me up? It's cold out, and I only have my bike."

Yes! We had a date!

My intuition had prevailed over my "Yeah, but. . . ." I was ecstatic.

You get to a point on the psychic pathway where you must either push ahead or really struggle with yourself. But the truth your soul gives you will stay with you. You will know it in the deepest part of your heart. When you let go of the "Yeah, but . . ." syndrome, you are free. You will lighten up, ease up, and relax.

To minimize your struggle with the "Yeah, but . . ." bug, take steps not to invite it into your life. Be very careful not to ask people who are not spiritually aware to comment or advise you. Guard your intuition. Don't subject it to an open forum. Protect the jewels of awareness your soul gives you, and honor your truth.

In fact, if you start having "Yeah, but . . ." attacks, you should be very excited. This means you are pushing through and almost completely free of the hold of the ordinary restrictions of illusion. You are approaching your full psychic level of consciousness. When "Yeah, but . . ." shows up, your full psychic breakthrough is at hand!

The next step on the psychic pathway is to surrender yourself to prayer. At this point you must let go of being in charge of yourself and let God become in charge of you. The next step—the final step, really—is the leap of faith! At this point you need to fully remove your sense of self from your false self-identity, your ego, and completely remember who you are.

Jesus said, "Ask and you shall receive."

"Yeah, but . . ." is a test of faith. To fully enter the world of truth, your awareness has to fully accept that you are a spiritual essence, a child of God. "Yeah, but . . ." tells you that you are mortal, you are ego, you are physical, and above all, you are not safe—not *ever*.

"Yeah, but . . ." is a lie. Truth is truth, and when you see truth, feel truth, and know truth, *embrace* truth with all your heart. Pray for courage, pray for comforting, pray for release from illusion, and embrace the truth completely and without compromise.

"Yeah, but . . ." sneaks up on you sometimes, but more often you invite it directly into your life. How? you wonder. By asking people who are not enlightened, who know nothing about the soul, who have no intuitive awareness, to advise you on whether or not to honor your intuition.

INSPIRATIONAL AND AUTOMATIC WRITING

A great way to stop a "Yeah, but . . ." is by using inspirational and automatic writing. If you've been keeping your journal, automatic and inspirational writing should come easily. You've already set up your subconscious mind to release psychic guidance from the higher planes of consciousness. This is just one more way for it to do so.

Here's how it works.

Inspirational Writing

The way I get it to work for me is to write a letter to my Higher Self. When you write this letter, tell your Higher Self the problem you're having and ask if your Higher Self or one of your guides will counsel you on what to do. Then, after a five-minute meditation, imagine that your Higher Self is writing out the answer. Many people say it feels awkward at first, but the more they write, the more inspired they become, and usually they end up writing very specific solutions that they had not consciously considered before. These solutions just flowed into their minds as they wrote.

The more comfortable you become with inspirational writing, the more exploratory you can be. Try writing out tomorrow's headlines or listing events that will take place next week. Try writing out the stock market trends, if this interests you, or new developments at work. Use this method to answer questions for yourself and for others. As always, the more sincere your attitude, the better the psychic channel. Automatic and inspirational writing give your psychic frequency a conscious outlet. Your psychic radar is always on. It's your attention that shifts. These writing techniques help shift your attention and focus it directly on your psychic channel.

Give these techniques a try and see if they feel right for you. Be patient. It will definitely take a little time. How much? Well, I don't know exactly, as each person is different. A day, a week, a month, maybe longer. Usually you will have better results if you begin practicing inspirational writing first, then move on to the automatic writing later. The important things to remember in developing this technique are:

- finding a quiet time to practice without interruption
- practicing two or three times a week for twenty-five to thirty minutes
- maintaining an attitude of receptivity and sincerity

Automatic Writing

Automatic writing is a little different from inspirational writing. It requires even more surrender from your ego because in automatic writing you are allowing your guides or Higher Self to borrow your hand to write.

To practice automatic writing, you just put yourself in a relaxed, trancelike state, usually through a short meditation exercise. When you are very relaxed, you take a pen in your hand and let it rest very gently on a blank sheet of paper, as if you are going to write. Imagine your Higher Self flowing through your arm and taking over your hand. Make no effort to write. Simply visualize your Higher Self taking over and writing for you. It usually helps to sit in a comfortable writing position and to keep your eyes closed, with the lids comfortable, not tense. Allow your hand to doodle gently or to scribble on the paper to ensure that no tension sets in and that your hand does not lock. Do not concern yourself with whether or not you are making words with the pen. Just let the pen move in any direction that it wants to across the paper. All the while, imagine that your Higher Self is writing. Even try letting the persona you imagined as your Higher Self come to mind. Ask your Higher Self questions and let your relaxed hand move gently across the paper.

The object of this technique is to allow the Higher Self to take over and write to you from the unconscious plane. In automatic writing you feel the sensation of your hand being maneuvered without your conscious direction. Messages, phrases, sometimes even long letters, come through in automatic writing. Very successful results have been noted if you try this technique upon first waking up in the morning, before starting the day.

This technique is very exciting, but it requires a patient, very receptive person to develop it. If you think you are the type, practice two or three times a week. Pick a time when you won't be interrupted and work on it for at least twenty-five to thirty minutes each time. After each automatic writing practice session, look at the paper and see if you can read any messages. Sometimes perfectly clear sentences will be spelled out, although you felt as if you were just doodling.

The more you practice, the more likely you are to succeed in developing this psychic channel. Patience is necessary. I worked on automatic writing for two years before I ever felt any real, strong pull in my hand. Once it did come through, however, it was very exciting. At first the messages were just short, fragmented words, but there were some names of people who turned out to be important in my life. I was never patient enough to perfect this technique, but I know several other physics who have. Each person is different.

Give automatic writing a try. Maybe it will be just the channel for you. Entire books have been written through automatic writing. Great inspirations have come this way, too. Some of the greatest composers and authors in history attributed their genius to a spontaneous flow of the pen, somehow beyond conscious thought. Who knows what inspiration you may sense?

EXPLORATIONS

Finding Your Desires

You *will* get what you dwell on.

Your desire doesn't have to be a grandiose and lofty one. Most likely it won't be. Look at what areas of your life are painful, frustrating, or unpleasant to you now. What tiny little change can you imagine would bring about a little pleasant relief? That should be the focus of your first goal.

To begin identifying your goals, follow these simple steps.

1. What is your most immediate need now? Write down in your psychic journal what it is you most lack or long for in your life.
2. Try not to be concerned over how, where, who. Just focus on what you wish were better, right now, and leave it at that.
3. Keep your list of desires in the beginning to a time frame of one, two, or three weeks—a month at most—and focus on the most immediate desires.

I find that when I focus on fulfilling my immediate life needs, it actually helps me to get closer to that greater future I long for.

My point is, sometimes you cannot see important connections between the immediate situation and your ideal future, so start by focusing on the immediate situation, however mundane and insignificant you may think it is. It may be the very catalyst to a much greater chain of events.

Ask the Experts

Begin this exercise by writing out a question. Sit for a moment, clear your mind, clear your aura, and ground yourself by imagining all the energy in your body is flowing into the earth. Then imagine the earth pouring clear, vibrant energy back into your freshly cleared aura. If possible, meditate for five to ten minutes. Also, be sure to pay attention to your breathing. When you feel grounded and clear, start writing down your question. For example: What is the problem in my relationship with _____? This physical action alone will provoke all sorts of thoughts. If you feel upset or disturbed, reground yourself, clear your aura, and just relax.

Visualize all your guides gathering together, with only one purpose in mind—answering your question. Now turn the question over to your imagination.

Imagine the guide who is an expert on your particular question guiding your hand as you write down an answer. Relax and allow it to flow. Continue to write as long as you feel like it. When your hand stops, be sure to thank your guide.

Now take a couple of moments to ground yourself again. When you feel grounded, go over the transcription. The wisdom—and simplicity— of the answers will often astound you. You will quickly feel this is not you yourself speaking. This is someone wiser and with a much better perspective!

Who Asked You?

Every time you start to talk about your life, make sure you are not talking to people who can sabotage you physically, emotionally, or mentally.

Go Home, Stay Put!

If you are feeling insecure, or need support as you let go of false perceptions, ground yourself and say an affirmation or a prayer asking God, the "powers that be," the universe, to give you the energy or courage to trust your soul.

Asking Your Own Experts

Write down your insecurities in your journal. Using inspirational or automatic writing, write down what your soul advises or guides you on.

Quieting the Yeah, But . . .

- Quiet the "Yeah, but . . ." chatter with meditation.
- Another excellent way to overcome a "Yeah, but . . ." attack is to get out of your head and start a project with your hands. Sew, paint, clean house, organize books, mow the lawn, draw a picture, play an instrument, or write in your journal. You are thinking too much! When you use your hands, you move your attention into your heart, which is the seat of the soul.

Be on the lookout for "Yeah, but . . ." and be ready to send it running!

CHARTING YOUR PROGRESS

Reflect on your experiences this week when answering these questions.

How many days this week did you meditate? Are you beginning to look forward to it?_____

_____

Have you remembered to ground yourself?_____

_____

Have you remembered to clear your aura?_____

_____

How many days this week did you make entries in your psychic journal? Surprised by how psychic you are becoming?_____

_____

What did you get unexpected guidance on?_____

_____

Which of your goals surprised you?_____

_____

What are you "waiting" to ask about?_____

_____

_____

What would you *love* to be helped with?_____

_____

Are you using your panel of experts?_____

_____

Did the "Yeah, but . . ." bug bite you? How did you stop it from messing
things up?_____

_____

Using Your Compass

Psychic tools assist you in studying the energy around you and help expand and extend your awareness even further as you move through life. They are like a compass, showing you the directions your energy may take you as you push forward creatively.

Psychic tools can also indicate a little about the energy patterns of others. This is what we mean when we speak of "doing a reading"—studying your energy or someone else's as it is being set up and then released into motion. This allows you to contemplate choices and reflect on potential outcomes, so that you can proceed or abandon your plans, whichever will bring the best possible end result. Using psychic tools prevents your ego from interrupting your psychic ability, because the tools are "irrational" or nonrational. The tools are the outward symbols of the language of the soul.

When you use rune stones, or I-Ching coins, or tarot cards, you tap into an awareness deep in your soul. These symbols are ancient and connect you to the collective unconscious. Your soul is ancient and recognizes these tools as familiar symbols. These symbols resonate with your deepest soul awareness, bypassing the logical mind and its limitations. They are like art pieces—they speak to you in a nonlinear way.

Not all symbols work for all people, however. Your soul may resonate with one set of symbols more readily than another. For example, you may look at rune stones and feel nothing. They will not elicit any spark of insight, and there will be no resonance with your soul. However, when you look at tarot cards, your soul may jump right out, bringing with it feelings or impressions or simply *telling* you what these images mean. Obviously, then, tarot would be a good tool for you, while rune stones would not.

How can you know which, if any, tool is appropriate? By doing what *always* works when engaging your soul. You play with them and trust your experience. Psychic tools are sold as games, and quite appropriately so. This is because it is play that brings the soul out of hiding. Remember, even though it's play, don't fall into the trap of thinking that it is unimportant or insignificant. Absolutely not! The play of the soul is some of the most important work you'll ever do, so experiment freely with these tools in the true spirit of play.

Tools are not necessary to have dialogue and contact with your Higher Self and guides. You may be a purist and prefer just to focus your attention inward. But if they do attract you, dive in and explore. Psychic tools are rich in meaning and history. As you explore them, they open further pathways to the realm of spiritual knowing.

For a while it seemed that everyone was wearing a crystal. Why? Was it just a fad? What about rune stones? Angel cards? Sacred path cards? Medicine cards? Or the Whack Pack? What is all this about?

The answer is simple. They are all basically telephone lines to your Higher Self and to your guides, and they very effectively bypass your mind and tap your consciousness into the sea of superconscious energy. Imagine each of these tools enabling you to "dial direct" to your guides and your Higher Self and giving you access to wisdom and guidance that you otherwise may not be able to reach. I would like to introduce the tools to you as simply as they were introduced to me.

THE PENDULUM
One day when I was studying with my teacher Charlie, he handed me a fishing weight dangling from a string and said, "Here, try this!"

"What's this?" I said jokingly. "Are we going fishing?"

"Yes," he said, "in a way. This is your first psychic tool. It's called a pendulum, and you fish for guidance from your Higher Self with it."

A pendulum is any small weighted object, dangling from a six-to-eight-inch string, able to rest perfectly balanced as you hold it steady—like this:

THE PENDULUM

Any small object will do. My first pendulum was an oval-shaped fishing weight, but you can also find pendulums made of crystals or cone- or diamond-shaped silver pieces on a chain. Some pendulums are very elaborate and expensive. But the pendulum's principle works equally well with a simple one. Your guides don't have a preference.

Once you make or find a suitable pendulum, wear it around your neck, preferably over your heart chakra, for a few days. While doing this, tell your subconscious mind that you *intend* to use this pendulum as a way to talk to your Higher Self and guides. Remember, the imagination opens the door to psychic knowing.

From the time you create a pendulum, don't allow anyone else to touch it. This pendulum will develop a specific vibration through your wearing it and infusing it with your intention over a period of days. It will be a clear channel to your energy, and anyone else's energy will interrupt this flow of vibrations like static or interference on a telephone line.

Here's how a pendulum works. You hold your pendulum perfectly still and ask your Higher Self or guides a question. The pendulum will swing in one direction to mean yes or positive and another to mean no or negative. To determine which direction your Higher Self wants the pendu-

lum to swing for the yes/positive answers versus the no/negative ones, get
a piece of paper and put a dot in the center of two axes.

PENDULUM AXES

Hold the pendulum perfectly still over the center dot, and ask your
Higher Self to swing in the direction for "yes." Let it indicate to you
whether "yes" is N/S or E/W. It doesn't matter what direction it moves.
Just always be sure to be consistent with the same axis to mean yes and
the opposite axis to mean no.

USING YOUR PENDULUM

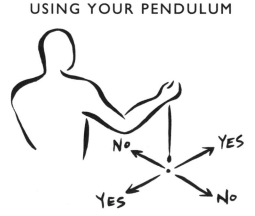

In the beginning your pendulum may not budge or may barely
move. Be patient. It will start to work after a couple of tries if you are sincere. I think it's a very good idea to ground yourself and clear your aura

before you begin to work with your pendulum. It's hard for your guides or Higher Self to work through sludge.

Remember, your energy flows best if it is clear. I also think you should say an affirmation to protect yourself from random negative energy, and even your own negativity, before you begin. For example:

> I ask my angels to remove all negative energy and all foreign energy surrounding me and send it into the light.

> I clear myself of all unwanted influences, and I become a clear channel to my Higher Self.

> I ask only the highest forces of God, my Higher Self, or my guides to work through this pendulum to offer me guidance.

> I am open and receptive.

Breathe in deeply, and then release. Now you are ready to begin.

Once you've established how the pendulum wants to answer "yes" and "no," hold it perfectly still and ask a question. The energy from your Higher Self and guides will flow into the pendulum, causing it to move and give an answer.

Start with simple, clear yes-or-no questions. It is important that you be sincere and not "test" or "trick" the pendulum. If you do, you are only testing or tricking yourself with the mind's attempt to seize control. Avoid this temptation, as you are only blocking your success.

When you use your pendulum, rest your elbow on a table so that the pendulum hangs directly over the center point of the diagram you made, but do not allow it to touch the center point. Then concentrate on your question and watch the pendulum move. At first the move will be subtle, but in no time you'll receive a definite sway. Start with questions that are not emotionally charged and are nonthreatening—ask, "Will I take a vacation trip this spring?" instead of "Is my girlfriend cheating on me?" It's important to get comfortable with the pendulum before you introduce emotionally charged questions. That way you can be certain that your fears don't override the system and give you false information.

Be certain that you are sincere and receptive. Your Higher Self does not need to convince you of its existence, and it will not engage in insincere activity. In other words, unless you are truly interested in receiving guidance, you won't—plain and simple. You decide on what are appropriate questions. Any question on which you are genuinely receptive to an answer is fine.

The pendulum can also be programmed to more individual needs. For example, one student, a nurse named Patricia, asked her Higher Self to guide her, through her pendulum, in choosing foods that were fresh and energy giving from the hospital cafeteria where she worked.

She held her pendulum perfectly still and asked her Higher Self to show her how it would indicate whether the food had any life-giving energy. The pendulum swung in big circles. She asked her Higher Self to indicate the movement that would show the food had no life-giving energy. The pendulum didn't budge.

Patricia tried the system at work. Sure enough, as she held her pendulum over each food she was considering for her lunch, the pendulum indicated by either circles or no movement whether each food would be good for her. This system was especially helpful when checking fruits or vegetables. Even though they looked good, if they weren't fresh, the pendulum didn't move.

Eventually Patricia used the same technique when shopping at the fruit-and-vegetable market. It was a simple, enlightening way for her to assure herself of eating energizing foods.

Another client of mine, an engineer named Tim, programmed his pendulum to help him lose weight. He asked his Higher Self to swing the pendulum on a "no" axis if the foods he was considering would upset his weight loss program. He also asked his Higher Self to swing the pendulum in circles if he was eating a portion that was too large.

In using this technique, Tim lost seventy-five pounds in seven months. The best part was that his technique was fascinating and rewarding to his spirit—not painful, frustrating, and self-defeating, as his past dieting efforts had been.

As a teenager and young adult, I consulted my pendulum on *everything,* from whether or not to buy a certain outfit to whether to accept a date with a boy. The best part was that in the spirit of consulting my pendulum, I got into the much more important habit of asking my Higher Self for guidance.

Be creative with the pendulum, as it is not limited to yes-or-no responses. Pay attention to any other impulses or feelings that pop into your mind as you ask. For example, you may ask the pendulum, "Is this apartment that I'm considering renting one that I'll be comfortable in?" Your pendulum may simply say "no," but you may also get the feeling as the pendulum swings that the neighbor across the hall is a drummer who likes to practice at midnight. The pendulum stimulates your psychic voice. With practice, it will give you a lot of insight and information. It can be used for yes-or-no answers and for confirmation about a psychic feeling. For example, you may ask, "Am I correct in feeling my sister is in danger and needs my help?" The pendulum can confirm your intuition and, as in this case, act as a built-in support system.

Here are a few sample pendulum questions:

- Is this potential job good for me?
- Am I on the right track . . . spiritually? creatively? physically?
- Is this car a good investment?
- Will I move this year? When? January? February? March? . . .
- Is eating meat necessary to my grounding?
- Is my investment in stock sound? Stay? Sell?

You get the idea. I suggest you write down your questions before you consult your pendulum, so that your question is clear and so that you are certain you want to know the answer. Then record the yes-or-no response and any other feedback your guides may put into your head. The pendulum is an excellent beginner's psychic tool because it's easy to make, is portable, and gives instant feedback; but the pendulum's simplicity does not limit its use. If you are stuck on the "Yeah, but . . ." fence, the pendulum will help you out by pushing you toward your intuitive self and freeing you from that harmful resistance.

When I was seventeen and living in Colorado, I had a very good buddy named Randy, who was eighteen. Randy was a handsome guy, but he was afflicted with a severe case of cystic acne, which was killing his self-esteem. Randy went to dermatologists for over two years, but he was not able to stop the breakouts. He was seriously depressed over his scarred complexion.

I had heard of a psychic woman named Doris who lived in Santa Fe and knew she'd had some success in diagnosing and treating people with health problems. Although I had never met her personally, I talked Randy into going to Santa Fe to see if she could help. He said yes, and we drove together to the health food store where she worked. When we arrived, we found her in the back of the store, with four or five people waiting to see her. We took our place in line and waited.

Doris was a Hungarian woman, about sixty years old. She was short, only five feet two or so, roly-poly, and the glowing picture of health and vitality—pink cheeks, bright eyes, and a clear white aura.

"She's got a lot of energy, Randy," I said. "I feel she'll be able to help."

We waited for a half hour, and then it was Randy's turn. The first thing Doris did was take a look at Randy's face and say, "Okay, I see."

Then she reached into her pocket and took out a pendulum. She held it over Randy's head as he sat on a chair.

"Umm . . . no," she said as she moved the pendulum down across his face.

"No, no," she kept murmuring as the pendulum stayed perfectly still. She lowered the pendulum to his chest—no movement.

"No, no," she continued to murmur. She lowered the pendulum to his abdomen; still no movement.

She walked around him to his back and slowly held the pendulum across his upper, then lower back. Nothing. The pendulum didn't move.

Finally she asked him to hold out his legs together in front of him, and when she held the pendulum over his legs, it swung wildly in circles.

"Ah-hah! This is it!" She smiled.

Then she closed her eyes as she continued to hold the spinning pendulum over his legs. "Did you have surgery on your legs?" she asked.

"Yes," he said. When he was young he had been bowlegged and had vein problems and had surgery on both legs at age six to correct them. Even I hadn't known that!

"You have staph infection in these bones," Doris said. "It's affecting the blood and causing your skin eruptions."

She recommended large doses of garlic and chlorophyll pills to kill the staph. She said, "It will take three to four months, but if you follow through on this, your skin will stop breaking out."

Randy had nothing to lose. He diligently gave her recommendations a go. It took longer than three months, more like six, but eventually the skin eruptions stopped and his face began to heal. It was amazing for him to actually get relief, and it was amazing to me to see how valuable a simple little pendulum could be.

PLAYING CARDS AND TAROT CARDS

I love cards! My mom taught me to read cards before I was ten years old. They are beautiful, mysterious, and very helpful in taking a general psychic feeling you may have and breaking it down into specific feelings. For example, all my life growing up, my mom had what we called her "vibes." Whenever she had vibes, something was the matter. Sometimes if she would relax and focus on her vibes, she would eventually figure out what her guides were warning her about. But in a houseful of seven children, being quiet and focusing was not always possible, so she would say, "Sonia, get my cards. Let's see what's wrong."

I'd get her deck of playing cards, kept in a special box by her bed and used exclusively for readings. She would shuffle the cards, then lay them out, starting with one in the center and building out, one at a time, in all directions until she had made a diamond pattern. She would study the layout, and depending on what cards she pulled, she would be able to find the problem or cause of her vibes.

I remember distinctly once when I was ten years old, while helping my mom make dinner, her vibes started. Something was wrong. I fetched the cards. She laid them out: nine of spades, ten of spades, ten of clubs, ten of diamonds, king of hearts, six of hearts reversed—my mom gasped.

"Something's wrong at home," she said. "I feel it's someone in my family."

I stared at the cards. I looked at the sadness in my mom's eyes. I knew it was true. I didn't know my mom's family, but I could feel the pain and anxiety in her heart.

She looked right at me and said, "Mark my words . . . something's terribly wrong."

She put away the cards, and we waited. At three-thirty in the morning, the phone rang. The ring woke me from sleep. It was my mom's sister on the phone from Bucharest. She told my mom that my grandfather —her father—had died. I remember my mother saying in Romanian, "I know. His spirit came to me and told me."

The cards had told her, too.

By the time I was twelve, I was an avid card reader. My best friend at the time, Sue Bosler, and I spent hours and hours doing card readings for the next five years. Every day I'd read her cards. She'd read my cards. We'd read about cards. We even made our own cards! We invented a deck with our own meanings. We called it the "all-knowing, this-is-the-real-story" deck. It was excellent for developing our imaginations and exercising our psychic abilities, and for two self-conscious, nerdy teenagers, this was terrific, incredible, delicious fun! It was never boring. It was challenging and exciting play.

When I was twelve, my mom gave me a beautiful deck of playing cards from Italy and told me they were my own reading deck. I did readings with that deck all through high school and college. Eventually they fell apart from years and years of use. I loved my cards. They didn't speak to me—they *sang* to me! The meanings of the cards sank deep into my subconscious mind and became a part of my psyche. Working with cards taught me to look for and understand the importance of symbols. Symbols unlock the door to the soul, where words can't reach.

Cards, whether they're a regular deck or tarot cards, have a rich, colorful history dating back to the Middle Ages, where lore has it that church repression began to force spiritual and mystical philosophies underground. In order to preserve ancient spiritual teachings, metaphysical adepts developed a set of symbols to relay visually each spiritual principle or law.

These symbols were drawn from the sea of our collective unconscious, where our souls connect. These pictures and symbols convey spiritual principles from soul to soul, regardless of background, somewhat like a spiritual alphabet. These symbols emerged disguised as what we now know as tarot cards.

Tarot cards are divided into two kinds: twenty-two major cards and fifty-six minor cards, called the major and minor arcana. An ordinary deck of playing cards is simply the minor cards of a tarot deck, minus a court card called the Page. The major cards represent spiritual laws of metaphysical growth. The minor cards represent the infinite ways your life circumstances may unfold for you to use the laws—in other words, everyday life. That is why so many psychics use regular playing cards for readings; they convey all possible everyday conditions.

Tarot symbols are strong and evoke a feeling of importance in the person who looks at them. People who don't want to or are not ready to look into life especially dislike tarot and playing cards. Others may not feel strongly about them one way or another.

I consider cards to be a workout room for the psychic voice, a gym for the psychic in you, where you can really stretch and strengthen your awareness, and strive to pull out more psychic information. The symbols on the cards focus your psychic awareness onto certain areas, but it is the soul that gives true meaning to the cards. As you learn the meanings of the cards, and have those cards fall into relationship with each other, it is your soul, your Higher Self, that looks into these images and pulls out the significant meanings.

Cards are naturally attractive to people who have the fifth and sixth chakras working. They work especially well for people who are visually oriented, who can imagine in pictures, and who can see images in their mind's eye when they meditate. If you don't naturally see images with your intuition, you may not be attracted to cards, but if you want to develop the sixth chakra, the "third eye," and improve your psychic imagery skills, cards are a great way to do it.

The soul understands cards—only the mind doesn't "get it." In the last five years there has been an explosion of new psychic cards on the market, as more and more soulful people reach out to those on the edge and pull them into the light. Cards wake up the creative in you. Cards speak to the feeling part of you, the artist and child in you, and as I said, they are *fun* to work with.

If you want to work with cards, there are many to choose from. For example:

The Rider Tarot
The Motherpeace Tarot
The Enchanted Tarot
The Shakespeare Tarot
Sacred Path Cards
Russian Tarot
Medicine Cards
Inner Child Cards
Whack Pack
Psycards

Each deck is a different trail to your inner self. Trust your impulses when choosing a deck. Your soul will let you know which one is appropriate for you. It will be the one you like most. I happen to like them all. They are like crayons and oils for the psychic artist. They create psychic art inside you.

One thing is important for successful reading of tarot or regular cards. You *must* know the meanings of the cards to set up the proper vibrational connection between your unconscious and the pack. Once you know the meanings, however, you are not obligated to adhere to their strictest definition in interpreting your layout. These cards are intended to stimulate clairvoyance and clairaudience and will provide a general guideline for your natural psychic channel to work on. The rule of thumb is to follow the general guidelines but to focus on your own psychic channels to provide a fuller, more complete explanation.

The general meanings of the cards are listed at the back of this book. Many books are available to give you a much more in-depth history, as well as more techniques for doing readings if you want to develop this psychic medium. Reading cards is not for everyone. If you have the right temperament, the cards will "start to talk to you." By this I mean that you will quickly pick up the meanings and get lots of impressions and feelings when you work with them. If you don't have the right temperament, the cards will leave you cold. If so, don't force it. Try other techniques until you find one that works.

THE *I-CHING*

When I began exploring psychic tools, I loved the pendulum and cards, but the *I-Ching* seemed too complicated for me. I ignored it until I was twenty-one and had just returned from a rather disappointing tour of southern France. I had moved there to find my independence and follow my spirit but ended up suddenly hospitalized with appendicitis, my great romantic journey cut abruptly short. I came home eight weeks later, needing counsel instead of prediction. My best friend, Lu, suggested that I study the *I-Ching,* the Chinese Book of Changes.

At first I was cool to the idea, but after having her explain it to me, I realized I had avoided using it only because I'd never been properly introduced to what it is and how to consult it. Lu helped me with that. She loved the *I-Ching* and showed me why. It not only indicates what kind of energy you are working with, but counsels you as to the proper spirit you should have in any undertaking. It's wonderful and *very* reliable.

The *I-Ching* is an ancient Chinese oracle, based on the significance of "chance" aspects of one's life. To the Chinese, the chance of a moment reveals the nature of a condition in its totality.

Here's how it works.

The *I-Ching* comprises sixty-four hexagrams, each representing typical situations in life. Each of the sixty-four hexagrams has a meaning and interpretation appropriate to the situation. To consult the *I-Ching*, one must pose a question and then toss coins or sticks six times. Each throw will determine a line in the hexagram. You can find *I-Ching* coins in metaphysical bookstores, but pennies work just as well.

To find out the meaning of the hexagram, you must consult the *I-Ching* (Book of Changes). This book has a complete list of all the hexagrams and their meanings.

To find the *I-Ching*, go to any bookstore and look in the philosophy or religion section. Usually you will find several versions of the *I-Ching*, as well as workbooks. Again, the hexagrams are designed to provoke thought and stimulate intuition about your situation. They will usually bring to your attention things that you overlooked or misunderstood. It is an excellent tool for developing psychic ability because it teaches you how to observe a given situation *correctly*. This is what psychic ability calls for—accurate and objective awareness of the world around you. The *I-Ching* not only offers useful guidance, but promotes the proper attitudes for psychic development.

I go back and forth with the *I-Ching*. There are times when I have no inclination to consult it. At other times I feel I would step on a land mine without it. The *I-Ching* is excellent when life is complex and great care is required to move forward. It is especially good to consult when beginning a new business, forming partnerships, ending partnerships, divorcing, dealing with hard-to-read people or powerful but difficult people, or when you are in a cycle of change, where you are unsure or vulnerable. I always travel, for example, with my *I-Ching* coins and book. It advises me beautifully when traveling.

A recent addition to the psychic panoply is Barbara Walker's *Feminist I-Ching*. Again, I would advise you to trust what feels appropriate for you.

RUNE STONES

Rune stones are a relatively newly discovered oracle. The runes come from the ancient Nordic people, and the stones indicate the spiritual cycles a person goes through. There are twenty-two rune stones. Each stone is about the size of a large postage stamp and a quarter-inch thick. They are marked with symbols on one side that have specific meanings. The best introduction to runes and their meanings is in Ralph Blum's *Book of Runes*.

I started using runes a little over ten years ago. I find they beautifully reveal the pathway of your life as your soul sets it up. They show you what your soul is requiring at this particular time. Rune stones have taught me that the soul is always true to itself in some way. It's always apparent in your life, if you have the eyes to see it.

A rune reading is simple to do: Just ask your Higher Self for guidance, then pull a single rune. This works for me. You can do a three-rune spread as well. Ask your Higher Self what the situation calls for, then pull the first rune. Ask what the situation must let go of, then pull the second rune. Finally, ask what's the best or ideal outcome. Then pull the third and final rune.

Write down your questions before posing them to the rune oracle; then, using the *Book of Runes*, study the text that corresponds to the rune reply. Some of you may find, as I have, that the runes themselves suggest their meanings clearly and directly. Trust this if it occurs. The book is meant only as a guide.

The best way to pose a question to the runes is to ask an open question, like "What does this situation call for, Higher Self?" as opposed to a question like "Should I continue . . . ?"

The Blum book and workbook are an excellent introduction to the runes and can be found at metaphysical bookstores everywhere. You can learn the meanings of the runes as you practice. You don't have to know them in advance to do a rune reading.

Another divination system is set forth in Nancy Blair's book *The Amulets of the Goddess*. Both gentle and informative, it is based on the symbolism of ancient goddess worship. Its divination system works very much like the runes but includes healing rituals to be performed as the reading suggests.

PSYCHOMETRY

Psychometry is the primary way I do psychic readings for clients. Psychometry is the psychic art of being able to pick up hidden information through holding or touching objects. The word *psychometry* is derived from two Greek words: *psyche,* meaning "soul," and *metron,* meaning to "measure." Psychometry was developed as a psychic art in the nineteenth century after an American geologist, Professor Denton, conducted many hours of testing with his sister, who could hold wrapped objects to her forehead and identify what they were or give some other information about them.

Further experiments were carried out by other doctors during the following years, and the results showed that there were indeed certain people who had the ability to sense the characteristics and qualities of present and future events concerning the person who owned or had handled the object being "read."

The reason one can pick up information from objects is that they absorb the vibrational patterns of those who carry them. The vibrations create an "aura memory" that reflects the circumstances surrounding the owner. These signals vary from weak to strong, depending on the owner's personality.

Charlie taught me how to do psychometry readings, and because I've very "feeling based," the technique came easily to me. If you empathize with others easily, this may work well for you, too.

To develop your ability to use psychometry, you have to do a little preparation. The first step is to begin paying much closer attention to the world around you. If you are not able to observe closely, psychometry will be difficult for you. If you can't see the concrete world very sharply, you won't be able to sense subtle psychic energies well, either. You'd be surprised how much one usually misses, observing some things yet blocking out others completely. The better you can train yourself to observe, the greater success you will have receiving subtle impressions from objects.

Practice some basic exercises to develop your powers of observation. Have one or two people stand in front of you for a moment. Then ask them to leave. Write down everything about them you can recall—what they were wearing in detail, everything. Then have them return and check your list.

Another exercise is to look around some familiar place and try to find things you've never noticed before. Do this on the way to and from work. Get into the habit of paying *attention* to what's happening around you, and don't just move unconsciously from moment to moment, hour to hour, day to day.

The best psychics are sharp, objective, and attentive, and they have trained their senses to work on highly acute levels. Practice looking closely at your surroundings, then closing your eyes and paying attention to the sounds around you. Next, focus on smells, then touch. Practice being *aware*. Describe your surroundings in as much detail as you can with your eyes closed.

After you sharpen your awareness a little, you can start practicing psychometry. First you'll need objects to hold. The best way would be to have a friend select a few things that are unfamiliar to you so you are not biased. Metal objects are good, and so are pieces of jewelry. Fabrics don't seem to work as well, possibly because they are constantly washed or cleaned. Although some psychics disagree with me, I prefer holding a key because it is usually carried by its owner every day.

A letter is another good object. Handwritten letters especially pick up some vibrations. In fact, if you are working on psychometry without the help of others, gathering a few letters to start with is a good idea. If you pick letters, put them in identical envelopes and seal them so you can't differentiate one from another while you are practicing.

If you are working alone, arrange your objects or letters on a table in front of you. Then sit on a comfortable chair and relax as much as possible. Being tense or nervous will block your ability to sense subtle ener-

gies, so concentrate on relaxing. Close your eyes and take one of the arranged objects or letters in your hand. Experiment with holding the object or letter first in one hand, then the other, if necessary. As you hold
the object or letter, put your full concentration *only* on the object. You
may also want to touch the object to your forehead.

Now, pay attention to the object and notice whether or not you
begin to sense anything about it. It may take a few moments, so just relax
into the exercise. Don't rush yourself. The vibrations will begin to rise to
your conscious attention. They may come in bits and pieces, rather
slowly, or you may get impressions so fast that it's hard to take it all in.
Each person varies, as does the vibration from each object. As the vibrations rise, just start talking as if you are with a friend, describing whatever impressions come through. If you are working alone, you may want
to use a tape recorder. There may be scenes, or you may get feelings or
sensations. Just express whatever comes to mind. Now is no time to intel-
lectualize as to whether or not it feels "certain." Nothing may feel very
certain in the beginning, because the impulses are so subtle. Some objects
may give you very distinct feelings, while others give you very little.

After you acknowledge and record your impressions, open the letters so you can see if your impressions are right. If someone has given you
objects to hold, ask for a list of each object and a description of its owner
so you can check your accuracy. With practice you will be able to pick up
vibrations from all objects.

Some objects may belong to highly emotional people. If you pick up
strong emotions, be certain only to *observe* and not *absorb* the vibration.
You do not want to be emotionally affected yourself. This is one reason
for the preparation exercises. You want to observe, not react. Even if you
pick up very good feelings, be sure only to observe. The objective of psychometry is to be able to pick up psychic vibrations and let them pass
through your conscious field of attention without permitting them to affect you.

With practice you can begin to fine-tune your psychometry ability.
When working with psychometry, tell yourself, once the flow of impressions stops, to disassociate from the object and shut down the connection.

When you are finished, it helps to shake your hands or even wash them to remove the impressions.

When you are practicing psychometry, feel free to experiment with all types of objects. You may discover that one type—a ring or a watch, for example—works better than, say, a key or a letter. However, here's a word of advice. Don't take people's belongings and do psychometry readings without their permission. I assure you that they usually don't appreciate it. Psychic advice, like any advice, is not wanted if it is unsolicited. Do, however, work with those who share your interest. In fact, it's very helpful to work with others.

When you are developing the technique of psychometry, work very hard to avoid emotional reaction in any way. Emotion can be very draining and upsetting. Do the exercises to balance the second chakra if necessary (see page 147). Take a *neutral* attitude, and simply observe what you pick up. If you do find yourself feeling drained, stop, wash your hands, and try another day. I have great success with psychometry and have been doing it for twenty years. After a while you too can learn to do the same and become equally skilled at it if you work hard enough.

PREDICTION VERSUS PROBABILITY

What about predicting the future? That's no big deal, either, really.

First of all, there are predictions and probabilities. Predictions are really projections—projecting how creative energy, set in motion, will play out on the physical plane. The difference between a prediction and a probability is that a prediction is based on energy already released, while a probability is a projection of energy that may be released but hasn't been yet.

Let me use an example. Suppose you are a baseball pitcher, and you have a ball in your hand. As you wind up to throw the ball, a person who can integrate all the elements involved (position, speed, height, point of release, and so forth) can project a probability of where the ball will fly if all the calculations follow through and the ball is thrown. The pitcher, however, may change his mind. The pitcher may not release the ball, for example, or shift and throw it elsewhere.

A prediction, however, will indicate where energy will go once it is released. In this case, if the ball has left the pitcher's hand, one can predict how it will move out into the universe. This trajectory is obvious, especially if you are psychic.

Psychic predictions are different from pure conjecture in that psychic predictions take into account hidden or unseen elements not obvious to the eye. For example, a client came to me last year and asked me if her new office location would prove beneficial to her law practice. I *predicted* that the move would ultimately be beneficial, but it would be seriously delayed because of plumbing problems and would initially throw her business into disruption.

She said, "No, you're wrong! I'm moving into a high rise in the Loop today. We don't have anything to do with plumbing."

"That's funny. It looks like it's underwater to me," I said. "Oh, well, perhaps I'm wrong."

Little did we both know that even as I was speaking, the great flood of the Chicago Loop was taking place. The Chicago River broke into an old underground system of tunnels and flooded basements of buildings in the entire Loop. Her building, along with the rest of the Loop, was closed for weeks because of serious damage to the electrical equipment. It was a prediction because the energy was already released. She called later that morning to tell me what had happened, and for her it was a two-month upheaval.

A probability is different.

A client named Carl came to me for a reading because he was having a terrible time making a marriage commitment to his on-again-off-again girlfriend of four years. He wanted to know how it would turn out if he forced himself to marry her; the guilt and frustration of this impasse was causing him great sadness, even depression.

My guides told me that he loved her dearly as a friend, and he really wanted to have her in his life because she was so loving and nurturing to him. But his love was platonic, almost maternal, and it lacked the chemistry of sexual union. My guides told me Carl was actually gay and was sexually attracted to men, but he was greatly afraid of the social and physical realities of following his natural inclination.

In his case, the *probability* of a happy marriage with his girlfriend was zero. He needed to be fair and tell her the truth: that he was not sexually compatible with her. It would then be up to her to decide whether she wanted to preserve their friendship. This woman wanted a marriage partner, and it was spiritually incorrect to give her the impression that he could be a genuine partner on an intimate sexual level.

Carl did marry his fiancée. He wasn't able to honor his true impulses because he was unsupported emotionally and was afraid he'd lose the love of his fiancée and his family. They had two children and for all the world looked like a happy family. Yet Carl's sexual nature was not to be repressed, and he found himself living a double life. He went to gay gathering places and eventually met and fell in love with a man named Rick. He now found himself in the infinitely worse situation of facing a divorce and leaving his two children. Needless to say, it was an emotional mess. Carl divorced, and the battles between Carl and his embittered wife rage on even today.

In Carl's case the probability played out, but when he came to me for a reading, he had not yet made a choice. He followed his fears, but ultimately he was forced to recognize and live within his true nature, which is good. Unfortunately he had incurred a lot more karma along the way and now had even more spiritual growth work to do.

Whether you are using psychic tools or psychometry, it's important to see that all these possibilities provide even more ways to get in touch with and experience the loving and uplifting benefits of your soul. They allow your Higher Self, your soul, to step in, take over, and take care of you. Whether you are examining probabilities or making predictions, think of all these avenues as ways of building up a relationship with the greatest person you'll ever know—*you*, the Highest You, your soul.

EXPLORATIONS

It is my feeling that all of the tools in this chapter are ongoing explorations. I urge you to move into the tools that feel most immediately attractive to you.

CHARTING YOUR PROGRESS

Reflect on your experiences this week when answering these questions.

How many days this week did you meditate? (By now it should be a habit!)_____

Have you remembered to ground yourself?_____

_____

Have you remembered to clear your aura?_____

_____

How many days this week did you make entries in your psychic journal? Did you record any readings you did with your tools?_____

_____

_____

What tool seemed immediately inviting?_____

_____

What tool intrigued you?_____

_____

Which tool, if any, intimidated you? _____

_____

Which tools have you used? _____

_____

Which tool will you try next? _____

_____

Welcome Home

One thing you'll discover when you begin to awaken your psychic voice is that more than ever before, you are being asked to listen to and truly honor who you really are. You are training yourself to focus on what is real for you. You will look inside and recognize the genuine self within. You will stop living by someone else's rules and values. You will stop looking for your reflection in the eyes of others. You will stop depending on the illusion of the material world for your identity. You become free of the tendencies to harm or repress your genuine needs, feelings, and desires. You develop what is called integrity. You will become deeply committed to loving yourself. I call this "coming home."

If you walk the psychic pathway, you will learn to have a loving, kind, and unwavering integrity with yourself. You will remember who you really are and protect it with all your heart. As you listen and live by the code of your true inner self, your life will begin to turn around. What was frightening, tense, or confusing will become more manageable. You will move away from the behavior that your ego and mind set up. If you walk the psychic path, you will naturally be attracted to what it is that you really require for your peace and your serenity. When you start to walk the psychic pathway, you begin your spiritual healing, and as you heal the wounds in your soul and recover the childlike joy you've lost, a breakthrough will occur. You will be able to love yourself in a deep and profound way. You will start to feel how magnificent you really are.

Psychic awareness lets you see the truth. It establishes an integrity with yourself that, with time and experience, becomes unwavering. If you have integrity with yourself, then you can also have a spirit of genuine integrity with others. You can free yourself from the snarls and traumas of trying desperately to manipulate others to love you, to admire you, to delegate power to you, to make you feel worthwhile. You won't need that kind of attention and recognition. If your heart heals and your soul is expressed honestly in your life, you will not feel the same sad, empty pain of the life lived in illusion—the pain that causes you to make harmful decisions and make desperate attempts to feel loved.

The psychic pathway opens your eyes to others in a way never before experienced. You will know if someone is honest with you. You will know if someone is good for you. You will know whether or not to trust someone. You will know who can be your real friends, and above all, you will know what you can and cannot expect from others, because your soul will let you know. You will also know whether or not something or someone is right for you and why.

As you treat yourself with loving integrity, it will become possible to treat others in the same fashion. If in the past you've been less than honest or fair, you will finally be able to stop that tendency in yourself. If you have been unable genuinely to love others, you will now be able to love them. As you become whole and free from illusion, you will be able to bring that loving energy to others and see in them wholeness and truth. This is an energy you didn't have available before. It's exhilarating. It's better than pleasure—it's bliss, and it won't go away.

You will also be able to walk away from people or situations that are less than honest or fair to you. You will begin to see how you always have choices and options for growth. You will begin to realize that you can be happy, that you can live safely in your heart's desire, and that you have all the help in the universe to do so. "The Kingdom of Heaven is within." That's the truth! Power, authentic, true power, comes to those who honor the code of the psychic path. "To thine own self be true."

This doesn't mean you won't be required to be flexible as you move in the ordinary world. You will become, if anything, much more flexible. You will be flexible enough to let go of anything and anyone that compromises your integrity or oppresses your spirit. You will no longer tolerate living a sad existence, nor will you try to compromise anyone else's freedom or integrity.

As you live in truth, you'll attract others who also live in truth. Interestingly enough, you will also bring out the truth and integrity in people who otherwise operate out of the ego. When you center your consciousness in your soul, you bring out the soul in others. It's amazing. Therefore, the quality of all your relationships, even with those people who know nothing of the soul, will improve dramatically.

There is no question that starting to walk the psychic pathway is a healing experience. It is an adventure, a discovery, a great awakening, and it is extremely amusing! God has a wonderful sense of humor and of timing. Life will float up to you instead of you having to scrounge and struggle to hold on to it.

There is only benefit to your awakening your psychic sense, yet no great leap has ever been made without a sacrifice. You will have to make sacrifices to walk the psychic pathway. You will have to sacrifice:

- being a controlling person
- being addicted to the approval of others
- being manipulative
- being dishonest
- being selfish at the expense of others
- being dramatic
- being "the victim"
- being vengeful
- being lazy
- being full of excuses
- being disorganized
- being abusive to yourself and others

Using the exercises in this book, you will be able to let go of this behavior naturally and gracefully.

Leading a spiritual life sounds restraining and oppressive to some people. To many people, leading a spiritual life sounds somber—depressing! Leading a spiritual life to many people means denying themselves pleasure or spontaneity.

In reality, nothing could be further from the truth. Being spiritual does not depend on what you eat, drink, smoke, wear, spend, consume, or desire. Being spiritual means, very simply, being loving and being kind—starting with listening to yourself and valuing yourself. If you walk the psychic pathway, you walk with a gentle heart, a joyous heart, the heart of a child. By giving your spirit a proper voice, you will also look for and hear the voice of truth in others. You will see each person as a soul—lost maybe, but precious!

Walking the psychic pathway brings light into your life and will thus help you bring light into the world. For that reason above all, it's *very* important to recruit as many souls as possible into the pathway of light. You see, the world has sadly become a very dark place. The voice of the ego has gone wild, because it's insatiable. The ego can't get enough. People have become totally detached from their souls, as from generation to generation the truth becomes more obscure, more lost, and finally disappears. People do not value themselves anymore. They no longer care about the human spirit. The ego, in pursuit of immortalizing itself, feeds off sensation—from drugs, sex, food, power, money, narcissism, and control—anything that distracts it from pain. Because all of these pursuits are in vain, providing no peace to the spirit, the ego in our society is becoming more and more manic. People are killing one another like flies, abusing one another without regard, crushing one another in unprecedented numbers. And it is breaking the heart and soul of the earth. We must reverse this course, because it is the collision course of catastrophe. The course of illusion is becoming the course of mass destruction.

As you begin to travel the psychic pathway inward to your soul, you begin to reverse the course. Being psychic will give you authentic power, power no one can ever take away, power that grows and grows. Being psychic transforms the drudgery of being human and barely surviving into a joyful and creative pleasure. Life will become happy. It will also bring you your heart's desire, as it did for me.

Let me tell you the rest of my story.

From our first date on, Patrick and I seemed to fit together like two birds of a feather. Just as I'd known, we became inseparable partners. We really clicked. We had so much fun together. We camped, we danced, we rode bicycles, we had picnics. He had the same spontaneous love of adventure as I did. We shared intimacy—or at least I thought we did.

One night, after a year of constant togetherness, I asked Patrick what kind of future he saw: I meant for *him* more than for us. It might have been a sensitive question or may have hit a sore spot. He was not fulfilled in his job. He seemed to be more artistic than service-motivated at the time, and I felt frustrated for him. He was turning thirty, was basically poor because of his lengthy travels abroad, didn't have much confidence, and was questioning his judgment about the career path he had chosen.

He said point-blank, "I don't know, but I don't plan on any big commitments, if *that's* what you mean."

It wasn't! (But I had been planning on big commitments at some point.) His saying he wasn't moving in that direction with me really shocked me. Up until then I believed we had an understanding about a future together. Could I have been this wrong?

I looked at him. He felt cold, detached, withdrawn, at that moment. I couldn't find a warm tone toward me anywhere. It was the night after Christmas.

I said angrily, "Well, that's good, because I wasn't talking about commitments with me. How presumptuous! I was talking about what you at thirty want to be when you grow up. You seem so miserable. I was just exploring how you could change that!"

"Oh," he said. "I don't know. I don't want to discuss it." He stopped talking. So did I. Patrick drove my car to his loft and asked me if I wanted to come up and stay with him.

"Me? Stay? With you?"

Let go, said a voice in my head. I really didn't want to be, but I *needed* to be alone. This guy was so unpredictable that even I couldn't read him very well. I left.

I felt such anger, confusion, and disappointment at his callous and flippant dismissal of any future commitment with me. I was only twenty-four, and I wasn't holding my breath to get married. But I thought our energy together was so well matched that it was obviously going to last forever.

I really loved Patrick. He was one of the most precious, creative, sensitive, sensual, energetic, wonderful people I had ever known. He wrote poetry! He made his own Christmas cards. And worked at soup kitchens. And met me with picnic baskets. And took me to strange little nooks and crannies in the city that I had never seen before. And cooked me dinner. And threw fun parties. And told great stories. And brought me flowers.

Also, early in our relationship we combined our talents and started teaching psychic development classes. Patrick had extensive ability in relaxation training, visualization, and guided imagery exercises and hypnosis. Between his skills and mine, we had successfully taught several workshops in sensory expansion, and I felt our work together was perfectly complementary. Between the two of us, people in our classes were able to have some very exciting personal psychic breakthroughs. Now, for the life of me, I couldn't figure out what his problem was. We were so good together. What should I do?

During the time I had spent with Patrick, I felt grounded, stable, safe, loved, and cared for. My psychic ability had soared. With my emotional state so peaceful, feeling so happy, I found my awareness and ability to concentrate on others magnified many times over. He made me feel protected. With him in my life as an emotional anchor, I found I could really open up, really reach out there. My readings for others were better than ever, and the number of people calling had multiplied quickly ever since I had started dating him.

I thought—no, I knew—that being loved played a tremendous role in expanding my intuition. It started to develop with the love and support of my parents, but in my time with Patrick it burst wide open. I could see places, name names, give very specific details that shocked and surprised my clients and helped them in very concrete ways.

I wondered if, by ending my relationship with Patrick, I would diminish my psychic ability. For a moment I even feared losing it. In any case, I sure felt at that moment that I'd lost interest. Why bother doing readings or anything?

I was so depressed. I cried myself to sleep.

The next day Patrick called. He asked if I wanted to get together after he got off work. I said sure. I was planning on telling him good-bye. I was in a peculiar frame of mind—neutral, neither happy nor sad. Probably numb.

I met him at the loft. We talked for a while about his day. He acted as if the episode in the car had never happened. Then I said, "Patrick, I really love you, but obviously you and I are not working toward the same goals in life. So I've decided to respect your need to be noncommittal. But I also have needs, so I am going to move on."

He looked taken by surprise. "You mean date other men?"

"Yes," I said. Of course the thought of dating someone else at this moment was repulsive, but I wanted to save face.

He was silent for a moment. Then he said, "Want to take a trip together before you move on?"

"What?" It was not the response I'd expected, but then again, he was the most unpredictable guy I'd ever met.

"Where?"

"To Egypt. Cairo."

"*Cairo?* You're kidding! You must be kidding!"

"No, really," he said. "I've never been to Africa. I'd love to go there with you. How about one last adventure?"

It was such a crazy idea. I thought about it. "When?"

"In two weeks. I get my vacation. Come on. Let's do it." He looked happy and sad at once. It was a classic Gemini look. He was such a romantic.

"Okay, sure. Why not end our great love affair in Cairo. But you plan it! Apparently my plans are way off. And I don't want to see you before we go. I've got to make plans to get along without you."

I left there totally puzzled. I wondered if Patrick had been working with schizophrenics too long. We had just broken up by planning a trip to Egypt. This ought to be good, I thought. For once I couldn't even begin to think what this experience would be like.

We met two and a half weeks later at O'Hare Airport and took a flight first to JFK, then on to Cairo. It was a very long flight. The plane was full, so we didn't get seats together, but I was relieved.

This was ridiculous. Why was I going to Cairo with someone who had basically disregarded me as a possible wife? I didn't know—curiosity, mostly. Not intuition, just curiosity.

Arriving in Egypt was stepping into pandemonium. It was a mob scene at the airport. I floated into the crowd half dazed. I had traveled extensively in Europe, but I had never seen anything as exotic as this. It was pungent, dense, loud, and overwhelming. A man rushed up and grabbed my suitcase out of my hand and started walking.

Patrick screamed, "Stop!" at him, and, "What are you *doing?*" at me. He rushed up and grabbed back my suitcase. "Sonia, never give someone your suitcase unless you know who it is. He could have stolen it right here in front of you!"

I was still trying too hard to absorb the culture shock to pay much attention. Patrick led me through a sea of beggars to a white taxi, an ancient, choking Datsun. In went our bags, and off we went to the hotel.

I had only been in Egypt thirty minutes, yet as we drove through the streets into town, I loved it. It was a filthy, run-down cacophony of sound and color. This was by far the wildest experience I'd ever had. Nothing was familiar. It was ancient and absolutely seductive to me.

We arrived at our hotel, the Sheraton on the Nile, truly an oasis in the middle of massive poverty. It was luxurious and elegant, and best of all, as Patrick said, "Only sixty-five dollars a day. What a deal!"

Our room overlooked the Nile. I looked out our window and saw the Great Pyramid at Giza standing in the setting sun. It was almost like déjà vu! I stared at the pyramid in awe. I knew this place somewhere in my bones, in my soul. I knew this place.

I looked at Patrick, and his face looked different to me. At first I thought it was the jet lag, but then I realized in that moment that he had the look of the old, wise face I'd seen in my dream. For just a moment that was his face.

I sat and stared at the sun going down. Suddenly the sound of the Muslim call to evening prayers burst out over loudspeakers all over the city. It was an eerie, soulful, sacred sound drifting to my ears as the sun faded into the night, leaving a star-studded sky. I was hypnotized. Neither Patrick nor I spoke.

Finally I took a shower. Jet lag kicked in like a tidal wave, and I couldn't stay conscious. I fell asleep.

Patrick woke me up in the middle of the night.

I jumped. "What? Now what? Are you all right?"

It was pitch black outside. I was still so tired, I felt drugged.

"Get up. We are going to the Pyramids!"

"Now?" I said. "Are you crazy?"

"Yes, yes, I am," he insisted. "Come on."

For a moment I thought I was dreaming again of the same wise old face saying, "Come on." I forced my eyes open. There was a knock at the door.

"Room service." It was a cup of coffee. I poured it down my semi-conscious throat.

"Why are you doing this to me?" I asked Patrick. "First you tell me you are not committed to a future together, then you drag me to Cairo to torture me! What is wrong with you?"

"Come on, Sonia. It's a full moon, and I want to watch the sunrise at the Pyramids. Come on. We can sleep later!"

"Go alone. Take pictures. I'm tired. You are really starting to bug me!" I buried my head in the pillow.

He kissed my hand. He kissed my neck. He kissed my cheek. Then he pulled me up on my feet and said, "Easy does it. Let's go."

I poured myself into clothes. I also put on a hat, scarf, and gloves because it was January, and even in the desert it was cold. There was a taxi waiting downstairs. Patrick was as happy as a bluejay. He looked almost like a little boy, grinning from ear to ear. "This is exciting," he said as we barreled into a pitch-dark night across the city toward Giza.

The taxi approached the Pyramids and parked about a half mile away. The driver agreed to wait for us as we bailed out into the crisp ebony night and started to walk. I was freezing, shivering, and complaining. Patrick seemed unfazed. He put his arm around me and said, "Isn't this amazing?" as we approached the huge black shape of the pyramid. I had to agree. This was awesome!

We walked slowly. The night sky seemed to lighten a moment at a time. By the time we reached the base of the pyramid, the first rays of sun broke like a song across the sky.

"Patrick," I gasped, "look at the sunrise against the Pyramids!" I swung around to grab him, but he was on bended knee.

"Sonia," he said, "I love you, and I couldn't think of a better place to ask you to be my wife!" The sky lit up as if on cue. The light of dawn was all around. "Will you marry me?"

I burst out laughing and crying at the same time. This guy was one in a million.

"Of course I will!" I shouted. "You are the most spectacular soul in the universe!"

We kissed until the sun rose high. I felt we were beginning again where we had left off.

As this (very long, but I love him) story shows you, if you take the leap of faith and let go of the ordinary point of view, you can see that anything you imagine and hold close to your heart in sincerity is possible.

Being psychic will lead you to your heart's desire, your true purpose in life. It will connect you to your pathway of genuine gratification and meaningful work. It will also connect you to your spiritual family and leave you with a profound sense of *real* security.

Being psychic is healing. As you come to love and honor yourself, you make it possible to forgive those who have hurt you and to understand and accept the value in all you've done in life. Your heart will heal, and the child in you, the creator, will come out and play again.

Being psychic will bring love back into the atmosphere, as well. You will become a crusader for the future of all of us. You will be part of the consciousness that will help return humanity back to the heart, to the center of balance and serenity, to its source of life!

Walking the psychic pathway is a challenge. Your mind will test you every step of the way. It is the great tempter, the voice of illusion, of fear, of distortion. But this voice can be tamed and trained to assume its rightful place. The voice of reason can be taught to support and protect the soul. The ego can be taught to respect and honor its source of love. That is the proper place for the ego—to serve the soul, not to dominate it or kill it off. This is the "sacred marriage," mind and soul working together.

The right use of reason is to be reasonable—to be respectful of your physical needs and limitations; to study what the physical and practical side of life requires and work to respect it, starting with the basics of your body. In the spirit of self-love, honor what this vehicle requires to do its job. Give your body proper nourishment and rest. Keep it clean and make it attractive out of love and respect for yourself. Be grateful for its service, and be appreciative of just how remarkable a vehicle it is.

- Give the emotions a rest.
- Ground yourself.
- Clear your aura.
- Balance your chakras.
- Pay attention to the energy coming into and out of your soul.
- Eliminate confusion by establishing your goals.
- Work on hearing your Higher Self.
- Identify and walk away from sabotage.
- Organize what is important to you.
- Simplify your day by doing only what you really can do in the spirit of love and caring.
- Stay away from "should" thinking and work toward "I would love to . . ." as you make choices.

Life is a precious but impermanent gift. The body gives out, and your soul is released. The real value of life is whatever value it is to your soul. Snap out of illusion! Strive to see the truth. It is so beautiful that it will make you laugh with joy. The truth is, you are a creation of God. You are safe. You are loved. You are truly magnificent! And you are moving steadily toward coming to know this and profoundly embracing this truth.

Welcome home!

EXPLORATIONS

Give Yourself a Star
Go to your psychic space. Light a stick of incense. Put on a tape of music you enjoy. Go back over your transformation, using your psychic journal entries.

Tell someone you are psychic. What are their reactions?_____

_____

_____

What are your reactions to their reactions?_____

_____

_____

How does it feel to completely honor who you are?_____

_____

_____

CHARTING YOUR PROGRESS

Reflect on your experiences this week when answering these questions.

How many days this week did you meditate? Boy, does time fly!

_____

How many days this week did you make entries in your psychic journal?_____

Close your eyes and ask yourself how it feels to be coming home.

_____

A Few Last Tips
for Travelers

It is my hope this book will start you on your way to successfully developing your psychic ability. It is an exciting natural resource and can greatly enhance your life and give you many opportunities to be helpful to others.

You should, however, be aware of the responsibility and ethical conduct that goes with psychic ability. Psychic awareness can give you many advantages, but it may not *ever* be used to control or manipulate other people. If you do use it in this way, it will bring you very unpleasant repercussions. There are universal laws that you must respect at all times. The most important of these is the law of karma.

Quite simply, this universal law states, "As you sow, so shall you reap." That is, whatever you do, whether it's good or bad, eventually comes back to you in kind. If you are considerate, honest, loving, and just, you will experience the same energy from others. If you cheat, lie, or treat others unkindly in any way, your actions will surely be turned against you and usually when you least expect it. You must *always* respect others' rights and not lose sight of this ethic.

Psychic ability will present you with many insights, and though you need not necessarily maintain a spiritual point of view to be psychic, it is necessary that you use the information that comes to you responsibly and with care.

Here are a few guidelines to ensure that you avoid potential trouble when you use your psychic sense and put the knowledge you gain to good use.

Never Offer Psychic Information Unless It Is Asked For

Sometimes, in overzealous enthusiasm, budding psychics will practice their abilities on anyone they come in contact with, offering free advice and psychic perceptions without being asked. This is a definite faux pas. Indiscreet use of psychic ability is an invasion of another's privacy and is most unethical. Besides, you will quickly learn that unsolicited advice, psychic or otherwise, is *unwanted!* If you pick up psychic vibrations from others without trying, just dismiss them. If these vibrations don't involve you, then let them pass. If it is not information pertaining to your life, and you retain it, it will interfere with your own energy. The danger in psychically intruding on others' thoughts and lives and concerning yourself with their problems is that you may absorb their moods, states of mind, emotions, and troubles, which is very draining and disruptive to your own psyche. Keep your attention on yourself and let what doesn't concern you pass you by.

Don't Brag about Psychic Ability

Bragging is boring. Bragging about psychic ability is downright obnoxious. It puts people on guard, makes them defensive, and will attract all kinds of negative feelings toward you. More important, bragging will interrupt your progress because your ego has to be silent to pick up psychic vibrations. The best policy is to be discreet. You should be happy with the progress you make, and if you have psychic allies, share your experiences with them freely. But beware of falling into the trap of thinking your psychic ability makes you special, more important, or more powerful than others. It's a natural ability, and possessing it in no way gives you special merit.

The other potential danger in bragging about your psychic ability is that you will encourage people to challenge you to demonstrate. Psychic ability works least well under pressure, and it is likely you will fail miserably. Spare yourself the embarrassment that bragging could bring about.

Don't Try to Manipulate or Control Others Psychically

This is not to suggest that this is your intention, but it may be tempting. An example of psychic manipulation would be finding yourself sexually attracted to someone and trying to coerce that person psychically into involvement with you. If you are lonely and desire a lover or mate, ask the universe to bring you the right one. (This may not necessarily be the one *you* think is right.)

It doesn't happen often, but sometimes students want to use psychic ability to manipulate others. They want to learn how to make others behave a certain way—to hire them, love them, or make their lives easier. Sorry, folks, but it won't work. People have free will, and you *must* respect this. If you want a new job, ask your psychic sense to direct you to the job that is best for you and in which you can contribute the most. If you want love, ask your psychic sense to guide you to someone who also wants love, so both of you can benefit mutually from each other's special qualities. We have a saying: "Tell the universe what you want, but don't tell it how!" Use your psychic ability to attract those situations and people that will best serve the higher interest of all concerned, not just of yourself.

Trying to control others psychically actually *attracts* trouble. You will gain far more by being open, flexible, and receptive to the many gifts and opportunities life offers, rather than trying to use any means, fair or unfair, to achieve your own often shortsighted desires.

Never Use Psychic Ability to Tell Someone When or How They Will Die

If it ever happens that you become psychically aware of someone's approaching death, you must keep it to yourself. If you see an accident, you can subtly suggest that the person who might be hurt or killed should be cautious, should slow down, or should be more aware. *Never* say, "I feel you are going to die."

It's tricky, especially if you feel an obligation to intervene and try to stop it, but death is something that is strictly between a person and the divine. If you pick up a feeling about death, respect it as a warning or as a method that your psychic sense may be using to prepare you emotionally. If your perception is that the death is the inevitable result of another's recklessness, you may suggest to that person that he or she be careful, but do not say, "My psychic sense tells me that if you are not careful, you will kill yourself." Say, "My intuition tells me that you should pay attention to what you are doing, and be careful." Nothing more.

It is not your job to save people. You will exhaust yourself trying. If your psychic sense tells you something that may protect another from harm, and if that person is willing to listen, you may share it. But if you don't know that your intended help will be welcome, just send love and prayers and hope that all will be well. Fortunately, even experienced psychics are rarely shown the untimely death of another. If you sense death, but it's not untimely, send love, prayers, and support, and don't interfere. Let that person enjoy whatever time is left without your casting a shadow on it.

Do Not Condemn or Judge Others' Behavior

Your psychic sense may make you aware of behavior you don't approve of. This does not give you the right to expose, condemn, judge, or criticize the guilty person publicly. This could be difficult, but you must respect this rule. Regardless of the way things may appear, you'll never know the total motivation behind other people's behavior. If you encounter something you don't approve of, end your association with that person quietly and carry on.

The law of karma sees to it that everyone answers for his or her own behavior. Of this you can be sure. Let the universe render justice. Be responsible for your own behavior, and be forgiving toward others. This is asking a lot, but we are all on this earth to learn to love and forgive. Just as you wouldn't appreciate anyone condemning you, you must refrain from condemning others.

Believe it or not, most people are neither deliberately foolish nor deliberately evil. They lead their lives as they feel they have to. This does not mean that you must approve of or condone wrong behavior. It just means that it may not be your job to correct it through a public exposé. If your psychic sense makes you aware of wrongdoing, protect yourself the best way you can and move along.

Be respectful of these rules and guidelines, and you can freely practice and exercise your psychic ability without any worry.

One final word. Psychic development can be very important to you, but don't approach it so seriously that you don't enjoy it. Take pleasure in exploring your own psychic potential. Laugh at your mistakes and go on. Have fun with the exercises. Most of all, *expect* results. You *are* psychic, and with a little practical effort your natural talent will grow and work for you in every aspect of your life. Wake up to your own potential! Challenge yourself to reach new levels of understanding. Somewhere along your psychic pathway, you will get a glimpse of your own *magnificence!*

Walk in peace.

Sonia

The Psychic Pathway workbook is offered in genuine love and support in guiding you on your personal pathway of the soul. It is not, however, intended for the professional practice of counseling.

If you are interested in being a facilitator of the Psychic Pathway Workshops, please direct your inquiries to:

The Psychic Pathway
PO Box 408996
Chicago, IL 60640-2820

HOW TO USE TAROT CARDS

The most important thing in working with a tarot deck or with regular playing cards of psychic guidance is to use them with a sincere attitude. This is the difference between divination and fortune-telling. Divination is when one seeks guidance and spiritual understanding, whereas fortune-telling is a much more irreverent and superficial look into the future.

Start by meditating to clear your mind so that the psychic pathways will open. Then, select one card to represent yourself, if the reading is for you, or the person you are reading for, if it is for someone else. This is the *indicator* or *significator* card.

The best way to select the indicator card is to choose a Page, a Knight, a Queen, or a King from the court cards that correspond to your astrological sign and the element of earth, air, fire, or water. If you are twenty or younger, male or female, choose the Page. If you are a male twenty-one to thirty, choose the Knight. If you are twenty-one or over and female, choose the Queen. If you are older than thirty and male, choose the King.

For example, if you are:

- Aries   Choose an indicator from
  Leo   *Fire*   the suit of Wands or
  Sagittarius   Clubs.

- Pisces   Choose an indicator from
  Scorpio   *Water*   the suit of Cups or
  Cancer   Hearts.

- Libra   Choose an indicator from
  Gemini   *Air*   the suit of Swords or
  Aquarius   Spades.

- Virgo
  Capricorn   *Earth*   Choose an indicator from
  Taurus   the suit of Pentacles or
                          Diamonds.

Place your indicator card in the middle of the table. Hold the deck in your right hand and mix with your left hand. Next, cut the deck face down into three separate piles and then place the cards back together in whatever order you wish. Now spread the deck out, still face down, and pull out ten cards.

Then lay them out according to the instructions that follow.

Step 1: The Indicator Card

First, select your indicator card and place it in the center of the table **face up,** like this:

Step 2: Placing the First Card

Next, place the first card **face down,** directly on top of your indicator card, like this:

Step 3: Placing the Second Card
Next, place the second card crosswise across the first, **face down,** like this:

Step 4: Laying Out the Other Cards
Then lay out the remaining cards face down, in this pattern:

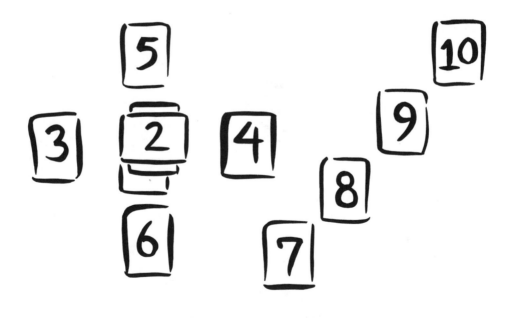

Step 5: Interpreting the Cards

Once you have your cards laid out, turn them over one at a time, in consecutive order, beginning with the first card on top of your indicator card. Then you can begin your reading.

Use the following list to interpret their position in your layout:

Indicator	(No interpretation)
Card 1	The force or condition at hand
2	The opposition or obstacles
3	The conditions leaving you
4	The conditions entering (immediate)
5	The motive or goal (hidden)
6	The tools to work with
7	Your attitude
8	Influences from the environment
9	Hopes and fears
10	Final result

This layout is known as the Celtic Cross and is used in answer to a specific issue.

Refer to the explanations following to help you interpret the meanings of the individual cards.

THE MINOR ARCANA OF THE TAROT

Minor Arcana	Regular Deck	Element
Wands	Clubs	Fire
Cups	Hearts	Water
Swords	Spades	Air
Pentacles	Diamonds	Earth

The Suits—General Information

Clubs or Wands	Choices, decisions, action, travel, words
Hearts or Cups	Usually concern emotional matters
Spades or Swords	Mental matters, business negotiations, usually difficult or challenging events
Diamonds or Pentacles	Money, material world

The Courts

The court cards usually represent people playing a role in the subject's life. Select cards that represent you one of two ways: (1) age and coloring, or (2) astrological sign (see page 270).

Court of Wands

King of Clubs	Brown, curly, wavy hair; green or blue eyes. Sign of Leo (fire).
Queen of Clubs	Brown, wavy hair; fair skin. Sign of Aries (fire).
Jack of Clubs	Young man/woman; brown hair; fair skin. Sign of Sagittarius (fire).
Page (tarot only)	Child; brown hair; fair. No sign.

Court of Cups

King of Hearts	Older man; strong, powerful; fair. Sign of Scorpio (water).
Queen of Hearts	Older woman; mother; future; fair. Sign of Cancer (water).

| Jack of Hearts | Young man/woman; blond; fair. Sign of Pisces (water). |
| Page (tarot only) | Young child; blond; fair. No sign. |

Court of Swords

King of Spades	Powerful man; strong; dark. Sign of Aquarius (air).
Queen of Spades	Powerful woman; strong; dark. Sign of Libra (air).
Jack of Spades	Young man/woman; clever; dark. Sign of Gemini (air).
Page (tarot only)	Young child; mischievous; dark. No sign.

Court of Pentacles

King of Diamonds	Down-to-earth man; solid worker. Sign of Taurus (earth).
Queen of Diamonds	Practical woman; intuitive. Sign of Capricorn (earth).
Jack of Diamonds	Young man/woman; serious; student. Sign of Virgo (earth).
Page (tarot only)	Young child; solemn; quiet. No sign.

Note that the cards have two meanings. They can be interpreted one way if right side up and another way if turned upside down. A card is upside down if the smaller number of symbols is at the top. Some cards are not clearly right side up or upside down. You can make a small mark on these cards to mark the "up" side.

Suit of Wands (Clubs)

Ace   A creative birth, starting a new path, new opportunity, new ideas.
Reversed—failure, opposition, obstacles.

Two   Attracting inspiration from new places, opening up to new beliefs, growth, good fortune, temporary gain, success.
Reversed—surprise, new elements coming into action.

Three   Temporary but correct use of time, learn by watching others, lasting success in business, short journeys.
Reversed—arrogance, close-mindedness, fixed attitudes.

Four   A settled home, job, stability, peace, valuable relationships.
Reversed—peaceful end, satisfaction, prosperous activity.

Five   Competition, struggle, quarrels, defending your principles, usually jealousy or sabotage.
Reversed—trickery, fraud, lawsuits.

Six   Important news coming, triumph.
Reversed—delay, disappointment, disloyalty.

Seven   A challenge, a threat to your position.
Reversed—embarrassment, anxiety, doubts.

Eight   Things move quickly, conclusions, new ideas start to sprout.
Reversed—quarrels in home, jealousy, guilty conscience.

Nine   Inner strength, new friendships, overcoming threats, recovery, protecting what is genuinely valuable.
Reversed—adversity, obstacles, betrayal.

Ten   Journey, voyage, period of hard work with progress.
Reversed—theft, loss, intrigue.

Suit of Cups (Hearts)

Ace — The home, the heart, the body, love affair, breakthrough in self-love and acceptance.
Reversed—changes, unwelcome news, disappointment in love.

Two — New romance, good marriage, friendship, union, genuine love.
Reversed—foolishness, silly behavior, divorce, end of relationship.

Three — Abundance, good luck, favorable outcome to anyone, time to celebrate, lighten up, play.
Reversed—excessive indulgence, end of job/project.

Four — Uneasiness about future, boredom, missing what is important, overlooking your source of support.
Reversed—a new relationship, job, friendship, home.

Five — Disappointment in love, broken plans, regret, isolation, loss.
Reversed—plans go bad, unexpected turn for worse.

Six — Desire beginning to materialize, friendship, support, learning to receive.
Reversed—something able to happen, revealed in surrounding cards.

Seven — Vice, guilty conscience, vanity, pleasure confused with true heart's desire.
Reversed—humility, decision about love.

Eight — Lack of interest, dissatisfaction, rejecting the superficial for deeper meaning.
Reversed—a proposal, an offer.

Nine — Wish card, wish come true, you manifest material gain.
Reversed—still favorable but delay.

Ten	Permanent success, spiritual peace, well-being. Reversed—disruption, violence, anger.

Suit of Swords (Spades)

Ace	Power, control, death (of a situation), feeling in charge. Reversed—definitely bad, accidents, destruction.
Two	Closed off to others, not receptive, defensive but need to be, protecting yourself. Reversed—false affection, separation, divorce.
Three	Sorrow, separation, divorce, betrayal of confidence, poor judgment. Reversed—caution, sensible, greed, or will.
Four	Return to health, solitude, convalescence, return to self, retreat. Reversed—disorder, confusion, mental imbalance.
Five	Setting your enemies back, temporary gain but still in danger. Reversed—loss, mourning, funeral.
Six	Success by hard work, improved situation, leaving the old and outgrown. Reversed—declaration of love, confession.
Seven	Compromise, negotiation, progress due to others' lack of awareness. Reversed—wisdom, good judgment.
Eight	Bad news, illness, hospitalization, abuse, oppression, emotional or physical danger. Reversed—danger, accidents.
Nine	Total depression, failure, possible death, grief, despair. Reversed—suspicion, loneliness, false friend.

Ten	Most difficult card in deck. Death, ruin, disaster, failure, betrayal—all steps in humiliation. Reversed—small chance of escape, still grim.

Suit of Pentacles (Diamonds)

Ace	Money, comfort, security, status. Reversed—materialism, stable situation, in a rut.
Two	Ups and downs, fears imagined, impractical. Reversed—pretense, simulated joy.
Three	A raise, promotion, status. Reversed—mediocrity, weak, mundane.
Four	Material success, no risks, immobile, attachment to material. Reversed—delays, annoyances, uncertainty.
Five	Too much concern over money, can't thrive, no support, wrong path (karma). Reversed—hardship, severe financial loss, poverty.
Six	Gifts, presents, help, generosity to others, assisting others. Reversed—envy, greed.
Seven	Taking care of what matters, hard work and slow but sure success. Reversed—loans, debts, gossips, slander.
Eight	Skill in business, clever, cunning, in right vocation. Reversed—dishonesty in business.
Nine	Financial gain, windfall, inner wealth, at ease. Reversed—deceit, bad business.
Ten	Great material success, but not necessarily peace of mind. Reversed—gambling, disputed inheritance or taxation.

THE MAJOR ARCANA OF THE TAROT

Fool

Folly, action without plans, naiveté, but in open spirit.
Reversed—apathy, recklessness, lack of vitality.

Magician

Initiative, concentration, choice, decision.
Reversed—vagueness, confusion, trickery.

High Priestess

Memory, secret, intuition, guidance.
Reversed—passion, seduction, stupidity.

Empress

Pleasure, creativity, fruitful project, imagination.
Reversed—inaction, mental sterility, disruption.

Emperor

Control, order, authority, organization.
Reversed—injury, poor judgment, chaos.

Hierophant

Inspiration, divine guidance, intuition.
Reversed—failure to listen to conscience.

Lovers

Good judgment, helpers, attraction, sex, balance.
Reversed—poor choices, fickleness, super-ficiality.

Chariot

Divine will, inner strength, success, feeling helped by God.
Reversed—disorientation, bad accidents, mis-guided.

Strength

Discipline, power, persuasion, commitment to true path.
Reversed—weakness, illness, embarrassment.

Hermit

Conquest, completion, understanding, power to influence.
Reversed—fear, ignorance, dishonesty.

Wheel of Fortune	Luck, wealth, gain desire, fate shift. Reversed—bad luck, loss, failure.
Justice	Balance in life, smart choices, seeing into a situation. Reversed—legal problems.
Hanged Man	Appearances deceiving, warning to look deeper. Reversed—humiliation, exposure, revelation.
Death	Ending, completion, end of cycle. Reversed—a birth, inertia, laziness.
Temperance	Good ideas, right choices, good health, faith. Reversed—too extreme, impatience, disputes.
Devil	Seduced by wrong things, temptation, too much emphasis on material. Reversed—blind and stupid, thus unfortunate.
Tower	Universe teaching lesson, disruption of present conditions for inner growth, painful progress. Reversed—a total change of conditions.
Star	Gifts, inspirations, charisma, inner vision. Reversed—bad luck, wrong desires, disappointment.
Moon	Inner work, spiritual contemplation, psychic, physical body. Reversed—moodiness, minor mistakes.
Sun	Success, prosperity, grace, marriage, health, and balance. Reversed—the same but lesser degree.
Judgment	All things in proper place in the end. Reversed—delay, postponement.

| World | Absolute success, travel. |
| | Reversed—no success, failure, fixation. |

These are very general meanings, but enough for you to get started. If you want to pursue this subject, refer to books on tarot and card readings in the Occult section of the nearest large bookstore.

It's important to recognize that cards are used to *stimulate* your psychic channels and are powerless in themselves. After you work with tarot or regular cards for a time, you should find that your psychic ability is improving and getting sharper.

Books are available on other tarot techniques. Three of my favorites are *Living the Tarot* by Amber Jayantri and *The Major Arcana* and *The Minor Arcana* by Rachel Pollack.

Tarot cards can be found where most regular playing cards are sold, as well as in many metaphysical bookstores. If you prefer to use a regular deck, that's fine. With either deck you should keep the cards wrapped in a piece of fabric (preferably silk) to keep the vibrations isolated and clear of negative energy, and they should be used only for readings, never for games.

You should also refrain from using the cards more than once for any one question. Asking a question repeatedly indicates that you are not sincere, that you are looking just for what you want to hear and not for genuine guidance.

HOW TO THROW *I-CHING* COINS

Take three pennies. Attribute the number 2 to the head side and 3 to the tail side. Now take the three coins in your cupped hands and shake them together while concentrating on your question. Next, drop the coins in front of you and add up their numerical value. For example:

Heads + Tails + Heads

or

2 + 3 + 2 = 7

Do this six times, each time recording the number. Each number corresponds to a line in the hexagram. The even numbers give you a broken line (____ ____). The odd numbers give you a solid line (_____). Starting at the bottom, work upward to build a hexagram.

Here is an example of a hexagram, built from the bottom up.

Throw	Results (Heads/Tails)	Lines
Last	2 + 2 + 3 = 7 (odd)	_____
Fifth	2 + 2 + 2 = 6 (even)	____ ____
Fourth	3 + 3 + 3 = 9 (odd)	_____
Third	2 + 3 + 2 = 7 (odd)	_____
Second	2 + 2 + 2 = 6 (even)	____ ____
First	2 + 2 + 2 = 6 (even)	____ ____

Your hexagram will correspond to a chart found at the end of the *I-Ching*. First, identify the hexagram, then look up the meaning in the main text. The meaning should apply directly to your question and usually offers specific advice on what course of action you should take, if any. The principle behind this method of divination is that you unconsciously throw the hexagram applicable to the issue, and the "chance" of the hexagram is exactly the one concerning your situation.

SUGGESTED READING

Below are some titles that I have found valuable in my studies. Perhaps you will, too. I have starred my particular favorites.

Andrews, Lynn. *Teaching Around the Sacred Wheel.* New York: Harper-Collins, 1990.

Andrews, Ted. *Healer's Manual.* St. Paul, Minn.: Llewellyn, 1993.

Baldwin, Christina. *Life's Companion.* New York: Bantam, 1991.

*Besant, Annie. *The Spiritual Life.* Wheaton, Ill.: Theosophical Publishing House, 1991.

Bolen, Jean Shinoda. *The Tao of Psychology.* New York: HarperCollins, 1979.

Borysenko, Joan. *Fire in the Soul.* New York: Warner, 1993.

*Bowers, Barbara. *What Color Is Your Aura?* New York: Simon & Schuster, 1989.

Castaneda, Carlos. *Tales of Power.* New York: Simon & Schuster, 1974.

*Dyer, Wayne. *You'll See It When You Believe It.* New York: Avon, 1992.

Fox, Emmett. *Power Through Constructive Thinking.* New York: HarperCollins, 1989.

Goldberg, Natalie. *Writing Down the Bones.* Boston: Shambala, 1986.

Hay, Louise. *The Power Is Within You.* Carson, Calif.: Hay House, 1991.

Johnson, Robert. *He.* New York: Harper, 1989.

———. *Inner Work.* New York: Harper, 1989.

———. *She.* New York: Harper, 1989.

———. *We.* New York: Harper, 1983.

Joy, Brugh. *Joy's Way.* Los Angeles: Jeremy P. Tarcher, Inc., 1979.

*Kabbat-Zinn, Jon. *Wherever You Go, There You Are*. New York: Hyperion, 1994.

Keyes, Ken. *Handbook to Higher Consciousness*. Coos Bay, Ore.: Love Line Books, 1989.

Khan, Hazarat Inayat. *Spiritual Dimensions of Psychology*. New Lebanon, N.Y.: Omega Pub., Inc., 1988.

*Millman, Dan. *The Way of the Peaceful Warrior*. Tiburon, Calif.: H. J. Kramer, Inc., 1984.

*Moore, Thomas. *Care of the Soul*. New York: HarperCollins, 1992.

———. *Soul Mates*. New York: HarperCollins, 1994.

Redfield, James. *The Celestine Prophecy*. New York: Warner, 1993.

*Roberts, Jane. *Seth Speaks*. San Rafael, Calif.: Amber Allen New World Library, 1994.

*———. *The Nature of Personal Reality*. San Rafael, Calif.: Amber Allen New World Library, 1994.

Roman, Sanaya. *Personal Power Through Awareness*. Tiburon, Calif.: H. J. Kramer, Inc., 1986.

———. *Opening to Channel and Spiritual Growth*. Tiburon, Calif.: H. J. Kramer, Inc., 1989.

Weiss, Brian. *Many Lives, Many Masters*. New York: Simon & Schuster, 1988.

*White Eagle. *Spiritual Unfoldment I, II, III, IV*. Marina del Rey, Calif.: DeVorss & Co., 1942, 1969, 1987, 1988.

Wilde, Stuart. *Affirmation*. Taos, N.M.: White Dove International, 1988.

———. *Miracles*. Taos, N.M.: White Dove International, 1983.

———. *Life Was Never Meant to Be a Struggle*. Taos, N.M.: White Dove International, 1987.

Young-Sowers, Meredith. *Spiritual Crisis*. Walpole, N.H.: Stillpoint Publishing, 1993.

*Zukav, Gary. *The Seat of the Soul*. New York: Simon & Schuster, 1989.

INDEX

I wonder, 125–126
  Repeat after me, 127
  Telephone, 127
Goals, 81–82, 225
Goodman, Charlie, 41–42, 45, 156,
   169–170, 230, 244
Grounding, 119–123, 125
Guides, 195–200

Heart chakra, 152–156
  foods, 155–156
Helpers, 191–193, 198
Hermatite, 122
Hide-and-seek game, 127
Hypnosis, 22

I am psychic game, 172–178
I-Ching, 241–242, 283
Image collection, 178–179
Imagination, 123–124, 125, 160–161
Indicator card, 270–271
Inspirational writing, 222–223
Intellectual censor block, 56–60
Intuition, 14–19, 56
I wonder game, 125–126

Jayantri, Amber, 282
Journal, 30–31
Joy, 60
Joy guides, 195–196, 200
Judging other's behavior, 268–269
Jung, Carl, 69

Kundalini, 164

Living the Tarot (Jayantri), 282

Major Arcana, The (Pollack), 282
Masters, 194–195, 200
Meditation, 27–30
Memories, 112–114
Metaphysical Research Society, 41
Metron, 244
Miller, Jack, 101
Minor Arcana, The (Pollack), 282

Miracles, 209
My Toy Box exercise, 106

Negative energy, 137
Negative images, 33–34

Obsidian, 122
Opinions, 79
Organization, 69, 73, 81

Pace of living, 73–79
Passive people, 53–54
Pendulum, 230–237
Playing cards, 237–241
Pleasure, 146–148
Pollack, Rachel, 282
Prayer, 162–163
Precognition, 9
Prediction, 5, 247–249
Pretending, 171–172
Probability, 247–249
Psyche, 7, 244
Psychic, definition of, 1, 7
Psychic attack, 131–132
Psychic awareness, 116, 129, 253
Psychic Awareness Study, 12–13
Psychic blocks
  disorganization, 68–73
  intellectual censor, 56–60
  religious training, 40–52
  ugly duckling, 52–56
Psychic closet, 179
Psychic development, 8, 14, 257, 269
Psychic dress-up, 178
Psychic energy, 10, 20–25, 135
Psychic events, 57–60
Psychic guidance
  acting on, 19–20
  being open to, 14–15
  expecting, 15–16
  trusting, 16–19
Psychic hearing, 156
Psychic information, 4, 266
Psychic journal, 30–31
Psychic manipulation, 267
Psychic pollution, 132